The Archaeology of Alcohol and Drinking

The American Experience in Archaeological Perspective

UNIVERSITY PRESS OF FLORIDA

Florida A&M University, Tallahassee
Florida Atlantic University, Boca Raton
Florida Gulf Coast University, Ft. Myers
Florida International University, Miami
Florida State University, Tallahassee
New College of Florida, Sarasota
University of Central Florida, Orlando
University of Florida, Gainesville
University of North Florida, Jacksonville
University of South Florida, Tampa
University of West Florida, Pensacola

The American Experience in Archaeological Perspective
Edited by Michael S. Nassaney

The books in this series explore an event, process, setting, or institution that was significant in the formative experience of contemporary America. Each volume will frame the topic beyond an individual site and attempt to give the reader a flavor of the theoretical, methodological, and substantive issues that researchers face in their examination of that topic or theme. These books will be comprehensive overviews that will allow serious students and scholars to get a good sense of contemporary and past inquiries on a broad theme in American history and culture.

The Archaeology of Collective Action, by Dean J. Saitta (2007)
The Archaeology of Institutional Confinement, by Eleanor Conlin Casella (2007)
The Archaeology of Race and Racialization in Historic America, by Charles E. Orser, Jr. (2007)
The Archaeology of North American Farmsteads, by Mark D. Groover (2008)
The Archaeology of Alcohol and Drinking, by Frederick H. Smith (2008)

The Archaeology of Alcohol and Drinking

Frederick H. Smith

Foreword by Michael S. Nassaney

University Press of Florida
Gainesville/Tallahassee/Tampa/Boca Raton
Pensacola/Orlando/Miami/Jacksonville/Ft. Myers/Sarasota

13   12   11   10   09   08   6   5   4   3   2   1

Library of Congress Cataloging-in-Publication Data
Smith, Frederick H. (Frederick Harold), 1966–
The archaeology of alcohol and drinking/Frederick H. Smith; foreword by Michael S. Nassaney.
p. cm.—(The American experience in archaeological perspective)
Includes bibliographical references and index.
ISBN 978-0-8130-3290-0 (alk. paper)
1. Drinking of alcoholic beverages—Barbados—Saint Philip—History. 2. Alcohol industry—
Barbados—Saint Philip—History.   3. Sugar plantations—Barbados—Saint Philip—History.
4. Distilleries—Barbados—Saint Philip—History. 5. Maroons—Alcohol use—Barbados—Saint
Philip. 6. Slaves—Alcohol use—Barbados—Saint Philip. 7. Excavations (Archaeology)—
Barbados—Saint Philip—History. 8. Saint Philip (Barbados)—History. 9. Saint Philip
(Barbados)—Antiquities. I. Title.
GT2853.B36S65 2008
394.1'309729819–dc22   2008025848

The University Press of Florida is the scholarly publishing agency for the State University System
of Florida, comprising Florida A&M University, Florida Atlantic University, Florida Gulf Coast
University, Florida International University, Florida State University, New College of Florida,
University of Central Florida, University of Florida, University of North Florida, University
of South Florida, and University of West Florida.

University Press of Florida
15 Northwest 15th Street
Gainesville, FL 32611–2079
http://www.upf.com

To Jane and Rachel

Contents

Illustrations

Foreword

For many, but by no means all, young Americans, experimenting with alcohol is a rite of passage. A relatively inexpensive and readily available legal drug, alcohol is widely advertised to a youthful target audience. Advertisers and popular culture glorify alcohol, while other equally influential voices vilify it. An attitude of ambivalence surrounds alcohol in many societies, though perhaps especially in America, despite its use for literally hundreds of years. This ambiguity has tended to thwart alcohol studies and has shifted scholarly attention toward the social, physical, and mental pathologies that excessive alcohol consumption may engender.

Alcohol—like other commodities such as coffee, tea, tobacco, and sugar—is a product that can be traced through time and space to illuminate changes in its use and the interconnections it has created in the modern world. Moreover, its materiality embodied in the paraphernalia of production, distribution, and consumption makes alcohol amenable to archaeological investigation. The expansion of alcohol use and its introduction to areas of the world that lacked a tradition of brewed, fermented, or distilled beverages accelerated after the sixteenth century and became associated with many of the global processes like colonialism, immigration, slavery, capitalism, and industrialization that are considered to be the hallmarks of historical archaeology. The archaeological record clearly shows that colonists, immigrants, the enslaved, capitalists, and laborers drank, albeit at different times and places and for various reasons.

In *The Archaeology of Alcohol and Drinking*, Frederick H. Smith presents a comprehensive account of the ways in which historical archaeology has contributed to our understanding of alcohol in the modern world and its impact on the American experience. Drawing on literature from social history and cultural anthropology, Smith constructs a framework that explains why the topic has been generally avoided and how it has been hindered by the prescriptions of the temperance movement beginning in the nineteenth century. This is not to deny the potentially deleterious effects of excessive alcohol use. Rather, he claims that if we refrain from demonizing alcohol, we are in a better position to explore its roles in alleviating anxiety, creating sociability, and promoting escape in particular sociohistorical contexts.

Of course, it matters what beverages were drunk, where they were consumed, and how they were imbibed. As with all social practices—and drinking alcohol is no different—conscious choices serve to create and reproduce
social distinctions based on class, gender, and ethnicity. To some extent,
"you are what you drink." Personal identities are often tied to the sacred and
secular rituals of drinking and even the avoidance of alcohol altogether. The
learned behaviors associated with alcohol production, distribution, and use
lead to distinctive patterns in the material record that historical archaeologists can use to interrogate the hidden meanings that alcohol had for its
makers and consumers.

Alcohol-related behaviors are notoriously difficult to ascertain, and any
study that claims otherwise is likely to have an explicit political agenda. Because of the ambiguous attitudes surrounding alcohol use, people of all ages
are likely to exaggerate, underestimate, or completely deny consumption
rates, often depending on the situation in which they are reporting. Historical archaeology, with its reliance on multiple lines of evidence, can be used
to create a cultural context for a better understanding of the motivations
and consequences of alcohol use. Though not without its methodological
challenges (for example, bottle refilling and recycling), the tangible record
of alcohol-related material culture provides a concreteness that often speaks
to chronology, contents, connections, consumption, and community that
other sources may lack. Through a careful synthesis of a substantial body
of literature, Smith draws together a broad compendium of alcohol-related
material culture that implicitly or explicitly reveals the centrality of drinking
practices in past societies. Although much of this evidence was ancillary to
the recovery of data to address other research questions, Smith convinc-
ingly argues that closer scrutiny of the bottle, can, punch bowl, and wine
glass detritus of the past 500 years can inform on a commodity with important social, political, and economic implications. His examination of Mapps
Cave in Barbados illuminates how enslaved individuals selected a marginal
communal space to escape temporarily from the bondage of slavery and
the role that alcohol played in that process. Smith uses alcohol as a prism
through which he views the social and political events that fomented the
1816 slave uprising, the largest slave revolt in Barbadian history.

This study opens the door to new ways of approaching alcohol-related
material culture in the archaeological record. Indeed, such materials are
extremely common on post-Columbian sites, as Smith clearly enumerates.
Moreover, these objects are good to think with. Suffice it to say that the
flip-tops, broken beer bottles, spigots, abandoned stills, taverns, saloons,

and other alcohol-related objects and features are valuable clues to the practices and ideologies associated with alcohol and drinking, both past and present. As Smith notes, the tendency in historical archaeology to subsume alcohol-related material culture under the heading of foodways or to treat alcohol-related materials as simply an expression of dietary habits "obfuscates the uniquely meaningful character of alcohol drinking." Perhaps it is the ambivalence with which society treats alcohol that characterizes the American experience of drinking. By employing a comparative framework to juxtapose drinking practices in the United States with other parts of the post-Columbian world we will be in a position to gain a better understanding of the varied roles that alcohol has played, and meanings it has held, for different segments of American society. Smith has begun to construct that framework and highlight the place of alcohol in American history and culture.

Michael S. Nassaney
Series Editor

Acknowledgments

I wish to thank Kathy Deagan and Marley R. Brown III for their comments on earlier drafts of this manuscript. Kathy and Marley have supported and guided my archaeological research from the earliest days of my graduate studies and provided valuable insights that contributed greatly to the completion of this book. I am also grateful to David Geggus, whose meticulous attention to style and detail enhanced my research and strengthened the focus of this study. I wish to thank Dr. Michael Nassaney for his support and guidance at Western Michigan University and for encouraging me to publish my book in his series.

The fieldwork for this project was conducted with the help and support of Dr. Karl Watson, senior lecturer in the Department of History at the University of the West Indies, Cave Hill Campus, Barbados. Watson has devoted his life to protecting, preserving, and celebrating Barbados' rich cultural heritage. He brought me to Barbados to pursue my graduate research in Bridgetown in 1995, and since that time we have worked side by side on numerous archaeological projects in the island.

In addition, I wish to thank Kevin Farmer, curator of Archaeology and History at the Barbados Museum and Historical Society, for his insights and encouragement over the years. Kevin represents a new generation of Barbadian archaeologists: his unique perspective on Barbadian heritage strengthened my understanding of alcohol use in colonial Barbados.

Martina Alleyne is also a pioneer in Barbadian archaeology, and she, too, offered many important insights into Barbadian heritage. Martina's deep understanding of Barbadian material culture, her dedication to expanding archaeological research in Barbados, and her meticulous field methods have contributed to the completion of this project. Karl, Kevin, Martina, and I have initiated a number of important collaborative programs that will no doubt help shape the future of archaeological research in Barbados.

I would also like to thank the many other friends and colleagues in Barbados who have helped facilitate my research over the years, including Thomas Loftfield, Allissandra Cummins, Charles Holder, Cherri-Ann Beckles, Richard Haynes, Penny Hynam, Larry Warren, Anna Warren, Simon Warren, Nicholas Forde, Morris Greenidge, Shaun Coombs, Andy

Tempro, Mary Archer, Milton Inniss, Ingrid Cumberbatch, Patrick Watson, Linda Watson, Steven King, William Bain, and Lindsay Corbin.

I wish to thank the Department of Archaeological Research at the Colonial Williamsburg Foundation, which supported my early fieldwork in Barbados. In particular, Marley R. Brown III was instrumental in securing funding that helped facilitate my research in Barbados. His conviction and commitment to the field of historical archaeology has launched the careers of many aspiring scholars.

The A. Curtis Wilgus Foundation at the University of Florida Center for Latin American and Caribbean Studies also provided seed money that made the early phase of my research possible. A Faculty Research and Creative Activities Award from Western Michigan University helped fund the later phases of my studies at Holetown and Mapps Cave. More recently, Guru Ghosh and Theresa Johansson at the Reves Center for International Studies at the College of William and Mary have been very helpful in the organization of my field programs. In addition, I wish to thank the dozens of field school students and teaching assistants who have worked so hard for me over the years, especially Christopher Crain, Brendan Weaver, Meredith Mahoney, Kathleen Mocklin, Kimberly Peck, Alex Menaker, Jessica Allred, Stephanie Bucker, Stephanie Crumbaugh, Leah Giles, Melissa Pocock, Sean Devlin, Bill Tucker, Nicole Lukaczyk, Sarah Muno, and Jennifer Yamazaki.

A number of other researchers have aided in the success of my Barbados program. Jerry Handler helped me identify a number of valuable sources for this book. Dan Mouer has also contributed to my focus in Barbados. In 1998 Dan and I collaborated on excavations at Mapps Cave, which led to the production of substantive articles and conference papers.

I would also like to thank Norman F. Barka and Kathleen Bragdon for their positive influence on my early academic career at the College of William and Mary. In addition, when I was an undergraduate at George Mason University, Barbara Little encouraged me to follow my heart and pursue my interests in historical archaeology. Mark Walker, Andy Edwards, Audrey Horning, and David Muraca have been inspirational and influential throughout my academic and professional career.

I also wish to thank Christina Kiddle and Meredith Mahoney for preparing and formatting numerous drawings for me over the years, as well as Kelly Ladd-Kostro and Marianne Martin from the Colonial Williamsburg Foundation for helping me locate a number of important images for this book. In addition, Mary Beaudry's insightful comments on earlier drafts of this manuscript helped me identify a number of key points about the contributions that historical archaeologists can make in explicating the role of alcohol in the American experience. Her observations greatly strengthened the focus of this book.

Most of all, I am indebted to my wife, Jane Wulf. In 1995 and 1996 Jane assisted in archaeological investigations in Barbados. In 1998 and 2000 she helped me search the Barbados Department of Archives for tax records, deeds, and other historical documents that would help improve our understanding of the archaeological discoveries we made. Above all, Jane has supported me throughout my academic career and encouraged me to pursue this project. This book would not have been possible without her assistance.

1

Introduction

Alcohol is the world's most widely used drug, and alcohol drinking is often a highly ritualized social event. Historical archaeology provides a unique opportunity to explore the production, distribution, and use of alcohol in the past. Although a number of archaeological studies have already addressed alcohol-related themes, archaeological investigations of alcohol are typically serendipitous by-products of fieldwork that had other emphases. In fact, despite the rich body of archaeological evidence for alcohol production, distribution, and use, archaeologists have generally overlooked the impact of alcohol on society. Moreover, few archaeologists have rigorously applied historical and anthropological theories to help them explain their alcohol-related discoveries, and an overview of archaeological approaches to alcohol has never been produced. This book explores the way in which historical archaeologists have investigated alcohol and drinking in different regional and temporal contexts and identifies alcohol-related themes that are most germane to historical archaeological study. Those themes provide the foundation for a case study of alcohol and drinking among enslaved peoples in Barbados. Drawing on historical archaeological evidence from Mapps Cave, a cavern and sinkhole complex in St. Philip Parish, the study seeks to understand how enslaved peoples in Barbados viewed alcohol and used it as a vehicle of escape from the challenges of life on sugar estates.

Alcohol studies is a general term for a broad range of research on the social, political, economic, and epidemiological impact of alcohol on society. While physicians and psychologists in the nineteenth and early twentieth centuries were quick to explore the impact of alcohol on society, the social sciences and humanities were slow to embrace alcohol studies. In part, the ambiguous nature of alcohol helped fuel their hesitancy. Societies have long viewed alcohol with uncertainty. Alcohol is an elixir of life and the cause of illness. It is a sacred fluid that opens the door to spiritual guidance and a profane substance that inhibits divine enlightenment. Alcohol enhances sociability, yet drinking also has the potential to disrupt otherwise stable social situations. In order to cope with these inherent contradictions, societies have created cautionary tales and instituted complex rules to govern drinking, which reflect the simultaneously feared and celebrated status of alcohol. For example, although the Prophet Muhammed described heaven as a place where wine flows freely, he stressed the importance of a rational mind and urged followers of Islam to refrain from drink. Positive notions about wine in Judeo-Christian thought are also tempered with warnings about excessive drinking and drunken vulnerability. Noah's drunken comportment after the great flood, for example, led to the divine curse of Ham, which the renowned scholar St. Clair Drake (1987–90, 2: 16–23; Genesis 9:20–25) argues was later used as a biblical rationale by Christian European slave traders and planters to help justify the enslavement of millions of Africans. And, despite the celebrated status of palm wine in Akan spirituality, Akan folktales warn of the dangers of drunkenness (Akyeampong 1996: 25–26). The study of alcohol therefore presents researchers with a series of complicated dichotomies, which appears to have produced an attitude of scholarly ambivalence.

Yet perhaps the greatest impediment to the rise of alcohol studies in academe has been the passionate rhetoric of temperance reformers. Since the mid-eighteenth century, reform-minded temperance advocates in Europe and North America polarized the meaning of alcohol and forced citizens to take a decisive stance on drinking. In Britain, in the 1730s, officials in Parliament sought to curb drunkenness through high taxes, strict licensing laws, and neighborhood informants (Warner and Ivis 1999). In Ireland, in the 1830s, Capuchin friar Theobald Mathew espoused temperance as a Catholic ideal and enrolled nearly 6 million followers in the Cork Total Abstinence Society (Bretherton 1997). In the late nineteenth century, socialists in Russia blamed the high levels of drunkenness in that country on worker alienation and urged their proletarian comrades to abstain from alcohol (Snow 1991). In Paris, in the nineteenth century, physicians and psychiatrists struggled to define the parameters of alcohol abuse in France (Prestwich 1997). Missionaries in Africa, Australia, the Caribbean, and the Pacific Islands condemned alcohol use, and colonial administrators passed legislation that sought to stamp out excessive drinking (Akyeampong 1996; Langton 1993; Marshall 1976; Marshall and Marshall 1975, 1979; Smith 2005: 168–93). Alcohol use among the indigenous peoples of North, South, and Central America was also a target of reformers and government officials (Mancall 1995; Mora de Tovar 1988; Taylor 1979).

Temperance reformers were most active in the United States. As early as the 1780s, doctors, including the eminent physician Benjamin Rush (1790), used medical knowledge and scientific inquiry to attack conventional beliefs about the salubriousness of drinking. Quakers, Methodists, and Baptists also began to encourage temperance among their congregants. These faiths gave birth to charismatic leaders who founded a number of reform-minded social organizations, including the Women's Christian Temperance Union, the Order of the Good Templars, and the Band of Hope (Blocker 1985; Bordin 1981; Epstein 1981; Murdock 1998; Pegram 1998; Tyrrell 1991). The abstemious middle class enthusiastically welcomed temperance and the Victorian notions of respectability it bestowed. The success of the temperance movement in the United States culminated in the passage of the 18th Amendment in 1919, which banned the sale of alcohol, except for medical, religious, and scientific purposes. The emotional discourse emanating from nineteenth- and twentieth-century temperance campaigns made the neutral and impartial study of alcohol nearly impossible and prompted many scholars simply to avoid alcohol studies (Barrows and Room 1991a: 3).

Modern social fears continue to shape the field of alcohol studies and compound the problem of scholarly ambivalence. College binge drinking, drunk driving, domestic violence, alcoholism, and other problems associated with alcohol overshadow the more dispassionate cultural and historical research. While the negative impact of alcohol on society is certainly a facet of alcohol studies, decades of research have challenged the one-sided view of antialcohol campaigns to show that drinking is more than simply a social ill or the basis for aberrant behavior. The alcohol business has helped revolutionize world trade and shape the course of global politics. Drinking patterns distinguish social boundaries, reinforce group identities, and circumscribe the parameters of masculinity and femininity. Alcohol use enhances sociability, defines periods of leisure, and provides a temporary avenue of escape from a variety of social pressures. Drinking reduces personal accountability; and, as a result, drunken comportment is often exempt from punishment.

Despite these obstacles, some cultural anthropologists were quick to discern the scholarly potential of alcohol studies and explore the complexities of drink. Donald Horton (1943) sought to explain the factors that influenced levels of alcohol use in different societies. Surveying the Human Relations Area Files (HRAF), Horton argued that high levels of drunkenness in a society corresponded with high levels of anxiety. He specifically addressed the *function* of excessive drinking among hunting and gathering groups. According to Horton, excessive drinking allowed hunters and gatherers periodically to release aggressive impulses brought about by the anxieties of an unstable food supply. Although researchers have challenged Horton's theory of anxiety in hunting and gathering societies, the basic premise of his model remains strong (Bacon et al. 1965; Barry 1976; Mc-Clelland et al. 1972). Horton essentially argued that an unpredictable existence leads to anxieties that are ameliorated by regular bouts of excessive drinking. Scholars have used Horton's anxiety model to explain excessive drinking in a number of historical and cross-cultural settings. For example, anthropologist James Schaefer (1976) used the HRAF to show that excessive drinking is common in societies in which spiritual belief systems consist of malicious deities and unpredictable ancestral spirits that cause arbitrary danger and commit random acts of violence.

The comparative model, as is evident in the work of Horton and Schaefer, has been pervasive in anthropological studies of alcohol. Mac Marshall (1979: 1) succinctly summed up the necessity of the comparative approach to alcohol: "The cross-cultural study of alcohol presents a classic natural experiment: A single species (*Homo sapiens*), a single drug substance (ethanol), and a great diversity of behavioral outcomes." Anthropologists soon began to look far beyond broad comparative cultural studies, however, to explore the nuanced differences in drinking patterns between social groups in larger pluralistic societies. In the United States, for example, researchers focused on identifying the forces that shaped the divergent drinking patterns of Irish and Jewish youth (for an overview, see Keller 1979). In India, anthropologist G. M. Carstairs (1979) compared attitudes toward alcohol use among different Hindu castes. And Carol Yawney (1979) compared the different drinking patterns of Afro- and Indo-Trinidadians.

Despite these early forays, some anthropologists remained skeptical about whether there was a substantive and legitimate scholarly interest in alcohol studies research. Dwight Heath (1976: 42) identified numerous instances in which anthropologists had addressed patterns of alcohol use but believed that "there can scarcely be said to exist any constituency of specialists or any subdiscipline of 'alcohol studies.'" According to Heath, ethnographic studies of alcohol production, distribution, and use were "unexpected by-products of broadly conceived research." Anthropological interest in alcohol continued to grow, however, and a decade later Heath (1987: 17) could happily claim that alcohol studies in anthropology were no longer just offshoots of other research designs. More recently, Michael Dietler (2006: 230) argued that, while "alcohol has remained a minority research field within anthropology, and anthropologists have never achieved more than a minority voice in the broader field of alcohol studies," anthropologists have made valuable contributions to our understanding of alcohol and drinking in society and played an important "subversive" role in challenging ethnocentric assumptions about drinking in other disciplines.

In the 1970s alcohol studies also became an important subfield within history departments. According to historians Susanna Barrows and Robin Room (1991a: 2–3), alcohol studies research coincided with the rise of social history and was closely tied to the social historians' interest in reconstructing "the lives and collective experiences of ordinary people." Some historians welcomed the thoughts of anthropologists, especially those of Horton. For example, William Rorabaugh (1979: 174) argued that excessive drinking in the early American Republic stemmed in part from the anxieties caused by the rapid pace of economic growth and the inability of Americans to live up to the Revolution's ideals of individualism and independence. Similarly, Emmanuel Akyeampong (1996: 2) attributed the excessive drinking of migrant wageworkers in the early-twentieth-century Gold Coast to the anxieties caused by a transitory lifestyle and hard labor. Peter Mancall (1995: 82–84), who explored the links between anxiety and alcohol use in Native North American societies in the early colonial period, also recognized the value of Horton's work for explaining drunken comportment among some eastern Indian tribes.

Explaining the impact of alcohol in different societies provides fertile ground for interdisciplinary research. The holistic type of inquiry that the study of alcohol in society demands has led to scholarly publications that often blur the lines between anthropology and history. Several edited volumes on alcohol and drinking highlight the breadth of alcohol studies research and the need for collaboration with colleagues in cultural, historical, psychological, sociological, economic, literary, and health fields (Babor 1986; Barrows and Room 1991b; Blocker and Warsh 1997; de Garine and de Garine 2001; Douglas 1987b; Everett et al. 1976; Ewing and Rouse 1978; Gefou-Madianou 1992; Goodman et al. 1995; Holt 2006; Jankowiak and Bradburd 2003; Marshall 1979; McClelland et al. 1972; McDonald 1994; Smyth 2004; Tracy and Acker 2004). Alcohol studies have been strengthened by the exchange of ideas among members of the Alcohol and Drug History Society (ADHS) through its journal, *Social History of Alcohol and Drugs*, and electronic listserv. The ADHS is an international group of scholars who represent a broad range of academic disciplines. Moreover, an increasing number of anthropology and history departments now offer alcohol-related courses, which suggests that alcohol studies research has become a more widely recognized subfield that will continue to grow in the future.

How has historical archaeology contributed to our understanding of alcohol and drinking in the modern era? James F. Deetz (1977: 5) defined historical archaeology in his typically eloquent prose as "the archaeology of the spread of European culture throughout the world since the fifteenth century and its impact on indigenous peoples." More recently, Charles E. Orser Jr. (1996: 26), focusing on the key processes that have shaped life over the past 500 years, embraced a pithier definition for historical archaeology and called it simply the archaeology of the "modern world." Alcohol provides a prism through which to view life over the past five centuries. Indeed, some of the most profound changes in the alcohol business and in alcohol drinking have occurred in the past 500 years, and a survey of historical archaeological studies reveals that historical archaeologists are uniquely positioned to explore alcohol-related themes and the modern processes that have dictated patterns of alcohol production, distribution, and use. The rise of wine making in new areas of the world, the commercial expansion of alcohol distilling, the beginning of the long-distance overseas alcohol trades, advances in medical science, and the emergence of temperance-reform movements are just a few of the major forces that have shaped alcohol and drinking in the modern era. These alcohol-related changes were driven by broader social, political, and economic processes that fall within the purview of historical archaeological interest. The focus on alcohol and drinking in this book is meant to expand the avenues of historical archaeological inquiry and, at the same time, provide a new disciplinary tool for alcohol studies researchers. Drawing on models developed in cultural anthropology and history, it seeks to provide coherency for historical archaeologists confronted with questions of alcohol. Each chapter addresses key themes in the historical archaeology of alcohol and drinking. The book concludes with a case study of alcohol production and drinking among enslaved peoples at Mapps Cave in Barbados, which serves as a model for historical archaeologists who may wish to explore and develop alcohol-related themes in their own research.

2

Alcohol-Related Material Culture

The production, distribution, and consumption of alcoholic beverages has given birth to a wide array and distinct assortment of material culture that archaeologists have used to interpret and date archaeological deposits. As early as the 1890s, classical Old World archaeologists developed seriational techniques for ceramic wine amphorae to help them date archaeological deposits associated with the great civilizations of the Mediterranean (Dressel 1899). For historical archaeologists, identifying the material culture of alcohol is often self-evident, due to the long-standing and current use of glass bottles, crystal wine glasses, and ceramic drinking mugs. Probate inventories, period paintings, museum collections, and architectural drawing have also helped historical archaeologists identify the more unusual objects used for the production, distribution, and consumption of alcohol. This chapter discusses alcohol-related material culture and examines the methodological contributions that they have made to historical archaeological research, especially in terms of dating archaeological deposits and interpreting site function.

In the age of European exploration and settlement of the New World, Iberian storage jars were one of the primary means of storing and transporting alcoholic beverages across the Atlantic. Although popularly referred to as Spanish olive jars, they were in fact used to store and transport a variety of liquid and solid goods. Archaeologists have applied the terms *tinajas*, *peruleras*, and *botijas* to these vessels, though archaeologists at the British colonial settlement site of Jamestown, Virginia, have adopted the more generic *botijas peruleras* (jars of the New World), based on Spanish colonial records (Avery 1997; Deagan 1987: 30–35; Goggin 1960: 8–11; Kelso et al. 1999: 36; Marken 1994: 117; Rice 1997). These large, egg-shaped utilitarian vessels have short constricted necks and were the successor of the amphorae used by classical civilizations. Some of the larger Iberian storage jars had a capacity of more than five gallons. They were produced in Spain and Portugal and are ubiquitous on Spanish colonial sites in the New World, especially on sites from the sixteenth to eighteenth centuries. They are also

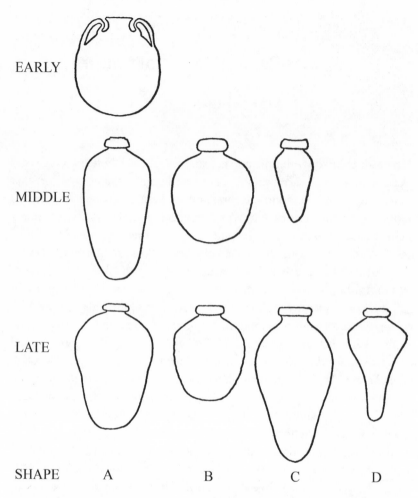

Figure 2–1. "Comparative vessel shapes of early, middle, and late style Olive Jars." From John Goggin, *The Spanish Olive Jar: An Introductory Study,* (New Haven: Yale University Press, 1960), 28. Courtesy of the Yale University, Department of Anthropology, New Haven, Connecticut.

quite common on early British colonial sites in the Americas (Kelso et al. 1999: 36–42; Smith 2004a: 54–55). Although they were used for holding a variety of liquids and solids, wine was one of the principal commodities stored and transported in these vessels.

Due to the painstaking work of a handful of archaeologists, Iberian storage jars have become excellent chronological markers (Avery 1997; Carruthers 2003; Deagan 1972, 1987; Fairbanks 1973; Goggin 1960; James

Figure 2–2. Type-B Spanish "olive jar" ca. 1630, from the British settlement site of Holetown, Barbados. Photo: author's collection.

1988; Lister and Lister 1976, 1987; Marken 1994). John Goggin (1960), for example, conducted some of the earliest and most comprehensive studies of these vessels found on New World archaeological sites. He analyzed the size, shape, wall thickness, and other morphological attributes of the jars to construct an elaborate typology that has served as the foundation for the functional and seriational analysis of these vessels. More recent studies have sought to refine Goggin's work. Analyzing a large sample of Iberian storage jars recovered from Spanish shipwrecks off the coast of Santo Domingo in the Dominican Republic, Stephen James (1988) argued that glazed varieties of these jars were more likely to have been used for wine storage and transport because the glaze would have reduced the chances of leakage and evaporation (see also Deagan 1972: 35, 1985). Although James was unable to find any direct correlation between the size and shape of these storage jars and their contents, Mitchell Marken (1994: 117), on the basis of shipping inventories and archaeological examples, suggested that the elongated Type A jars were primarily used for wine transport and storage (see also Lister and Lister 1987: 131–33). More recent analysis by George Avery (1997) has documented the emergence of centrally organized workshops for the production of wine-transport vessels and revealed a strong relationship between the size and type of Iberian storage jars and their alcoholic contents.

Prudence Rice and Sara Van Beck (1993) studied the kiln technology and local production of ceramic storage jars known as *tinajas* and *botijas*, which were utilitarian vessels used on *bodegas* in the Moquegua Valley in Peru during the early colonial era. *Tinajas* were very large earthenware jars, in some cases more than a meter in diameter, used for the fermentation of grape wine produced at the *bodegas*. Some had a capacity of 375 gallons. *Botijas*, in contrast, were small storage vessels that usually held only a few gallons and were similar in size and shape to the imported Iberian storage jars. Unlike the large fermentation jars, *botijas* were used for holding the finished alcoholic products, wine and brandy (Rice 1997). According to Rice and Van Beck, the local production of *tinajas* and *botijas* reflected the transfer of Iberian ceramic traditions of wine making and transport to the Spanish colonies in the Americas. Occasionally, seals embossed with the date of manufacture were applied to the bodies of these vessels, which have helped researchers track the morphological changes in these jars over time. In the mid-eighteenth century, the production of *botijas* declined in the Moquegua Valley, as goatskin bags (*odres*), coated on the interior with tar, began to replace the large and cumbersome earthenware jars for wine storage and transport. Perhaps the rugged terrain of the Moquegua Valley made lighter and flexible goatskin bags more appropriate for wine transport than the heavy and breakable *botijas* (deFrance 1996: 25; Rice 1997: 463). In Cuenca, Ecuador, Ross Jamieson (2000: 184–85) also distinguished the functional uses of *botijas* and *tinajas*. As at the Moquegua *bodegas*, Jamieson found that *tinajas* were more likely to hold molasses, the fermentable waste product of sugar making, while *botijas* were used to store the finished product, rum. In addition, Jamieson believed that Andean women typically used the small *botijas*, rather than *tinajas*, to brew *chicha* beer, perhaps reflecting the household scale of *chicha* brewing.

The Spanish and Spanish colonists were not the only ones to use and produce ceramic vessels for alcohol storage and transport. In the sixteenth to eighteenth centuries, German potters, especially in the towns of Frechen and Cologne, produced stoneware bottles for the storage and transport of alcohol as well as jugs and tankards for individual alcohol consumption. The iron-oxide slip used to coat these vessels before firing gave these bulbous vessels a distinctive pitted texture and mottled brown color. For years these storage bottles have misleadingly been called Bellarmines because of the supposed association between the characteristic bearded facial motif applied to the neck of these vessels and the Tuscan-born Jesuit Cardinal Roberto Bellermino. David Gaimster (1997a), in his exhaustive study of the German stoneware industry from 1200 to 1900, prefers the term "Bartmann bottle," after the German *Bartmannkrug*. Gaimster (1997a: 209) believes the facial motif (*Bartmaske*) "originated from the popular tradition of the Wild Man, a mythic creature who features prominently in northern European folklore." These bottles had a capacity ranging from one pint to five gallons and were used for the storage and transport of a variety of commodities. Archaeological examples of sealed Bartmann bottles recovered from seventeenth-century shipwreck sites have been found to contain mercury and perhaps animal fats and cooking oils (Gaimster 1997b: 125; Kleij 1997: 188–89; Vlierman 1997: 163–65). The widespread presence of Bartmann bottles illustrated in English and Dutch tavern scenes from the sixteenth and seventeenth centuries, however, indicates that these vessels were frequently used to hold wine and spirits. Moreover, court records and merchant accounts reveal that wine traders, such as Pieter van den Ancker, an Anglo-Dutch merchant in London in the mid-seventeenth century, purchased large numbers of Bartmann bottles from Frechen presumably for the storage, transport, and sale of his wine (Haselgrove and Van Loo 1998). Bartmann bottles are found especially on early British, French, and Dutch colonial sites throughout the Americas. In the early years of Atlantic trade, Dutch shippers, who had direct access to German goods as well as wine and brandy from southern Europe, were largely responsible for transporting these vessels to the New World (Boiten and van Vuuren 1982: 246–47; Wilcoxen 1987: 75–76).

As with Iberian storage jars, the morphology of Bartmann bottles changed over time, giving archaeologists another tool for dating archaeological deposits. Gaimster's (1997a) analysis of Bartmann bottles provides archaeologists with a clear and detailed understanding of the form and function of these vessels. Early Bartmann bottles from the sixteenth and early seventeenth centuries were round and squat with elaborately designed *Bartmasken*. Sprig-molded rosette medallions and the coat-of-arms of the city of manufacture or the city where these vessels were to be marketed

Figure 2–3. Bartmann bottle from the British settlement site of Jamestown, Virginia. Courtesy of the APVA Preservation Virginia.

were occasionally applied to the body. Gaimster (1997a: 209) viewed these applied motifs as an early art form but noted that they also served as a medium for the expression of political thought. German potters also produced Bartmann bottles with applied personalized medallions for merchants, and, for example, Bartmann bottles bearing the seal of wine trader Pieter van den Ancker have turned up at seventeenth-century archaeological sites in Ireland, Virginia, and elsewhere in the British Atlantic World (Haselgrove and Van Loo 1998: 58–59). By the mid-seventeenth century, Bartmann bottles had become more pear-shaped. The molded faces with long flowing beards had also given way to stylized faces with crude linear beards. In addition, the rosettes and coats-of-arm had become simplified, and some medallions were merely apocryphal symbols (Noël Hume 1969a: 57). Many of the applied medallions on Bartmann bottles were embossed

Figure 2–4. Bartmann bottle with applied medallion bearing the date 1661 from a mid-seventeenth-century domestic site in Bridgetown, Barbados. Photo: author's collection.

with the year of manufacture, which increases their chronological utility for archaeologists. Gaimster's (1997b) study of the lifespan of Bartmann bottles (the lag time between the production of these vessels and their deposition in the archaeological record), however, raises questions about their usefulness as a seriational tool. According to Gaimster, many of these vessels remained in use for decades before being lost, broken, or discarded.

While German potters were leaders in the early stoneware industry, the English began producing their own variety of stoneware bottles in Fulham in the late seventeenth century. The English stoneware bottles, especially those produced at John Dwight's Fulham pottery, were similar in size, shape, and color to the Bartmann bottles made in Frechen and Cologne. Early Fulham potters imitated their German counterparts and applied decorative *Bartmasken* and elaborate medallions to their bottles, but that practice had largely ceased by the end of the seventeenth century. English

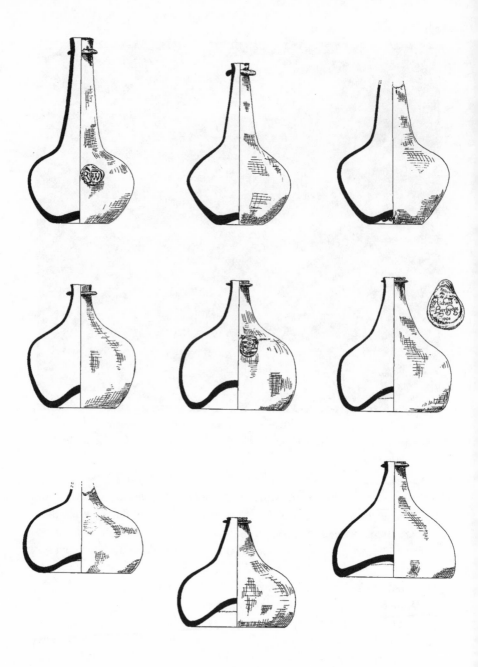

Figure 2–5. Illustrated hand-blown glass bottles from Ivor Noël Hume, "The Glass Wine Bottle in Colonial Virginia," *Journal of Glass Studies* (1961). Courtesy of Ivor Noël Hume.

stoneware bottles found on late-seventeenth- and eighteenth-century sites, therefore, are generally plain vessels that lack any elaborate applied motifs (Green 1999: 109–24). The rise of the English stoneware industry in the late seventeenth century also helped launch the widescale production and use of English brown-stoneware jugs and drinking mugs, including those with sprig-molded hunting scenes (Hildyard 1985; Noël Hume 1969a: 112; Paddock 1992)

In the sixteenth and seventeenth centuries, hand-blown glass bottles began to surpass ceramic vessels as the primary means of alcohol storage and transport. While the color of these bottles usually ranges from a light green to a very dark olive, glass specialists typically refer to them as black glass bottles. The art of glass blowing emerged in the Roman Empire in the first century BC, and classical archaeologists have recovered evidence of hand-blown glass bottles from ancient sites in and around the Mediterranean that were probably once used to hold wine (Tatton-Brown 1991; Whitehouse 1997). The commercial expansion of glass industries in England in the mid-seventeenth century was no doubt spurred by the increasing demand for alcohol in the British New World colonies. Archaeological investigations at seventeenth- and eighteenth-century glasshouses, such as those excavated by Denis Ashurst in Yorkshire, England, have helped shed new light on the architectural design of glasshouses, the materials used in glassblowing, and the wide variety of bottle forms produced at glasshouse sites (Ashurst 1970, 1987). The enormous output of English glass industries in the seventeenth and eighteenth centuries has helped make fragments of hand-blown black glass bottles one of the most ubiquitous artifacts found on postcontact period archaeological sites, especially in the British colonial world. Yet, while the English were major producers and suppliers of hand-blown glass bottles in the sixteenth to nineteenth centuries, they are frequently found on non-British colonial sites (Deagan 1987: 130–36).

By correlating the shape of hand-blown glass bottles with known dates from stamped bottle seals that were occasionally applied to the bodies of these vessels, Ivor Noël Hume (1961, 1969a: 60–71) developed an elaborate and complex chronological sequence for English hand-blown black glass bottles that has greatly helped historical archaeologists date archaeological deposits from the mid-seventeenth through the early nineteenth centuries. Detailed analyses of bottle rim and neck changes, as well as subsequent morphological studies by antique bottle collectors, have helped expand and refine Noël Hume's sequence (Dumbrell 1983; Jones 1971, 1986; Noël Hume 1974; Pittman 1990). The most obvious change is that early hand-blown glass bottles were globular but gradually became more straight-sided over the course of the seventeenth and eighteenth centuries. According to William Pittman (1990), English hand-blown black glass bottles became less globular and more straight-sided over the course of the seventeenth and eighteenth centuries to accommodate the increasingly common practice of binning (storing bottles on their side to keep the base of the cork soft and moist). Binning reduced the likelihood of evaporation and therefore helped promote long-term wine storage, which was growing in popularity among the British and British colonial elite. While dated bottle seals on hand-blown glass bottles have helped archaeologists track the temporal changes to these vessels, personal bottle seals, bearing surnames or initials, have occasionally enhanced our understanding of the temporal and functional attributes of archaeological sites. In particular, when coupled with documentary evidence such as land titles and wills, the personal bottle seals have from time to time helped archaeologists identify the owners of particular properties in the past and thus allowed them to date more precisely archaeological deposits recovered from those sites (Hudson 1961; Kelso 1984: 168–69).

To a lesser degree, the Dutch and French also produced hand-blown glass bottles. In 1989 Parks Canada published one of the most comprehensive studies on hand-blown glass bottles, including information about non-English varieties (Jones and Sullivan 1989; see also Brown 1971). In addition, Olive Jones (1971) examined the morphology and evolution of pontil marks and push-ups, which provided an additional means to identify and date hand-blown glass bottles, including those produced in France. Many of the imported French glass bottles from the eighteenth century are represented at French colonial sites, such as Fortress Louisbourg in Nova Scotia (Harris 1979). Yet not all hand-blown glass bottles were imported from Europe. Colonists in New Spain probably produced hand-blown glass bottles in the sixteenth century and may have even exported them to other areas of the Spanish colonial world (Deagan 1987: 129). In North America, a seventeenth-century glasshouse at Jamestown, Virginia, may have also produced hand-blown glass bottles for early Chesapeake colonists (Harrington 1972: 31–36).

Dating techniques have also been developed for late nineteenth- and twentieth-century mold-made and machine-made glass beer and liquor bottles. In short, the molds and the industrial machines used to make glass bottles changed over the course of the nineteenth and twentieth centuries, and each change in bottle-making technology left its distinguishing marks

Figure 2–6. Examples of stamped bottle seals from hand-blown glass bottles. Courtesy of the Colonial Williamsburg Foundation, Department of Archaeological Research.

on glass bottles (Fontana 1968; Hull-Walski and Walski 1994; Jones 1986; Lorrain 1968; Miller and Sullivan 1984; Olsen 1965; Schulz et al. 1980; Switzer 1974; Walker 1996). In addition to glass bottles, archaeologists have also investigated the design and seriational contributions of tin beer cans (Busch 1981; Maxwell 1993; Shanks and Tilley 1994: 172–240).

What can historical archaeological methods tell us about the original contents of alcohol-related vessels? Chemical analysis of vessel residues has helped archaeologists identify the alcoholic content of containers at ancient sites in the Old World. For example, infrared spectroscopy of residue deposits recovered from pre–Bronze Age ceramic jars from the Near East revealed high levels of tartaric acid, a principal residue of grape wine (Badler et al. 1990). Such elaborate methods are not always necessary for the historic period, as alcohol itself is occasionally recovered. For example, in 2000 underwater archaeologists with the Netherlands Institute for Ship and Underwater Archaeology recovered wine from a glass bottle found on a Dutch warship that had wrecked in the Wadden Sea off the coast of Holland in the early seventeenth century. The wine may originally have come from Portugal or Spain, and laboratory testing showed that the alcohol content was 10.6%, similar in strength to modern wines (Harrington 2000). In the 1970s and 1980s Donald Hamilton and Robyn Woodward (1984: 45) recovered sealed glass bottles from underwater sites in Port Royal, Jamaica, which may have still possessed remnants of their original alcoholic content (see also Link 1960). And wine has been recovered from sealed Iberian storage jars from Spanish shipwrecks off Bermuda (Marken 1994: 117).

Historical archaeologists have speculated about the original contents of hand-blown black or green glass bottles. For example, Noël Hume (1974) suggested that darker-hued glass bottles were used to hold beer and ale while glass bottles of a lighter hue were used to hold wine. However, it is probably impossible to determine the original contents of individual glass bottles. Many were simply shipped empty and filled with various liquids upon arrival in the colonies (Adams 2003: 58; Otto 1984: 115; Pittman 1990). Similarly, until the first half of the sixteenth century, Iberian storage jars were often shipped empty and filled once they arrived in the Americas with wine, which was transported in separate wooden casks (Lister and Lister 1987: 135). Using newspaper advertisements from the eighteenth and nineteenth centuries, Jones (1993) studied the history of different storage containers, including wooden casks, earthenware jars, and glass bottles, and found that such vessels were typically used to hold both alcoholic and non-alcoholic contents. Moreover, once in the market, glass bottles and other storage containers were reused and recycled for a variety of alcoholic and nonalcoholic purposes. For example, William Kelso (1984: 157) recovered several hand-blown black glass bottles from an eighteenth-century well at the Bray's Littletown site in Virginia. One of the bottles was corked and still contained remnants of its last contents, milk.

Although glass bottles can be good chronological markers, the reuse of bottles for many years can make archaeological sites appear older than they really are. James Deetz (1993: 61), for example, recovered hand-blown glass bottles from late-seventeenth- and early-eighteenth-century sites at Flowerdew Hundred, Virginia, which possessed seals from the London taverns for which they had originally been produced. The presence of glass bottles with London tavern seals on British colonial sites in Virginia suggests that they were reused for long periods of time before entering the archaeological record, thus undermining their value as chronological markers. William Adams (2003: 59) stated simply: "Wine bottles clearly have some serious problems when it comes to using them to date an archaeological assemblage." In regard to black glass bottles from the early nineteenth century, Adams wrote:

> These bottles had been filled in Europe and consumed abroad. They came [to the Americas] not only as intentional cargo but also as ballast from China, Africa, Europe, and every major port in the world. The empties would be collected and placed on ships as ballast. At the next port, they might be washed, refilled, cellared awhile, and then emptied again. The process could be repeated for decades before the bottle was broken.
>
> (Adams 2003: 58)

Jane Busch (1987: 68) investigated eighteenth- and nineteenth-century bottle recycling practices and also concluded that "bottles could be kept for decades before they were discarded." Busch argued, however, that the number of nicks and scratches on a glass bottle might give some indication as to its lifespan.

As with hand-blown glass bottles, mold-made and machine-made glass bottles of the mid-nineteenth and twentieth centuries were also reused and recycled. Sarah H. Hill (1982), analyzing nineteenth- and twentieth-century samples from the Edgewood Dump in Atlanta, Georgia, and from various sites in Silcott, Washington, found that the lag time from manufacture to deposition in the archaeological record for glass bottles generally ranged from six to sixteen years, depending on the type and function of the bottle. Hill attempted to understand the particular processes that affect the lifespan of glass bottles, such as cost, in order to refine methods for using glass bottles to date archaeological deposits (see also Adams 2003: 58–59; Fontana 1968: 53; Jones 1993: 33). Certainly, the rise of a sophisticated secondhand bottle business in the nineteenth and twentieth centuries has complicated historical archaeologists' efforts to use these vessels to date archaeological deposits accurately (Crane 2000; De Cunzo 1995; Hull-Walski and Walski 1994; Walker 1996). Yet, despite the time-lag problems associated with reuse, glass bottles are generally good chronological markers for dating archaeological deposits because they often had a shorter lifespan than other diagnostic artifacts, such as ceramics, and because they are usually abundant on historical archaeological sites.

Archaeologists have also scrutinized the methodological potential of ceramic drinking vessels. For example, Anne Yentsch (1990: 41) argued that the use of leather drinking vessels in the seventeenth-century Chesapeake reflected continuity with English folk traditions (see also Beaudry et al. 1983: 25). In the late seventeenth century, however, ceramic drinking vessels began to replace those made of leather. According to Yentsch, the adoption of ceramic drinking vessels revealed a mid-seventeenth-century shift toward fashionable foodways practiced by elites in Europe. In particular, Yentsch (1990: 42) argued that tin-glazed earthenware drinking vessels became popular in the seventeenth century and were an economical way for lower classes to emulate the wealthy, who typically drank from pewter and silver drinking mugs. Multihandled posset and syllabub drinking pots were also popular, and they highlight the communal nature of alcohol consumption in the seventeenth-century Chesapeake. In a creative linguistic study of seventeenth- and eighteenth-century probate inventories from the Chesapeake, Mary C. Beaudry (1981) showed that Chesapeake colonists clearly understood the alcoholic function of cups and pots and therefore did not feel the need to assign modifiers (such as wine-cup or beer-pot) to express their alcoholic purpose.

Glass drinking vessels have also been the subject of historical archaeological inquiry. Noël Hume (1968) studied glassware, especially stemmed wine glasses, from archaeological assemblages recovered at several different sites in Port Royal, Jamaica. He established a sequential chronology for stemware drinking glasses and used this information to show that Port Royal, although partially submerged by an earthquake in 1693, remained an active port town well into the eighteenth century. In addition, the stemware chronology supported Noël Hume's contention that many of the ar-

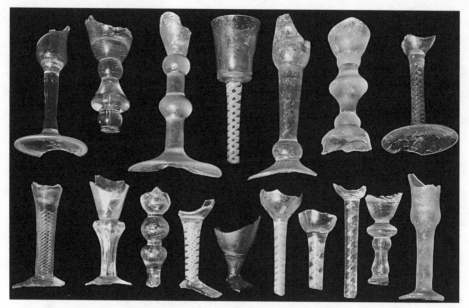

Figure 2–7. Examples of colonial stemware from Virginia. Courtesy of the Colonial Williamsburg Foundation, Department of Archaeological Research.

chaeological deposits from the pre-earthquake period were not submerged underwater. Olive Jones and E. Ann Smith (1985: 35–57) also rigorously investigated the extensive variety of British lead-glass tumblers and stemware from British military sites in North America in the eighteenth and early nineteenth centuries. As with attempts to distinguish the specific alcoholic content of black glass bottles, Jones and Smith sought to discern whether different glass drinking vessels were meant for specific alcoholic beverages. Despite painstaking documentary research, they were unable to identify any direct relationship between the type of drinking glass and its particular alcoholic purpose. Noël Hume (1968), however, felt more confident about his ability to link specific glassware to specific alcoholic beverages. The study of English drinking glasses from museum collections has no doubt complemented our understanding of the chronological and functional attributes of these vessels (Bickerton 1984; Haynes 1959). Some seventeenth-century glass drinking vessels found in museum collections show signs of repair suggesting the resourcefulness of the original users and perhaps the personal attachment people had toward particular drinking vessels (Willmott 2001). Jones and Smith also shed new light on the variety of lead-glass decanters and punchbowls used on British military sites. Barrel-shaped glass tumblers, air-twist and enamel-twist stemware, and engraved glass decanters from eighteenth-century domestic dwellings and taverns in Colonial Williamsburg have been the subject of extensive archaeological inquiry (Noël Hume 1969b). More recently, Kelly J. Dixon (2005: 99–111) meticulously cataloged the vast range of glass drinking vessels available to saloon-goers in Virginia City, Nevada in the nineteenth century.

Wooden casks and barrels represent another facet of the material culture of alcohol. Lester Ross (1985) examined Spanish Basque coopering techniques, drawing on an estimated sixty-two to eighty-five staved wooden casks recovered from a sixteenth-century shipwreck at the Red Bay site in Labrador. Although the wooden casks were used for storing and transporting whale oil, his study outlined early cask-making practices that are relevant for understanding the production of staved containers for alcohol storage and transport. Historical archaeologists have recovered other examples of staved wooden containers. In 1686 the *Belle*, the ship of French explorer René Robert Cavelier, Sieur de La Salle, wrecked in the Gulf of Mexico off the coast of what is today Galveston, Texas. Documentary sources indicated that six wine casks had been loaded on the *Belle* before it embarked on its final voyage. Archaeologists recovered four wooden casks from the shipwreck, which may have been used to hold wine (Arnold 1996: 80–83). Iron barrel hoops, indicating the presence of staved containers for alcohol storage, have also been recovered from eighteenth-century sites in Williamsburg, Virginia, and from the wine cellars of Vergelegen, a late-eighteenth- and early-nineteenth-century estate in South Africa (Markell et al. 1995: 26; Noël Hume 1969a). Even when wooden barrels and iron barrel hoops are absent, other artifacts indicate the presence of staved containers. For example, archaeologists in Colonial Williamsburg recovered wine cocks and spigots made of copper alloy from Wetherburn's Tavern and Charleton's Coffeehouse, two eighteenth-century drinking establishments (Levy et al. 2007; Noël Hume 1969a). Cocks, spigots, and faucets used to tap alcohol-filled wooden casks have also been recovered from a nineteenth-century fur-trading post in Wisconsin, a sixteenth-century English shipwreck, and mining-town saloons in Alaska and the western United States (Bowers and Gannon 1998; Dixon 2005: 77; Ewen 1986; Redknap and Besly 1997: 198).

The material culture of alcohol was sometimes recycled in practical or nonalcoholic ways that have the potential to complicate discussions about site function. For example, archaeologists working on Spanish colonial sites

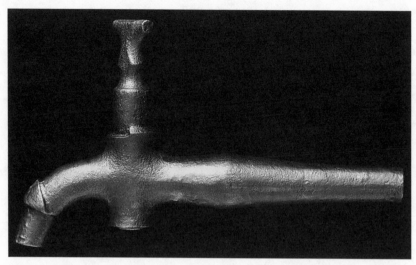

Figure 2–8. Copper-alloy spigot from Wetherburn's Tavern, Williamsburg, Virginia. Courtesy of the Colonial Williamsburg Foundation, Department of Archaeological Research.

in the Americas have found that *pipas* (wooden casks) used to store and transport wine were commonly employed in well construction (Deagan 1985: 15; South et al. 1988: 191–99). Ceramic Iberian storage jars were also sometimes used as architectural elements in the Spanish Americas, especially to fill in arched cellars (Lister and Lister 1981; McEwan 1992: 104). Moreover, they were used in food storage and preparation activities. Julia King (1984), for example, examined Iberian storage jar fragments from three seventeenth-century Spanish colonial sites in St. Augustine, Florida. King found that the use of aboriginal ceramics for cooking and storage became increasingly common in the seventeenth century, while the use of Iberian storage jars for cooking and storage decreased. She attributed the increase in aboriginal ceramic use in part to the inability of St. Augustine residents to afford imported wine. As a result, aboriginal wares replaced Iberian storage jars when access to wine, and the Iberian storage jars that carried wine, declined (King 1984: 79; see also Deagan 1983: chapter 11). The practical uses of plants themselves also have the potential to complicate discussions about alcohol. In Buenos Aires, Argentina, for example, grape-vines (*Vitis vinifera*) were used around homes and patios for shade; thus, ethnobotanical remains of grape seeds may indicate evidence of shade and covering rather than evidence of wine making (Schávelzon 2000: 150).

Glass bottles were also recycled to serve nonalcoholic purposes. Aileen Agnew (1995: 70) discovered seventy hand-blown glass bottles adjacent to a late-eighteenth- and early-nineteenth-century domestic site in Portsmouth, New Hampshire. She argued that the bottles reflected not high levels of alcohol use by the residents but rather the purposeful deposit of bottles to aid drainage around the property. Adams (2002) found that alcohol bottles have been reused and recycled to construct paths and mark planting beds in parts of Melanesia and Micronesia. Similarly, researchers working at the Peyton-Randolph House in Colonial Williamsburg and Bacon's Castle in Surry, Virginia, found that residents reused glass bottle fragments to pave asparagus planting beds (Edwards 2001; Edwards et al. 1988; Luccketti 1990).

Historical archaeologists have identified the production of tools from bottle glass on a number of native and contact-period sites. For example, projectile points, scrapers, and cutting tools made from bottle glass have been found at Powhatan contact-period sites at Jamestown (Cotter 1958; McCary 1962), late-eighteenth-century Qikertarmiut Eskimo sites in Rus-

Figure 2–9. Bottle-lined planting beds at Peyton-Randolph House, Williamsburg, Virginia. Courtesy of the Colonial Williamsburg Foundation, Department of Archaeological Research.

sian-controlled areas of Alaska (Crowell 1997: 182), Spanish-Indian mission sites in Florida and the Orinoco Delta region of South America (Scaramelli and Tarble 2003: 169; Smith and Gottlob 1978: 14), contact-period Aborigine sites in Australia and Tasmania (Allen 1973; Williamson 2004: 83–87), and early-nineteenth-century Koasati Indian sites in Texas (Perttula 1994: 70). It was not just bottle glass, however, that was recycled to serve traditional indigenous subsistence purposes. The indigenous peoples of Argentina, for example, were known to fashion spear points from iron barrel hoops and straps that were once used to secure Spanish wine casks (Virginia Pineau, personal communication, November 2007).

Enslaved Africans and Afro-Creoles in the Americas also recycled and knapped bottle glass fragments. According to Laurie Wilkie (2003), the recovery of retouched bottle glass from the nineteenth-century Lucretia Perryman site in Mobile, Alabama, indicated evidence of traditional female healing practices that were handed down from mother to daughter. Theresa Singleton (2006: 281) found scrapers made of bottle glass at the El Padre slave village in Cuba that may have once been used for splitting straw, palm, or cane for basketry. And enslaved peoples at Oakley Plantation in Louisiana may have also retouched bottle glass fragments to use as shavers in lieu of razor blades (Wilkie 1996). Using ethnoarchaeological evidence from peasant villages in Greece, Curt Runnels (1975, 1976) distinguished between knapped tools made from bottle glass and what he called "opportunistic implements." Based on his criteria, not all of the retouched bottle glass implements that historical archaeologists have recovered fit cleanly into his understanding of "tools."

Bottles also served spiritual purposes unrelated to alcohol use. For example, at Juan de Bolas Plantation in Jamaica, Matthew Reeves (1996) recovered two partially intact black glass bottles standing upright adjacent to a former slave dwelling. Reeves interpreted these bottles as "obeah bottles" and believed that they functioned as spiritual objects associated with that religious belief system. Similarly, Patricia Samford (1996: 107–9) argued that the presence of bottles at slave and postemancipation African American dwelling sites in the U.S. South sometimes represent spiritually charged vessels, or conjurer bottles, associated with the ongoing practice of Bakongo religious beliefs (see also Wilkie 1997: 88–89). Bottle trees (trees decorated with hanging glass bottles) were also common around the dwellings of enslaved peoples and served both spiritual and aesthetic functions (Thompson 1984: 144–45). Thus, bottle glass found in the assemblages of enslaved peoples may occasionally reflect spiritual and aesthetic rather than alcoholic uses (see also Heath and Bennett 2000: 43; Mouer and Smith 2001).

However, the ritualistic use of bottles was not limited to the sites of enslaved peoples. Archaeologists have recovered "witch-bottles" from a number of early modern domestic sites in Britain. Glass and stoneware vessels often served as witch bottles and were buried beneath the hearths of houses to ward off witches and to counter the ill consequences of evil spells (Gaimster 1997a: 139–40; Merrifield 1955, 1987). One such example described by Matthew Johnson (1996: 161–62) was a Bartmann bottle that contained pins, fingernail clippings, and traces of urine. According to Gaimster (1997a: 140), the malevolent facial expression of the *Bartmaske* may have made Bartmann bottles suitable vessels for such magical purposes. Similarly, archaeologists in Reigate, a town just outside of London, recovered a seventeenth-century hand-blown glass bottle that probably also served as a witch bottle. The bottle contained traces of urine and nine tiny brass pins, each bent into an L-shape (Harrington 2000). In the New World, archaeologists have recovered witch bottles from eighteenth-century domestic sites in Virginia and Pennsylvania associated with the spiritual beliefs and magical practices of Anglo-Americans who lived at the sites (Becker 1978, 1980; Painter 1980).

Historical archaeologists have creatively used the material culture of alcohol production, distribution, and consumption to help them date and interpret archaeological deposits. While the morphological changes to alcohol-related materials have provided archaeologists with fundamental methodological tools, we know much less about the social, political, and economic forces that fueled those modifications. For example, how did the expansion of alcohol industries, especially distilled spirits industries, in the seventeenth and eighteenth centuries stimulate the industrial expansion of English glass industries, German stoneware industries, and Spanish coopering industries? Moreover, while binning may explain the shift from round to straight-sided hand-blown glass bottles, it does not explain why binning became an increasingly popular practice in the eighteenth century. Perhaps the escalating levels of alcohol production and the growing sophistication of alcohol consumers in the seventeenth and eighteenth centuries stimulated an increasing desire for aged (binned) alcoholic beverages. Moreover, drinking binned wines and spirits, as well as having the cellars and racks available to bin wine and spirits, may have been merely another way for elites to distinguish themselves from poorer classes.

Perhaps the tall, straight-sided bottles with narrow bases were simply more appropriate for long-distance transport, because they required less surface space per volume of alcohol than did short, globular bottles with wide bases. If that is the case, then the shift from globular to straight-sided bottles may purely reflect the merchants' desire to reduce shipping costs by filling the horse carts headed for rural districts or the hulls of ships headed across the Atlantic with narrow bottles that were easier to pack and used less surface space. Perhaps the increasing use of concentrated high-alcohol-content distilled spirits and fortified wines in the seventeenth and eighteenth centuries also made small glass bottles more suitable as beverage storage containers than the large bulky ceramic storage jars. Thus, changes in alcohol production may help explain morphological changes in alcohol-related materials. Indeed, historical archaeologists have investigated a number of sites of alcohol production, which have helped shed light on the social, political, and economic changes that have shaped life in the modern world.

3

The Historical Archaeology
of Alcohol Production

The key step in making alcoholic beverages is fermentation, the breakdown of simple sugars into ethanol (H2H60) by the action of yeasts. Because fermentation occurs naturally, the first societies to produce alcoholic beverages probably discovered them accidentally. Archaeological research tells us that the practice of making alcoholic beverages developed independently in different regions of the world, and archaeological evidence has greatly contributed to our understanding of the origins of alcohol production. For example, the acclaimed archaeologist Robert Braidwood was one of the first to suggest that the desire for beer spurred the rise of intensive farming in the Near East 10,000–12,000 years ago (Braidwood 1953; see also Kahn 1996; Katz and Maytag 1991; Katz and Voigt 1986). Archaeologists have also investigated early beer brewing at Cerro Baúl, a pre-Incan site in southern Peru. The beer produced at Cerro Baúl was made by an elite group of noblewomen, and beer drinking at the site played a central role in feasting rituals and may have helped cement alliances between regional chiefdoms (Williams 2001, 2004, 2005; Williams et al. 2000). In Europe and the Mediterranean, archaeologists have used historical texts, chemical residue analysis of ceramic jars, and ethnobotanical remains to trace the emergence of grain-beer and grape-wine making (Badler et al. 1990; Dietler 1990; McGovern 1998, 2003; Renfrew 1996; Sherratt 1991). In South Asia, F. R. Allchin (1979) found distinctive ceramic pots at 2,500-year-old village sites in northern India and Pakistan that he believed may have been used as alembics (distilling apparatuses for making concentrated alcoholic beverages from fermented compounds). If Allchin's hypothesis is correct, the pots would represent the earliest evidence of alcohol distillation in the world. Although the major technological advances in alcohol production—brewing, fermenting, and distilling—developed long before the age of European exploration and settlement of the New World, the commercial expansion of alcohol production occurred in the modern era, and historical archaeological research has helped provide new insights into these endeavors.

Beer brewing was one of the earliest industries in colonial America. At Jamestown, the site of the first permanent British settlement in North America, John Cotter (1958: 102–9) excavated an early-seventeenth-century brew house. According to Cotter, the structure possessed distinguishing architectural features and artifacts, including circular brick fireboxes and a portion of a copper kettle, which reflected a semi-industrial complex associated with beer brewing. In Québec City, Marcel Moussette (1996: 13) also uncovered the remains of a seventeenth-century brewery that included "a floor of limestone flagstones bordered by thick masonry walls." Moussette noted that the limestone floor was used as an area where barley was allowed to germinate and dry before becoming the malt needed for beer making. He argued that the brewery used advanced brewing techniques and was probably too large for a city the size of Québec, implying that some of its product was for regional export. Beer making at the site ended in the 1670s, and the building was renovated. It was used as the first Intendant's Palace and later as a storehouse. In the mid-nineteenth century, however, the building was once again used as a brewery, and beer making at the site continued well into the mid-twentieth century (Moussette 1994, 1996). In the Chesapeake, archaeologists working at a seventeenth-century domestic site in St. Mary's City, Maryland, used regional probate inventories to identify the remains of a small-scale beer-brewing operation (Gibb and King 1991: 111; King 1990: 27; King and Miller 1987: 51). At Millwood Plantation in South Carolina, Charles E. Orser Jr. (1985) investigated the function of a small nineteenth-century outbuilding that was probably used to brew a type of beer from plantation-grown sorghum. And a prerevolutionary brewery in Newport, Rhode Island, that produced beer for local and Atlantic markets has also been the subject of archaeological investigation (Dubell 2002).

Ethnobotanical remains have helped archaeologists locate and identify brewing operations. Cheryl Holt (1991), for example, recovered hops from a nineteenth-century farmstead in Greenwich Township, New Jersey, which may have been used for brewing beer. According to Holt, alcohol production at archaeological sites would often go undetected without the help of such characteristic ethnobotanical evidence. At Richneck Plantation, a seventeenth-century tobacco plantation in Virginia, David Muraca recovered charred wheat seeds among archaeological deposits, which he interpreted as evidence that beer brewing may have been taking place at the site (David Muraca, personal communication, January 2007). The discovery of barley seeds from a mid-nineteenth-century gold rush store in Sacramento, California, led Elizabeth Honeysett and Peter Schulz (1990: 102) to similar conclusions.

In parts of Europe, Africa, and the Americas, women were often the primary producers of brewed alcoholic beverages. Archaeologists have explored the links between women and brewing in a number of historical settings. James Gibb and Julia King (1991: 113), for example, argued that beer making was a supplemental economic activity on small farms in the Chesapeake, and they attributed the rise of household-brewing operations in St. Mary's City, Maryland in the seventeenth century to women (see also Bennett 1996; Johnson 1996: 163). According to Anne Yentsch (1991: 134), brewing operations in the Chesapeake began as a female domain but were often taken over by men once the operations began to make substantial contributions to household revenues. In Cuenca, Ecuador, indigenous Andean women typically supervised *chicha* beer-brewing operations. Although imported Spanish ceramic vessels began to replace the indigenous ceramic vessels traditionally used for beer brewing, Andean women continued to be the primary producers of *chicha* after Spanish colonization (Jamieson 2000: 96, 184–85). Ross Jamieson, the archaeologist who investigated the Andean ceramic collections, wrote:

> Women's use of Spanish imported ceramics to create the quintessentially Andean drink, and then to sell it in public markets, must make us question any strict line between Native and Spanish ethnic groups. Such activity crossed the lines between public and private spheres and also challenges the assignation of ceramic vessel forms to particular ethnic groups.
> (Jamieson 2000: 207)

Although early colonial brewing in North America was largely a cottage industry, experimentation and technological advances led to changes in beer making that accelerated the shift toward large-scale brewing operations. One of the main factors that spurred the shift to large-scale beer brewing in North America in the mid-nineteenth century was the influx of German immigrants, who introduced innovative brewing techniques and specialized forms of yeast for producing lager beer (Rorabaugh 1979: 109). At the same time, technological change and the increasing regimentation of labor helped expand industrial brewing practices. In Harpers Ferry, West Virginia, for example, Deborah Hull-Walski and Frank Walski (1994) showcased the layout and efficiency of a late-nineteenth- and early-twentieth-century industrial brewery and bottling plant. In addition, they used documentary evidence to investigate the lives and living conditions of brewery workers. Hull-Walski and Walski provided details about the embossed Harpers Ferry brewery bottles and sought to explain the paucity of the brewery's bottles in the contemporary privies of Harpers Ferry residents, arguing that it reflected the success of bottle-recycling practices. If Harpers Ferry had a returnable bottle system, however, they felt compelled to explain why any of the brewery's bottles were found in the town's privies. They considered a number of possibilities, including theft by workers seeking free beer and laziness on the part of local residents. Given the harsh working conditions that brewery workers faced, Paul Shackel (2000: 111) contended that "sabotage" by disgruntled employees is another plausible explanation. There were also bottles from other regional breweries in the privies of Harpers Ferry residents, which according to Hull-Walski and Walski probably reflected the difficulty involved in returning bottles to distant breweries. Indeed, bottle recycling was an important factor in the success of some industrial breweries. Mark Walker (1996) conducted archaeological investigations at a nineteenth-century industrial brewery in Alexandria, Virginia, that possessed numerous bottles from other local and regional breweries. The great diversity of bottle forms and types found at the site allowed Walker to expose one of the key challenges facing some industrial breweries: having enough bottles to retail their product.

Archaeologists have also examined the spread of wine making in the modern world. While the tremendous numbers of Iberian storage jar fragments recovered by Maria Salamanca-Heyman (2007) at the major Spanish colonial port of Nombre de Dios in Panama attest to the enormity of Spanish wine exports to the Spanish colonies in the New World, the rise of wine making in the Spanish American colonies makes it clear that Spain could not meet the alcoholic demands of its colonists. Wine was a central feature of Spanish dietary habits and Catholic religious activities, and wine making emerged in the Spanish colonial world to fill these needs. Prudence Rice and Greg Smith (1989), for example, surveyed Spanish colonial *bodegas* in the Moquegua Valley region of Peru. They and their colleagues identified over 130 winery sites, and the research has served as the basis for a number of wine-related studies (deFrance 1996; McEwan 1992; Rice 1996a, 1996b, 1997; Rice and Van Beck 1993; Smith 1997; Van Buren 1999). Rice and Smith (1989), for example, conducted extensive excavations at a seventeenth-century winery at Locumbilla, where they interpreted the specific functions of winery buildings and even tried to estimate the level of wine production for the Moquegua Valley based on the number of ceramic storage vessels recovered from the site. In South Africa, Ann Markell et al. (1995) examined archaeological deposits at Vergelegen, an eighteenth- and early-nineteenth-century Dutch farmstead on the Cape Coast. At least part of Vergelegen was devoted to viticulture, and the estate probably produced wine for the regional and world export markets. Excavations at the Vergelegen wine cellar revealed unique architectural details consistent with documentary reports about the technology of early South African wine making and storage. Not surprisingly, artifacts associated with alcohol production and storage, such as glass bottles and iron barrel hoops, were present in the artifact assemblage from the Vergelegen wine cellar. James Schoenwetter and John Hohmann (1997) also focused on the impact of viticulture on land-use patterns at the original nineteenth-century settlement site of Las Vegas, Nevada. According to Schoenwetter and Hohmann (1997: 52), soil core samples produced palynological evidence that revealed changing land-use patterns in the nineteenth century associated with the need to irrigate vineyards, which produced grapes for local wine makers.

Ethnobotanical remains have also been used to identify wine making. At eighteenth- and early-nineteenth-century Russian fur-trade sites in southern Alaska, Aron Crowell (1997: 215) recovered elderberry seeds, which may represent attempts by traders to ferment their own wine. The elderberry wine would have offered a cheap alternative to the expensive vodka and brandy imported from Russia. Maria Franklin (1997: 211) argued that persimmon and honey locust seeds recovered from the root cellar of an eighteenth-century slave quarter in Williamsburg, Virginia, reflected evidence of wine making at the site. The presence of dandelion pollen from eighteenth-century privies in Newport, Rhode Island, has also been interpreted as possible evidence of dandelion-wine making (Reinhard et al. 1986: 34). Noël Hume (1969a: 21–26) recovered hundreds of cherry pits, leaves, and whole cherries from hand-blown glass bottles found at the eighteenth-century Wetherburn's Tavern site in Colonial Williamsburg in Virginia. Cherry-filled bottles were also unearthed at Thomas Jefferson's home, Monticello (Kelso 1982). Cherries from these bottles were probably used to produce sweet fermented drinks, such as cherry bounce, which was a popular specialty drink in North America in the seventeenth and eighteenth centuries (Noël Hume 1969a: 26; see also Dudek et al. 1998: 67).

As with beer brewing, wine making possessed a distinctive material culture and a unique division of labor. At the Moquegua Valley wineries in Peru, Prudence Rice and Sara Van Beck (1993) studied the kilns located on

Figure 3–1. Ivor Noël Hume excavating cherry-filled bottles from Wetherburn's Tavern, Williamsburg, Virginia. Courtesy of the Colonial Williamsburg Foundation, Department of Archaeological Research.

winery properties, which produced large earthenware *tinajas* for wine fermentation and small earthenware *botijas* for wine storage and transport:

> Kilns are an important part of the technological complex associated with viticulture that was transferred to the Andes by the Spanish colonists. Like the wine industry itself, the kilns retain many elements of their Spanish and Moorish and earlier Roman heritage.
> (Rice and Van Beck 1993: 78)

Susan deFrance (1996) examined faunal remains from the Moquegua Valley *bodega* sites in order to explicate the role of animals in winery operations. She found faunal evidence for the widespread presence draught and pack animals, such as llama, oxen, and mules. These beasts of burden were an integral part of winery operations, turning wine presses and transporting wine to distant markets located across the rugged terrain.

The archaeologists investigating the winery sites in the Moquegua Valley have also explored the lives of winery workers. Mary Van Buren (1999), for example, studied ceramic assemblages from the domestic sites of workers at the Moquegua Valley wineries and found that Spanish colonial winery workers in Peru embraced indigenous Andean ceramic forms and designs and were more likely to adopt indigenous pottery styles in their households than their Spanish colonial counterparts in the Caribbean. Attempts have also been made to discern the influence of African potters on ceramic vessels at the Moquegua Valley winery sites. It appears, however, that the utilitarian nature of winery ceramics, such as *tinajas* and *botijas*, muted any distinctly African influence on the form, function, or aesthetics of ceramic vessels produced at the wineries (Smith 1997: 78). While winery workers incorporated indigenous Andean ceramics into their material world, deFrance (1996) used faunal evidence to show that Andean dietary habits were less likely to penetrate traditional Iberian foodways. Drawing on evidence from Spanish colonial sites in Florida and Hispaniola, Kathleen Deagan (1973, 1996) argued that *mestizaje* (the blending of Spanish and indigenous cultural traditions) greatly shaped Spanish colonial dietary habits in the early colonial era. According to Deagan, the Spanish colonists' adoption of indigenous foodways reflected the strong influence of Indian women in the domestic household sphere. Perhaps the more limited evidence for indigenous Andean dietary habits at domestic sites at the Moquegua Valley wineries reflects the more limited influence of Andean women in male-dominated winery activities.

Distillation represents the most complex form of alcohol production. The production of distilled spirits requires not only fermentation but also the added step of heating and regulating the fermented compounds in an alembic or still to produce a concentrated alcoholic beverage with a high alcohol content. Distilleries and distilling operations have been the focus of historical archaeological inquiry, and the evidence has helped increase our understanding of these endeavors. For example, at Martin's Hundred, a seventeenth-century Virginia settlement destroyed in the Powhatan Indian uprising of 1622, Noël Hume (1982: 101–2) recovered a ceramic alembic head, the top portion of an alembic used to collect the vapors that rise from the heated fermenting compound in the lower portion of the alembic known as the cucurbit. Its odd shape initially puzzled researchers, though Noël Hume was able to locate an example in Randle Holme's *The Academy of Armory*, a three-volume encyclopedia published in 1688 that illustrates an enormous range of objects encountered in daily life in the seventeenth century. *The Academy of Armory* has been an invaluable tool for archaeologists working on seventeenth-century British colonial sites. The alembic

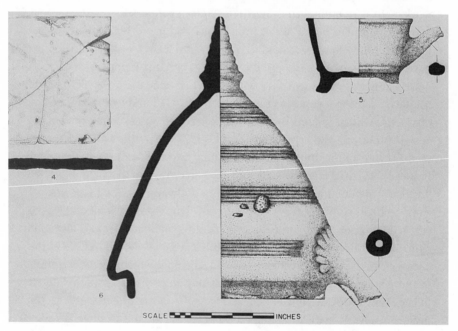

Figure 3–2. Illustration of an alembic head from an early seventeenth-century context at Martin's Hundred, Virginia. Courtesy of the Colonial Williamsburg Foundation, Department of Archaeological Research.

Figure 3–3. Distilling flask from an early-seventeenth-century context at James Fort in Jamestown, Virginia. Courtesy of the APVA Preservation Virginia.

head recovered at Martin's Hundred was made of unglazed red earthenware and appears to have been produced by colonists at the site. At nearby Jamestown, Audrey Horning (1995: 166) identified an earthenware alembic from a mid-seventeenth-century context, and recent excavations at James Fort in Jamestown by William Kelso (2006: 103–5) and his team have unearthed more distilling equipment, including an earthenware cucurbit, a distilling flask, and part of a glass alembic head (see also Kelso and Straube 2000: 39).

The researchers who made these discoveries, however, have tended to downplay the use of the alembics in the production of distilled alcoholic beverages. Noël Hume (1982: 102), for example, highlighted the role of alembics in the production of "medicinal curatives and essences," while Kelso (2006: 103–5) stressed the use of the alembics for the production of sulfuric acid, a principal ingredient in metalworking. Their emphasis on medicines and metalworking is probably justified. The art of alcohol distillation was still relatively new at the start of the seventeenth century, and the secrets of alcohol distilling had only recently been seized from the physicians and apothecaries of Europe (Underwood 1935). The consumption of distilled spirits in Britain for convivial purposes at the time was also very limited (Wilson 1975). As late as 1688, for example, Britain's Parliament levied a duty on only a half-million gallons of gin (Clark 1988: 64). Although distilled spirits were of limited use in seventeenth-century Britain, this does not mean that the alembics recovered from Martin's Hundred and Jamestown were not used to distill alcoholic beverages. In fact, the archaeologists investigating these sites, to their credit, do not entirely reject the possibility that the alembics were used for that purpose. Given the relative novelty of alcohol distillation in the early seventeenth century and the rather limited consumption of distilled spirits in Britain at this time, however, Noël Hume and Kelso are probably justified in emphasizing the medicinal and metallurgical uses of the alembics recovered from Martin's Hundred and Jamestown.

While distilling industries were slow to develop, they expanded in the mid- to late seventeenth century. The rise of distilling industries was driven in part by the expansion of sugar production in the Caribbean, which provided an enormous amount of base material (molasses) for local Caribbean distillers as well as distillers in Europe and North America. Historical archaeologists have investigated rum distilling at a number of sites in the Caribbean. For example, Conrad Goodwin (1994) surveyed Betty's Hope Plantation, an eighteenth- and early-nineteenth-century sugar estate in Antigua, and recorded the central placement of the estate's rum distillery within the larger sugar plantation complex. Betty's Hope had an unusual double windmill system that underscores the immense scale of sugar production on the estate. The low elevation at which the windmills were set, however, probably required workers to develop a complex system of troughs and gutters for getting the freshly squeezed sugarcane juice to the sugar cauldrons and fermentation vats in the main factory. Indeed, the process of rum distilling and the layout of the natural terrain dictated the location of structures on Caribbean sugar estates. For example, at St. Nicholas Abbey Plantation in Barbados, the estate owner constructed the main factory downhill from the estate's windmill so that the sugarcane juice squeezed from the rollers in the windmill could flow quickly and easily down gutters into the estate's copper sugar boilers and fermentation vats (Devlin and Smith 2007). In Tobago, Christopher Clement (1997) conducted an extensive survey of sugar estates in the island and recorded details about the location of rum distilleries on the plantation landscapes. According to Clement, the need for water, a key ingredient of rum making, determined the placement of sugar factories on plantations in Tobago:

> Of the 22 sugar factories encountered during the survey, 19 are located adjacent to a water source sufficient to provide water for rum production . . . This reliance on water for rum-making resulted in the confinement of factories to valley bottoms, broad vales, or locations that could be reached by canal in areas of high topographic relief.
> (Clement 1997: 95–96)

Figure 3–4. Windmill Wall, sugar factory, and rum distillery at St. Nicholas Abbey, Barbados. Photo: author's collection.

Figure 3–5. Feeding sugarcanes into the grinding mill at St. Nicholas Abbey, Barbados. Photo: author's collection.

Several other archaeological and architectural surveys in the Caribbean have produced plan drawings of sugar plantation boiling houses and rum distilleries (Barka 1993; Craton and Walvin 1970; Goodwin 1982; Higman 1988, 1998; Pulsipher 1982; Pulsipher and Goodwin 2001; St. John's Historical Society 1999).

Rum distilleries have also been investigated at colonial and postrevolutionary sites in North America. In Bristol, Rhode Island, for example, Richard Greenwood (2005) detailed the industrial signature of an early-nineteenth-century waterfront rum distillery that produced rum from imported Caribbean molasses. In Albany, New York, in 2001, archaeologists unearthed a sizable mid-eighteenth-century rum distillery that possessed no less than twenty-one wooden fermentation vats. Two of the wooden vats were in an incredibly good state of preservation, and they have provided insights into early North American woodworking and vat construction techniques (DiVirgilio 2003). Nancy Seasholes (1998) also identified an eighteenth-century rum distillery at the Mill Pond site in Boston, Massachusetts. Unlike the factory-in-the-field operations found in the Caribbean, rum distilling in early New York and New England was an urban industrial enterprise that used imported Caribbean molasses as its fermentable base material. Seasholes explained how the Boston distillery relied on a nearby pond to dispose of distillery waste. Thus, as in Tobago, proximity to water may have helped determine the placement of rum distilling operations in eighteenth-century Boston.

Historical archaeologists have explored other types of alcohol distilling. At a late-eighteenth- and early-nineteenth-century farmstead in Greenwich Township, New Jersey, Amy Friedlander (1991: 20) and Cheryl Holt (1991: 47) used ethnobotanical evidence to identify whiskey distilling at the site. According to Friedlander, distilling supplemented farm revenues and helped establish a web of social and economic relations that strengthened the farm owner's position in the community. Archaeologists have also excavated a whiskey distillery at George Washington's home, Mount Vernon. Washington's distillery was probably engaged in commercial levels of production, which helped supplement the estate's revenues. Eleanor Breen (2004), one of the key investigators at the site, argued that whiskey distilling was not simply a cottage industry at Mount Vernon but operated at a semi-industrial level. More recent investigations at the Mount Vernon whiskey distillery by Breen and Esther White (2006) have produced a complete and detailed plan of the distillery and uncovered items directly associated with distilling, including a copper alloy tap and cock used to regulate the flow of liquids in the distillation process.

While whiskey distilling was an ancillary economic activity in the bucolic setting of Mount Vernon, it was the primary economic focus of the industrialized Gravel Springs Distillery and Bottling Works outside of Jacksonville, Illinois, a half-century later. Water was a necessary ingredient in whiskey making, and the company located its operations near the Gravel Springs to take advantage of natural water resources. Kenneth Farnsworth (1996), the archaeologist who investigated the site, detailed the marketing strategies of the distillery owners, who touted their whiskey as an elixir of life because it was made with water from the salubrious Gravel Springs. The wide range of embossed glass bottles recovered from the Gravel Springs Distillery and Bottling Works underscores the complex and industrial nature of distilling and bottling operations as well as the sophisticated marketing techniques of the owners.

Figure 3–6. Reconstruction of George Washington's whiskey distillery at Mount Vernon. Courtesy of the Mount Vernon Ladies' Association. Photograph by Bob Creamer.

While whiskey distilling continued to expand in the nineteenth century, not all distilled whiskey was made legally. Audrey Horning (2002: 141–43), for example, identified moonshine whiskey stills at late-nineteenth-century sites in Appalachia. According to Horning, the illegal moonshine stills generated cash that supplemented the wages of coal miners and brought money into the local economy. In the early twentieth century, farmers in the Finger Lakes region of New York also produced moonshine whiskey that supplemented farm revenues. The illicit distilling operations there challenged the temperance ideologies of local public officials and corporate attempts to monopolize regional alcohol markets (Delle and Heaton 2003: 105–8; see also Adams 1977: 48). The archaeological signature of a moonshine operation is usually somewhat limited because small-scale distilling technology is rather simple. Moreover, as illicit operators, moonshine makers probably possessed a sparse material world, since they had to be ready to flee and move to new locations quickly. For example, a moonshine distillery investigated by archaeologists in northern Alabama consisted of little more than a few shards of stoneware pots and a handful of metal pieces from used fuel oil cans (Blitz 1978).

Brandy, made from distilled grape wine, has also been the subject of archaeological investigation. At Vergelegen estate in South Africa, Ann Markell et al. (1995) conducted archaeological excavations at the estate's wine cellar, which confirmed documentary reports of brandy distilling at the site. The archaeological evidence helped the researchers identify the location of the Vergelegen brandy still and show the architectural signature of a brandy-distilling operation. Daniel Schávelzon (2000: 85–86) excavated a nineteenth-century brandy distillery in the urban context of Buenos Aires, Argentina. As with the rum distilleries in New York and New England, the brandy distillery in Buenos Aires was an independent operation that distilled raw base material imported from distant locations, especially from rural vineyards and wineries located outside of the city. The brandy distillery operated within a congested urban landscape of Buenos Aires and was part of a larger commercial and residential complex that included the owner's house and a general store.

While historical archaeologists have successfully identified and described alcohol production in the modern world, a number of alcoholic beverages have escaped historical archaeological inquiry. For example, the archaeological signature of cider making, a key fixture on many farms in New England and the Mid-Atlantic, has yet to be tackled in the historical archaeological literature. Michael Lucas (2007) used account books to explore the relative importance of cider at ordinaries in Prince George's County, Maryland, and James Garman (1998) used probate inventories from East Bay, Rhode Island, to show the way cider making shaped the labor regimen of enslaved Africans and Afro-Creoles in southern New England. Yet the material culture of cider presses, their location on the landscape, and cider's contributions to local and regional economies remain an obvious gap in the historical archaeological literature on alcohol. Moreover, while ethnohistorians have investigated the indigenous production of fermented alcoholic beverages in Mesoamerica (such as *pulque* and *mescal*) and the Caribbean (such as *qüicou*), historical archaeologists have yet to explore the way in which European expansion and colonization transformed the meaning of these particular indigenous drinks (Bruman 2000; Smith 2006; Taylor 1979). Similarly, how did European expansion and colonization transform palm wine and grain beer production in West and Central Africa?

As for distilled alcoholic beverages, the archaeology of tequila, arrack, vodka, and sake production has yet to be written. The lack of archaeological evidence from early northern European gin distilleries and southern European brandy distilleries is especially troubling since these industries represent the Old World antecedents to New World distilling operations. One notable exception comes from Carrick Castle in Argyll, Scotland, where post-medieval archaeologists uncovered a simple copper-alloy still worm, as well as grain pollen, from a seventeenth-century context, which may help shed new light on the Old World precursor to New World whiskey distilling practices (Haynes et al. 1998). In addition to the gaps in our knowledge of specific alcoholic beverages, there seems to be a glaring need to understand the material culture used in alcohol production. I suspect that future archaeological investigations at breweries, wineries, and distilleries will lead to the increase in that database.

Historical archaeological research has shown that alcohol production emerged in nearly every corner of the colonial world from the earliest days of European expansion. What were the social, political, and economic forces that fostered the growth of those industries? As discussed later, the general desire to re-create Old World drinking patterns and the need to confront colonial anxieties helped spur alcohol making in the New World. Other factors, however, were more specific to the locations where alcohol making emerged. The rise of wine making in colonial Peru, for example, was no doubt driven by the high cost of imported Spanish wine and the inability of Spanish traders to meet the alcohol needs of Spanish colonists in the Americas. Environmental forces also may have determined where and when alcohol production was feasible. While economic profit was the primary motivation behind rum making in early New England, the colonists' desire to counter the cold New England winters may have been an added incentive.

Historical archaeologists must question the political-economic conditions that transformed alcohol production from a cottage industry that supplemented household incomes into an industrial science that produced a primary alcoholic commodity on a large scale. Did the installation of bottling plants at the Harpers Ferry brewery and the Gravel Springs Distillery reveal the owners' desire to turn regional alcohol businesses into large-scale industrial complexes that catered to distant markets? Can we gauge the expansion and contraction of rum distilling in the Caribbean by the increasing and decreasing demand for alcohol in the Atlantic World? Indeed, the demand for alcohol has shaped trade patterns in the modern world, and historical archaeologists have contributed to our understanding of the alcohol trade.

4

The Historical Archaeology of Alcohol Trade and Transport

Alcohol is a volatile fluid. If not consumed immediately after production, it must be stored in durable airtight containers. Alcohol has also been a valuable commodity and a prominent item of trade. The volatile and valuable nature of alcohol has led to the production of a rich material culture for its storage and transport, including glass bottles, ceramic storage containers, and ironbound wooden casks. These containers not only served the immediate purpose of alcohol storage and transport but also tend to survive well in the archaeological record and have helped archaeologists identify patterns of trade. Some of the most prolific archaeological research on the alcohol trade comes from classical archaeologists working at ancient sites in Egypt, Greece, and Rome who have used ceramic amphorae to trace the extent of the Mediterranean wine trade (Arthur 1986; Bass et al. 1989; Dressel 1899; Fulford 1987; Galliou 1984; Peacock and Williams 1986; Pulak 1998; Williams 1989). However, the evidence for alcohol trading is not limited to the classical world.

During the late Middle Ages, wine making expanded in southern Europe and advances in distillation technology led to the commercial production of distilled spirits. The increasing output of wine and spirits helped generate state revenues, fuel the growth of national economies, nurture the rise of long-distance trade, and bring together disparate parts of Europe (Braudel 1981; Unwin 1991). In the age of European exploration and settlement, alcoholic beverages were introduced to areas of the world with no prior history of alcohol production and use, such as North America and Oceania, and European traders brought new alcohol consumers into the emerging global economy. In areas of the world with prior histories of alcohol production and use, such as West Africa and South America, European-introduced alcoholic beverages were incorporated in preexisting drinking patterns. Alcohol-related artifacts are ubiquitous on contact-

Figure 4–1. *Manner of Instructing the Indians.* In William Apess, *Indian Nullification of the Unconstitutional Laws of Massachusetts Relative to the Marshpee Tribe; or, The Pretended Riot Explained* (Boston, 1835). Courtesy of the American Antiquarian Society.

period sites throughout the world and attest to the momentum and energy of the expanding capitalist system.

In colonial North America, alcoholic beverages played an integral role in creating and sustaining the European-Indian fur and skin trades (Mancall 1995: 29–61, 2003). Although North America was one of the few areas of the world that did not produce alcoholic beverages prior to European contact, Native North Americans quickly embraced European-introduced alcoholic drinks. They incorporated alcohol into traditional social and spiritual activities and used it to cope with the unsettling changes that accompanied European colonialism. More importantly, alcohol was key to the economic success of merchants and traders in the early colonial frontier, including Native Americans who themselves sometimes became intermediaries in the alcohol trade.

Historical archaeologists have recovered glass bottles and ceramic storage jars from Native North American sites that highlight the extent to which Native North Americans were engaged in the global alcohol traffic. For example, at eighteenth-century Creek and Cherokee sites in the southeastern United States archaeologists found glass bottles and ceramic storage jars, which testify to the prominent role of alcohol in the fur and skin trades (Fairbanks 1952; Sears 1955). Alcohol was one of the principal items that early Rhode Island colonists sold to local Narragansett Indians, and glass bottle fragments from Cocumscussoc, the site of Roger Williams' trading post in the 1640s, confirm the importance of the alcohol trade there (Rubertone 2001). British colonists in Rhode Island also sold alcohol to the Wampanoag, and archaeologists working at Burr's Hill, a seventeenth-century Native American cemetery, unearthed hand-blown glass bottles and ceramic drinking mugs, which demonstrate the significance of the British-Wampanoag alcohol trade (Baker 1980; Brown 1980; Gaimster 1997a: 100–101; Johannsen 1980). In the Chesapeake, glass and ceramic bottles appear at British-Powhatan contact-period sites (Hodges 1993: 35–41; Mouer 1993: 136). Archaeologists at Fort Toulouse in Alabama and Fort St. Joseph in Michigan have found numerous glass bottle fragments, which underscore the prevalence of alcohol in the French-Indian trades in the seventeenth and eighteenth centuries (Heldman 1973: 168; Nassaney et al. 2004). And fragments of bottle glass and Iberian storage jars are among the most common artifacts found at forts and missions in the Spanish colonial world, especially in Florida (Deagan 1972; Fairbanks 1978: 172–73; Lewis 1978: 41; Smith and Gottlob 1978: 16). The discovery of alcohol-related materials at these and many other Native North American sites illustrates the magnitude of the European-Indian alcohol trade and shows that Native North Americans were active participants in the emerging Atlantic economy.

Yet the alcohol trade with Indians was not limited to North America. As with their Native North American counterparts, the Taino of the Bahamas and the Greater Antilles had no history of alcohol production or use before European colonization. Archaeological investigations at La Isabela in the Dominican Republic, the site of the first Spanish town in the Americas, uncovered bottle glass and Iberian storage jar fragments that attest to the early wine trade with the Taino (Deagan 1992, 1996; Deagan and Cruxent 2002). Indeed, the discovery of "many fragments of green glass" at the Long Bay site in the Bahamas, the site of Christopher Columbus' first landfall in the Americas, suggests that alcohol was a key component of trade between Europeans and native groups from the very onset of European penetration into the New World (Hoffman 1987: 242).

Unlike their Taino cousins, Carib Indians in the Lesser Antilles had a strong tradition of alcohol production and use prior to European intervention in the Caribbean. European wine and spirits, therefore, entered a preexisting Carib social structure that embraced alcohol drinking (Smith 2006). Lennox Honychurch (1997) investigated the presence of European bottle glass at contact-period Carib sites in Dominica in order to show the extent to which alcohol stimulated trade between Europeans and Caribs in the early years of colonial expansion. According to Honychurch (1997: 299), the Caribs added commercial production to subsistence production in order to tap the emerging European trade. For example, Caribs increased their production of tobacco and sold it to European traders in exchange for alcohol. It was through this sort of informal exchange that Caribs acquired European alcoholic beverages.

Historical archaeological evidence of alcohol trading has been used as an index of culture change in Native American societies, especially in North America. While traditional acculturation studies in historical archaeology have given way to more sophisticated Creolization models, early acculturation studies in historical archaeology have provided a launch pad for exploring the processes involved in culture change and have raised questions about the agency of Native American groups in postcontact situations (Lightfoot 1995). The study of alcohol was a key component of that early acculturation research in historical archaeology. For example, Paul Farnsworth (1992) developed a system for measuring culture change among Native Americans at late-eighteenth- and early-nineteenth-century Spanish colonial mission sites in California. According to Farnsworth (1992: 25), the presence of glass bottle fragments at mission sites showed that Native Americans in California adopted "new [Spanish] cultural elements," which he interpreted as evidence of acculturation. Despite the presence of imported glass bottles, the Native Californians continued to produce and use indigenous materials, especially pottery. This convinced Farnsworth that missionized Indians in California were able to hold onto many aspects of their traditional culture despite Spanish intervention in the region (see also Hoover 1992: 41). Similarly, Timothy Perttula (1994) argued that the discovery of wine and liquor bottles at late-eighteenth- and early-nineteenth-century Koasati Indian sites in Texas reflected the penetration of western cultural elements into traditional Koasati society. Yet glass bottles are not the only alcohol-related materials to show the Native Americans' use of European goods. Marley R. Brown III (1980: 57) contended that the presence of ceramic drinking vessels and a German stoneware Bartmann bottle at Burr's Hill illustrated the Wampanoag's embrace of European alcohol drinking. At the Drake's Bay site in northern California, Edward Von der

XIIII. Capittel.

Wie sie ihre Getrenck machen daran sie sich truncken

Als Weibßvolck machet die Geträncke/sie nemen die Wurtzel Mandio-
ka/vnd sieden grosse Döppen voll/ weñ es gesotten ist/ nemen sie es auß ᵀʳᵃⁿᶜᵏ.
den Döppen/giessens in einander Döppen oder Gefeß/ lassens ein we-
nig kalt werden/denn setzen sich die jungen Mägde darbey/vnd keiwen es mit dem
Munde/vnd das gekeiwete thun sie in ein sonderlich Gefäß. Wenn die gesottenen
Wurtzeln alle gekeiwet seyn / thun sie das gekeiwete wider in das Döppen / vnnd
giessen es widerumb voll Wassers / vermengens mit den gekeiweten Wurtzeln/
L ij   vnd

Figure 4–2. *How the Tuppin Ikins Make and Drink Their Beverage.* Carib women of the Orinoco Delta region of South America masticating cassava and producing *oüicou.* In Hans Staden, *Americae tertia pars memorabilè provinciae Brasiliae historiam continès* (Frankfurt, 1592). Courtesy of the John Carter Brown Library at Brown University.

Porten (1972) recovered a Japanese sake cup made of porcelain, which may shed light on the extent of the sixteenth-century Manila galleon trade in the Pacific and the adoption of Asian ceramics, and perhaps Asian alcoholic beverages, by Miwok Indians.

The introduction of large quantities of alcohol into a volatile environment of colonial domination disrupted traditional indigenous social structures, even in areas with long-standing traditions of alcohol use. For example, before the arrival of Europeans, fermented alcoholic beverages made from cassava played a central role in the social and spiritual worlds of the indigenous peoples in the Orinoco Delta region of South America. Regular drinking festivals helped build alliances between regional groups in the Orinoco. More importantly, these fermented alcoholic drinks facilitated communication with the spiritual world. Through libations and offerings, alcohol helped the native peoples of the Orinoco propitiate angry spirits and elicit spiritual assistance in worldly endeavors. In the sixteenth and seventeenth centuries, European-introduced alcoholic beverages began to penetrate the Orinoco region. Franz Scaramelli and Kay Tarble de Scaramelli (2005) found that fragments of European glass bottles and ceramic storage containers, once used to hold European-introduced alcoholic beverages, represented a substantial part of the artifact assemblages from contact-period indigenous sites along the Orinoco River. In a skillful analysis of alcohol-related material culture in the Orinoco Delta, Scaramelli and Tarble de Scaramelli showed how European-introduced alcoholic beverages and the European alcohol trade upset the traditional sexual division of labor in indigenous Orinoco societies. In particular, they argued that the importation of European wine and spirits weakened the powerful domestic role of indigenous women in the Orinoco, who were the traditional producers of fermented alcoholic beverages made from cassava. The drinks made by these indigenous women were necessary for initiating interactions with the spiritual world and thus securing spiritual guidance. According to Scaramelli and Tarble de Scaramelli, foreign wine and spirits entered the Orinoco region in large amounts in the seventeenth century and began to replace locally produced alcoholic drinks. As a result, the traditional indigenous social structure in the Orinoco was set off balance as the onslaught of European-introduced alcoholic beverages denied indigenous Orinoco women access to the symbolic capital that alcohol production bestowed (see also Scaramelli and Tarble 2003).

Yet the presence of alcohol containers at contact-period sites represents more than simply the Europeans' desire to trade with native peoples and bring them into the emerging global economy. Colonial officials, missionaries, and merchants used the alcohol trade to establish political alliances with particular indigenous groups, maintain their loyalties, and entice them into colonial agendas. Moreover, the colonists, unfamiliar with their new physical surroundings, used the alcohol trade to acquire the knowledge and assistance of indigenous peoples, who could help settlers grow food and survive on the colonial frontiers. Thus, for example, the discovery of alcohol bottles on contact-period Aborigine sites in Australia shows that the alcohol trade penetrated the far reaches of the colonial world. The bottles also represent attempts by British military commanders to build political alliances with the Aborigine, gain access to food resources for British troops, and "seduce" the Aborigine into colonial compliance (Allen 1973; Langton 1993; Veth and McDonald 2004). Similar arguments may explain the presence of glass bottle fragments at European forts in southern Madagascar (Parker Pearson 1997). Historical archaeologists have also recovered glass alcohol bottle fragments from Native Alaskan sites at late-eighteenth- and early-nineteenth-century Russian fur trade outposts, which highlight the participation of Native Alaskans in the global alcohol trade (Crowell 1997: 229–35). However, the bottles may also indicate the need to appease Native Alaskan leaders, who could help ensure successful trade relationships. Bottle glass evidence from Fort Ross suggests that Russian fur traders used alcohol to pursue similar agendas with Native Californians (Lightfoot et al. 1993: 171). Virginia Pineau (2007) interpreted the presence of iron barrel hoops and bottle glass at early-nineteenth-century sites in rural areas of La Pampa province in Argentina as evidence of Spanish colonial political maneuvering. In particular, Pineau argued that the alcohol-related materials represent attempts by Spanish colonial official to insert themselves into indigenous political affairs and establish *tratados de paz* between the Spanish and Indians in the region. Similarly, alcohol played a central role in gift-giving ceremonies in Amazonia, and alcohol bottles found at indigenous sites in the Orinoco may reflect attempts by Dutch traders and officials to secure indigenous allies against the Spanish. The Dutch had to compete with the Spanish missionaries, however, who also used alcohol to "entice" the indigenous peoples of the Orinoco to come to missions (Scaramelli and Tarble 2003: 169). And the discovery of bottle glass and Bartmann bottle fragments at seventeenth-century Dutch military outposts along the Cape Coast of South Africa by Carmel Schrire (1991, 1995: 100) may not only offer insights into the Dutch alcohol trade with the local Khoikhoi herders but perhaps also demonstrate the Dutch colonists' dependence on the Khoik-hoi for cattle for meat.

Yet indigenous peoples were not the only groups with whom European colonists wished to trade and build alliances. The discovery of glass bottle fragments at Fort Mose, an eighteenth-century free black town in the shadow of Spanish St. Augustine, indicates that even marginalized social groups within larger colonial settings were integrated into the global alcohol trade (MacMahon and Deagan 1996: 58). In addition, the bottles from Fort Mose may reflect Spanish attempts to strengthen alliances with groups that opposed British incursions into the region. Similarly, while the fragments of bottle glass found at eighteenth-century maroon sites in Jamaica show the maroons' participation in the broader Atlantic economy, they are also expressions of the British colonists' need for allies in times of slave revolt and rebellion (Agorsah 1993: 190).

Historical archaeologists have also used the material culture of alcohol trade and transport to explore the rise of long-distance overseas commercial networks in the emerging colonial world. For example, the overwhelming presence of glass alcohol bottles at seventeenth-century domestic sites in Newfoundland led Peter Pope (1989, 1997, 2004) to investigate the fish-for-alcohol trade between North America and Europe. According to Pope, the alcohol trade to Newfoundland followed patterns established in medieval Europe, in which fishermen in England exported fish to France in exchange for French wine and brandy. The high demand for fish in Europe and the direct nature of the Newfoundland fish-for-alcohol trade meant that lowly fishermen at the periphery of the Atlantic World had ready access to expensive alcoholic beverages typically reserved for metropolitan elites. Similarly, the great number of German Bartmann bottles recovered from the wreck of the *Batavia*, a ship of the Dutch East India Company that sank near the Wallabi Islands off the coast of Western Australia in 1629 while on its way to Jakarta, highlights the role of alcohol in the Dutch spice trade with merchants in Indonesia (Stanbury 1974; see also Gaimster 1997b: 124–26). Archaeologists have also recovered evidence of the emerging colonial alcohol trade from the *Kennemerland*, a ship of the Dutch East India Company that sank off the coast of Scotland in 1664. Salvage and shipping records revealed that alcohol, probably destined for merchants and workers in the Dutch settlements in the East Indies, represented a major part of the *Kennemerland*'s cargo (Muckelroy 1976). Moreover, the archaeologists excavating the *Kennemerland* recovered glass bottles and wooden casks that escaped the hands of early salvors. Using shipping records from the Port of Annapolis, Mechelle Kerns-Nocerito (2003) demonstrated the extent of trade networks between Anne Arundel County, Maryland, and the Caribbean in the mid-eighteenth century. The trade records showed that Marylanders exported tobacco and maize to the British colonies in the Caribbean, especially Barbados, in exchange for one of the only products readily available from British Caribbean merchants: rum. Steven Pendery (1999) also argued that the presence of Portuguese tin-glazed earthenware at seventeenth-century British colonial sites in New England revealed the ancillary use of ceramics in the Portuguese wine trade with North America.

The recovery of Iberian storage jars at Spanish colonial sites also highlights the enormity of the Spanish wine trade with Spanish colonists in the Americas. Some of the storage jars found at Spanish colonial sites in Florida may originally have brought wine to Spanish colonists in Cuba and other parts of the Spanish Caribbean. Once emptied of their original content, they were filled with locally made Caribbean rum and re-exported to Spanish colonial outposts in Florida. Caribbean rum, according to Amy Bushnell (1981), was reported to be one of the main items of trade with Native Americans who lived near St. Augustine in the seventeenth century (see also Fairbanks 1978: 167–68; Hoffman 1997: 26). The broken bits of Iberian storage jars on Spanish colonial sites in Florida therefore reveal an intricate web of trade relations and show the extent to which the alcohol business connected disparate peoples spread throughout the emerging Spanish Atlantic World (Ewen 2001).

The modern western perception of alcohol as a profane fluid has often been evoked to amplify the insidiousness of European slave trading. According to Cuban anthropologist Fernando Ortiz (1947: 25), rum "was always the cargo for the slaver's return trip, for with it slaves were bought, local chieftains bribed, and the African tribes corrupted and weakened." Historian Eric Williams wrote:

> Rum was an essential part of the cargo of the slave ship, particularly the colonial American slave ship. No slave trader could afford to dispense with a cargo of rum. It was profitable to spread the taste for liquor on the coast. The Negro dealers were plied with it, were induced to drink till they lost their reason, and then the bargain was struck.
> (Williams 1944: 78)

Figure 4–3. *Interior View of a Boiling House.* In William Clark, *Ten Views in the Island of Antigua, in Which Are Represented the Process of Sugar Making* (London, 1823). Courtesy of the John Carter Brown Library at Brown University.

Yet the reality of alcohol's part in the African trades is more mundane than the images so passionately depicted. Before the arrival of European explorers and traders, West and Central Africans had a long history of alcohol use. They were therefore already familiar with the potentially disastrous effects of regular excessive drinking, which precluded the type of disruption to traditional social structures that accompanied the alcohol trade to peoples with no prior histories of alcohol use, including Native North Americans and Australian Aborigine (Langton 1993; Mancall 1995; Smith 2004b).

Archaeologists have uncovered evidence of alcohol use in the African slave and commodities trades. For example, at Oüidah, one of the main departure points for enslaved peoples destined for the French Caribbean, Kenneth Kelly (1997) found fragments of European glass bottles that verify the scope of the European-African alcohol trade. According to Kelly, the bottles were frequently associated with the homes of African elites, suggesting that imported alcoholic beverages were reserved for wealthy African traders who used foreign drinks to demonstrate their political and economic power. The British abolition of the slave trade in 1807 curtailed the slave traffic. Yet the alcohol trade to West Africa expanded in the mid-nineteenth century as the European demand for gum, peanuts, rubber, cocoa, palm oil, and other West African commodities increased (Akyeampong 1996; Ambler 2003; Eltis and Jennings 1988: 955). Intrasite comparisons at Makala Kataa in northern Ghana allowed Ann Stahl (1994, 2001) to identify dramatic increases in European trade in the region in the nineteenth century. Perhaps the increasing frequency of European bottle glass at later sites in Makala Kataa reflects the increasing role of alcohol in the West African commodities trades.

Historical archaeologists have also used the material culture of alcohol storage and transport to trace regional alcohol trade patterns within the Americas. For example, Prudence Rice and Greg Smith (1989) explored the seventeenth- and eighteenth-century Peruvian wine trade with New Spain, Panama, and the Potosi silver mining regions in present-day Bolivia. According to Rice and Smith, the Moquegua Valley produced between 60 and 90 percent of the wine and brandy consumed in the Potosi region in the eighteenth century. Their analysis relied heavily on ceramic vessel evidence, especially locally made and stamped earthenware jars used to transport Peruvian wine and brandy throughout South America. Most of the jars dated to the eighteenth century, suggesting that the increasing demand for alcohol in the growing Spanish colonial world probably fueled the expansion of the wine and brandy trade from the Moquegua Valley at that time.

The archaeological investigation of shipwrecks has provided insights into the regional alcohol trade in the United States. For example, in 1865 the steamboat *Bertrand* sank on the Missouri River twenty miles north of Omaha, Nebraska. In 1968 archaeologists with the National Park Service excavated the *Bertrand* and recovered more than six thousand glass and ceramic bottles, many of which had been used to store and transport alcoholic beverages. Among the collection were forty-eight bottles of schnapps, twelve bottles of bourbon-whiskey, and numerous bottles of wine, champagne, ale, and bitters (Petsche 1974; Switzer 1974). The *Bertrand* and its cargo were headed for frontier mining settlements in the West, and the bottle evidence highlights the scale of the alcohol trade in the early years of westward expansion in the United States. Moreover, many of the bottles included the names of manufacturers, which helped the archaeologists identify the departure points of goods headed west and thus explicate alcohol trade patterns in the early American Republic. Similarly, shipwreck excavations off the coast of Australia attest that alcohol represented a significant portion of cargoes headed for that frontier colony, and archaeological investigations at nineteenth-century households in Melbourne have uncovered numerous embossed wine and liquor bottles from Europe and Asia that demonstrate the breadth of early Australia's alcohol imports (Davies 2006; Staniforth 2003: 108–9).

Embossed bottles have indeed been extremely useful in identifying emerging regional trade networks in the nineteenth and twentieth centuries. Robert Schuyler and Christopher Mills (1976: 71–72), for example, recovered numerous alcohol bottles with embossed makers' marks from a nineteenth-century sawmill site in rural eastern Massachusetts. The makers' marks indicated that many of the embossed bottles were coming from Lowell and Boston, thus allowing Schuyler and Mills to identify the sources of alcohol and trace the extent of regional marketing networks (see also Adams 1977: 48–50). The extensive study of embossed wine and liquor bottles has also allowed archaeologists working at nineteenth-century sites in Sacramento, California, and nineteenth- and early-twentieth-century sites in Silcott, Washington, to follow the regional alcohol traffic as well as situate the citizens of these communities within broader international spheres of trade (Schulz et al. 1980; Adams 1977).

Historical archaeologists have been successful at demonstrating the reach of the global alcohol trade and tracing the movement of alcoholic beverages through marketing networks. The evidence they have gathered raises important questions about modern processes that have fueled and constrained the alcohol trades. What conditions spurred the indigenous demand for alcohol in North America and the Pacific, and what were the colonial agendas that allowed the alcohol trade with indigenous peoples in these areas to thrive? What did local officials, church leaders, and national governments do to facilitate and curtail the alcohol trades with indigenous groups? And, with the rise of industrial breweries and distilleries, how did the corporate nature of the modern alcohol industry dictate trade patterns? By placing archaeological evidence of the alcohol business within the proper historical context, historical archaeology can initiate discussions about the sweeping and pervasive role of the alcohol traffic in the modern world. Moreover, alcohol-related material culture at particular sites provides an opportunity to elucidate not only the broad patterns of alcohol trading but also the intricacies of exchange networks. In addition, historical archaeology must deliberately address the factors that fueled the demand for alcohol and investigate the impact of alcohol drinking in different historical and cross-cultural settings. Indeed, the beliefs and behaviors surrounding alcohol consumption have become a chief focus of historical and anthropological literature. Given this rich body of knowledge from which to draw, historical archaeology can thoughtfully contribute to our understanding of alcohol drinking in the modern world.

5

The Historical Archaeology
of Alcohol Consumption

The cultural anthropological study of alcohol consumption has generated a sizable body of scholarly literature that has been largely focused on distinguishing the drinking patterns of different social groups, interpreting drunken comportment, identifying the way in which specific alcoholic beverages create social boundaries, and exploring the various functions of drunkenness. In general, cultural anthropologists have sought to articulate the fundamental reasons why people drink. Unlike other disciplines, which emphasize the pathological aspects of alcohol use, the anthropological study of alcohol has tended to highlight the normative, constructive, and culturally mediated outcomes of drinking (Heath 1987: 19). Anthropological interest in alcohol has also been driven by the desire to untangle the complex meanings that societies attach to alcohol consumption. In particular, anthropologists have struggled to explicate alcohol's simultaneously feared and celebrated status. Indeed, societies have often viewed alcohol drinking as concurrently salubrious and deadly, sacred and profane, and harmonious and discordant. More importantly, alcohol drinking performs seemingly divergent escapist and integrative functions. It is escapist in that it provides a temporary respite from the troubles of the world, and it is integrative in that it heightens sociability among friends and strangers (Douglas 1987a; Gusfield 1986, 1987; Horton 1943; MacAndrew and Edgerton 1969). In addition, the study of alcohol drinking has provided anthropologists with a useful prism through which to view broader social processes of power, resistance, sociability, accountability, spirituality, health, and social relations (for an overview, see Heath 1976, 1987, 2000).

Although archaeological research has often been overlooked in anthropological surveys of alcohol, a recent synthesis of anthropological approaches to alcohol by Michael Dietler (2006) outlined some of the key contributions that archaeologists have made to our understanding of alcohol drinking in society. Dietler's valuable overview emphasized archaeological research on alcohol at ancient and classical Old World sites, no doubt reflecting his primary area of study. Classical archaeologists and prehistorians have certainly increased our understanding of alcohol consumption in a number of temporal and regional settings. For example, Solomon Katz and Mary Voigt (1986) argued that the psychopharmacological effects of alcohol drinking elevated the social and sacred value of beer in Natufian societies and thus spurred the rise of intensive farming in the Near East 10,000–12,000 years ago. Drawing on evidence from royal tombs in ancient Egypt, Patrick E. McGovern (1998, 2003) examined how the life-giving qualities attributed to wine fueled wine consumption throughout the Mediterranean. Dietler (1995), exploring colonial encounters in Iron Age Western Europe, showed that colonized peoples often embrace the alcoholic beverages of the colonizer and modify the use of those new beverages to fit traditional drinking patterns. At Cerro Baúl in Peru, archaeologists investigated the architectural structures of the Wari people that were specifically designed for the social and sacred consumption of *chicha*. The researchers argued that the ritual consumption of alcohol that took place at these buildings was meant to strengthen social bonds between members of the community (Williams 2001, 2004, 2005; Williams et al. 2000).

Historical archaeologists have also investigated the social and sacred forces that have shaped patterns of alcohol consumption in the modern world. They have helped shed new light on the types of alcoholic beverages that people consumed and illuminate the way in which social distinctions based on class, race, and gender fostered different drinking patterns. Historical archaeologists have identified the conditions that spark alcohol drinking and provided important contextual information that has enhanced our understanding of the circumstances that motivate individuals to drink. In general, historical archaeologists have successfully addressed many of the same themes as their colleagues in cultural anthropology as well as in classical and prehistoric archaeology. Historical archaeology, however, as the archaeology of the modern world, has dealt with its own particular set of alcohol consumption issues, which this chapter seeks to define.

Alcohol and Foodways

At a rudimentary level, historical archaeologists treat alcohol drinking, though not always explicitly, as part of the foodways subsystem. The historical archaeology of foodways concentrates on the material culture of beverage and food use, usually within the context of formal dining. The study of foodways has been especially popular at British colonial sites in North America. James Deetz (1973), for example, examined ceramic assemblages from Plymouth, Massachusetts, from 1620 to 1835 in order to show changes in British North American drinking and eating habits. Analyzing ceramic drinking and eating vessels, he distinguished three successive phases operating at Plymouth (1620–60, 1660–1760, and 1760–1835), which represented gradual changes in foodways. Deetz argued that differences in ceramic use in each phase revealed a shift from a communal to a more individual pattern of drinking and eating, which was representative of a broader ideological change occurring in the emerging British Atlantic World known to historical archaeologists as the Georgian world view. According to Deetz, ceramic drinking and eating vessels were both rare in the early (communal) phase but became increasingly common over time to accommodate a growing trend toward individualized foodways. An analysis of New England probate inventories by Marley R. Brown III (1973) supported his contention that the trend toward individualized foodways was first evident in the colonists' increasing use of individual drinking vessels. Although Deetz and Brown did not specifically address alcohol use, they examined the role of drinking in British colonial foodways and asserted that the varying frequency of ceramic drinking vessels on historical archaeological sites over time was an expression of ideological change.

In the Chesapeake, seventeenth-century probate inventories contradicted the pattern that Deetz and Brown identified in Plymouth. For example, Mary Beaudry et al. (1983) challenged the Deetz model of communal foodways and argued that it overlooked pewter flatware, rare on archaeological sites but prevalent in probate inventories (see also Martin 1989). In fact, they found a paucity of drinking vessels in the probate inventories, which, in contrast to Deetz, indicated that drinking patterns, rather than eating patterns, exhibited a greater tendency toward communalism. Moreover, Beaudry et al. (1983: 25) showed that class differences had little influence on the number of drinking vessels per household and that "the number of drinking vessels remained consistently small across the economic continuum." Further, the particular scarcity of pewter drinking vessels in the probate inventories led the researchers to conclude that "drinking vessels were being shared." In a separate study, Beaudry (1981) showed how the terms and qualifiers used in the probate inventories to describe alcohol-drinking vessels highlighted the convivial and communal nature of drinking in seventeenth-century Chesapeake society.

Garry Wheeler Stone (1988) identified a similar scarcity of drinking vessels in seventeenth-century probate inventories from St. Mary's City, Maryland. According to Stone, the small number of pewter drinking vessels listed in the inventories indicated that colonists were engaged in communal drinking. Moreover, Stone (1988: 75) identified drinking vessels specifically designed for sharing and wrote that "these shared vessels were relics of a medieval European economy of scarcity, when not just cups, but architectural space, tools, draft animals, and land were shared intensively." Stone (1988: 75) argued that shared drinking vessels contributed to the creation of "cultures with distinctly corporate characteristics." Anne Yentsch also stressed the communal nature of seventeenth-century drinking in the Chesapeake. According to Yentsch (1990: 41), "until the early eighteenth century, men often drank using a communal vessel, euphemistically known as 'the social bowl.'" Yentsch interpreted communal drinking practices as part of a "folk" tradition and argued that the shift toward individualized drinking had to await expansion of British stoneware industries, which produced individual drinking mugs, in the late seventeenth century. However, the recovery of numerous expensive Chinese blue-and-white porcelain wine cups and *façon de venise* stemmed glassware from seventeenth-century archaeological sites in the Chesapeake (such as Jamestown and Jordan's Journey, Virginia, and St. Mary's City, Maryland) may challenge the argument that all classes in the Chesapeake, especially elites, regularly engaged in communal drinking in the seventeenth century (Grulich 2004; Kelso et al. 1999: 47–50; Mouer et al. 1992). Similarly, discoveries of fine Chinese porcelain wine cups at early-seventeenth-century domestic sites in Bridgetown, Barbados, and among the cargo of the *Witte Leeuw*, a ship of the Dutch East India Company that was sunk by Portuguese in 1613 off the coast of St. Helena, also seem to attest to the early and widespread use of individual drinking vessels in the emerging Atlantic World (Smith and Watson 2007: 190; Van der Pijl-Ketel 1982). In the final analysis, however, Yentsch, like Deetz, believed that the increasing desire for individualized drinking vessels reflected a growing shift in social habits from communal to individual and an increasing preoccupation with social differentiation.

Yet the communal nature of drinking was not restricted to early colonists in the British Atlantic World. For example, ceramic and glass assemblages from British settlement sites in Sydney, Australia, revealed a pattern of communal drinking similar to that found in the Chesapeake. According to Grace Karskens (2003: 50), "Communal drinking and glass sharing reaffirmed established friendships and signaled new ones." Perhaps life on rugged and unpredictable frontiers throughout the expanding British colonial world necessitated the creation of community support networks, and communal alcohol drinking helped foster a cooperative spirit. As in British North America, the early pattern of communal drinking in Sydney appears to have given way to a greater emphasis on individualism over time.

More enumerative methods have also been used to identify the role of alcohol in the foodways subsystem. Stanley South (1977), for example, developed a system of artifact patterning that addressed drinking in a similar foodways model. South considered glass bottles and ceramic drinking vessels part of an artifact category known as the "kitchen artifact group." According to South (1977: 99), the ceramic and glass vessels included in this group were associated with food preparation, storage, and consumption or "behavioral activity primarily centered on the kitchen." As a result, South's model subsumed the act of drinking within a broad artifact category, which ostensibly obscured the possibility of understanding specific patterns of alcohol consumption within the foodways subsystem. South believed that artifact categories should be modified, however, to identify and isolate certain activities, including alcohol use. For example, by viewing bottle glass fragments as a percentage of the entire artifact assemblage at Fort Moultrie (a Revolutionary War period site in South Carolina) and comparing the results with nonmilitary archaeological assemblages, South (1977: 149–51, 178) was able to make the case that soldiers garrisoned at the fort engaged in relatively high rates of alcohol use. Thus, the quantitative study of ceramics and glassware has allowed historical archaeologists to isolate alcohol drinking in the foodways subsystem and treat it within a broader comparative cultural framework.

Sociality and Sociability

Teapot and teacup fragments recovered from British colonial sites are evidence of a meaningful symbolic activity known to historical archaeologists as the tea-drinking ceremony. According to Deetz (1977: 60–61), tea drinking reflected the order, control, and symmetry of the Georgian mindset, which stressed the primacy of the individual and subordinated the communal. Yet, despite his emphasis on individualism, the tea ceremony was in fact a communal event. Participants procured tea from a communal pot and drank together from matching cups and saucers. Alcohol drinking, like tea drinking, was also usually part of a larger social performance. Communal punchbowls and multihandled drinking cups underscore the links between alcohol and sociality. Moreover, the construction of buildings specifically designed for the group consumption of alcoholic beverages, such as town taverns and corner saloons, reinforced the social and sociable nature of drinking events.

Historical archaeologists have indeed devoted much attention to describing structures designed for alcohol consumption. Taverns, inns, ordinaries, saloons, cafés, fraternity houses, and other sites of social drinking provide archaeologists with enormous opportunities to explore alcohol use and its role in generating the appropriate atmosphere for sociability. In addition, drinking establishments provided public space for the socialization of male peer groups and the display of masculine ideals. For example, in her study of North American saloon culture in the late nineteenth and early twentieth centuries, folklorist Madelon Powers (1998: 30) wrote: "for many working-class men, the test of true manhood was peer recognition for being a reliable ally and comrade in the volatile street culture of urban America." Alcohol drinking was often the pretext for such tests, which were intimately tied with notions of male honor. Treating male comrades to drinks, engaging in games of strength and chance, commiserating over the challenges of life and love, pooling financial resources, avowing group loyalty, and speaking and singing in the conflated language of "men" were all elements of public drinking places (Powers 1998; Salinger 2002; Spradley 1970; Tlusty 1997; Wilson 1973). Moreover, alcohol drinking loosened inhibitions, which enhanced feelings of male camaraderie and increased the fraternal value of these male-oriented spaces.

Taverns, in particular, have been a popular focus of historical archaeological inquiry, and researchers have used alcohol-related ceramics and glassware to interpret and verify the location of tavern sites. Erik Eckholm and James Deetz (1971), for example, used bottle glass, pipe stems, and faunal evidence to identify a specialized tavern for shore whalers on Great Island near Cape Cod in the late seventeenth and early eighteenth centuries. In Jamaica, Ivor Noël Hume (1968) wrote extensively on the assortment of tavern glassware recovered from Port Royal and used it to outline the archaeological signature of tavern sites. Donald Hamilton and Robyn Woodward (1984: 45) also conducted underwater archaeological excavations at a tavern site in Port Royal, which possessed an elaborately decorated tankard and sixty hand-blown black glass bottles. And Yolanda Courtney (2000) used pub tokens, another aspect of the material culture of tavern life, to define regional marketing networks in England and Wales in the eighteenth and early nineteenth centuries.

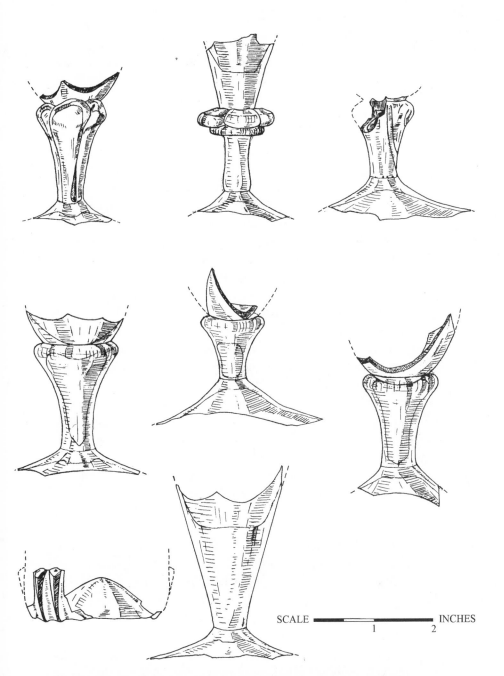

SCALE ▬▬▬▬▬▬▬▬▬ INCHES
        1   2

Figure 5–1. Illustrated glassware from Port Royal, Jamaica. From Ivor Noël Hume, "A Collection of Glass from Port Royal, Jamaica, with Some Observation on the Site, Its History, and Archaeology." Copyright The Society for Historical Archaeology 1968. Reprinted by permission from *Historical Archaeology*, Vol. 2.

Historical archaeologists have compared tavern artifact assemblages with those from domestic sites. For example, in Plymouth, Massachusetts, Kathleen Bragdon (1988) compared a seventeenth- and eighteenth-century tavern artifact assemblage with the domestic assemblage of a yeoman farmer of the same period. According to Bragdon, the high number of mugs, tumblers, and other drinking vessels recovered from the tavern site showed the primary function of the tavern as a place that dispensed alcoholic beverages. In contrast, the yeoman domestic site possessed a much more varied ceramic assemblage. Bragdon's study also showed that the tavern site possessed an especially high frequency of clay tobacco pipes. Deetz (1993: 104) made similar observations about the high number of clay tobacco pipes recovered from an eighteenth-century tavern site at Flowerdew Hundred in Virginia. Bragdon concluded that occupational differences had a greater influence on ceramic assemblages than did economic status. Thus, although the yeoman domestic assemblage had a higher concentration of coarse earthenware ceramics associated with food storage and preparation and a smaller overall number of ceramic drinking vessels, wine glasses, and specialized glassware, the variation reflected the occupational differences of the owners rather than the economic standing of the residents at the two sites.

Julia King (1988) compared domestic and tavern assemblages at the seventeenth-century St. John's site in St. Mary's City, Maryland. As with Bragdon, King found a higher percentage of drinking vessels during the tavern phase at the site. The tavern assemblage also contained a relatively high percentage of artifacts associated with food storage, however, suggesting that the tavern served a wide range of functions. Julia King and Henry Miller (1987) also conducted intrasite comparisons at the Garret van Sweringen site in St. Mary's City. The van Sweringen site consisted of a late-seventeenth- and early-eighteenth-century domestic structure and outbuilding. King and Miller investigated the spatial distributions of artifacts at the site, which revealed functional differences between the main house and outbuilding. The outbuilding assemblage possessed a large number of drinking vessels and clay tobacco pipes and a low percentage of dining vessels, which led King and Miller to conclude that the outbuilding assemblage probably represented van Sweringen's coffeehouse. Artifacts from the outbuilding were similar to those recovered from tavern assemblages, and documentary sources confirmed the presence of a coffeehouse at the site. Although the building was called a coffeehouse, alcohol appears to have been one of the primary drinks served there.

Historical archaeological evidence has helped shed light on the placement of taverns on the landscape. For example, Henry Miller (1988) examined the urban landscape of St. Mary's City and showed an orderly baroque design in what was previously thought to have been an unplanned and poorly organized urban center. Three of the four buildings located in the center of this baroque-designed city were taverns. Although they were not elaborate or high-profile buildings, they were located in the center of town. Mark Leone and Silas Hurry (1998) interpreted the layout of St. Mary's City in their investigation into the expression of power in the panoptic layout of urban space. Although not explicitly addressed in their study, the taverns in St. Mary's City were located in the center of town, perhaps as part of a conscious effort by clerics and town officials to subject social drinking to a greater level of surveillance and control. In a separate study, however, Leone (1995: 259) overtly identified the relationship between panoptic architecture and levels of alcohol consumption among urban residents of early Baltimore, Maryland. The concentration of taverns in the center of towns appears to have been a common practice in early British colonial settlements. John Cotter (1958: 46, 53–57), for example, also discovered two centrally located ordinaries in seventeenth-century Jamestown. Russell Handsman (1981: 15) conducted archaeological investigations at the Lawrence Tavern in Canaan, Connecticut, to show that taverns often served as centralized social anchors for members of dispersed agrarian communities in rural New England in the eighteenth century. However, the archaeological deposits indicated that, as Canaan developed into a nucleated urban village in the nineteenth century, the community became "highly differentiated and specialized and individuated"; and the Lawrence Tavern eventually served as a boardinghouse for young women in this increasingly industrialized landscape.

In contrast to the centralized location of taverns in St. Mary's City, Jamestown, and Canaan, tavern life in the eighteenth-century Moravian town of Salem, North Carolina, moved from its central location to the town's periphery. Moravians were a German-speaking religious sect. According to Brian Thomas (1994: 19), moving tavern life from the center of town to the periphery reflected the Moravian leadership's desire to create distance between Moravian residents and Anglo-American neighbors and visitors who frequented the town's tavern. Having a tavern in their community made Moravians part of the larger American society; yet, by placing tavern life at the town's periphery, Moravian leaders were able to manage outside influences and reduce cultural contamination. Thus, according to Thomas, the peripheral location of the tavern ensured that social interaction between Moravians and Anglo-Americans was restricted to the edge of town. Thomas (1994: 15) believed that relocating tavern life to the edge of town revealed a broader Moravian social strategy of "inclusion and exclusion."

Historical archaeologists have also examined the functions of different types of taverns. For example, Diana Rockman and Nan Rothschild (1984) modified South's artifact categories to identify distinct differences between rural and urban taverns in seventeenth-century North America. According to Rockman and Rothschild, artifact assemblages from urban taverns possessed a greater proportion of smoking- and drinking-related artifacts, indicating that urban taverns were specialized places for socializing. In contrast, rural-tavern assemblages possessed a wider variety of ceramic forms, indicating that rural taverns were less specialized places where travelers could simply receive a range of accommodations, including food, drink, and lodging (see also Salinger 2002: 63–65). Perhaps the rural location of the St. John's tavern in Maryland investigated by King explains the more varied artifact assemblage recovered from that site. Yet some rural taverns in colonial Maryland clearly excelled in the exclusive and outright sale of alcoholic beverages, including scarce and expensive wines and spirits imported from all over the Atlantic World (Kerns-Nocerito and Mintz 2000).

Tavern owners were occasionally forced to maximize space in dense urban settings. In Charleston, South Carolina, for example, historical archaeological investigations revealed that taverns sometimes served the dual purpose of drinking establishment and domestic dwelling in the eighteenth and early nineteenth centuries. According to Martha Zierden and Jeanne Calhoun (1986: 37), lots and buildings in Charleston were frequently used for both residential and commercial purposes "in response to the physical constriction and high cost of desirable land in the commercial core of the city." Similarly, Elizabeth Peña and Jacqueline Denmon (2000) investigated a nineteenth-century boardinghouse site in Buffalo, New York, that also operated as a saloon. Life for workers at the dual-purpose boardinghouse/saloon in Buffalo differed from life at corporate-owned boardinghouses, such as the Boott Cotton Mill boardinghouses in Lowell, Massachusetts, where employers established strict antialcohol codes that were meant to regulate the drinking habits of workers.

Several eighteenth-century taverns have been excavated in Colonial Williamsburg. For example, in 1965–66 Noël Hume (1969a) examined Wetherburn's Tavern, which was one of the first major archaeological studies of tavern life. He recovered an incredible amount of information about the

Figure 5–2. Archaeological excavations at Wetherburn's Tavern, Williamsburg, Virginia. Courtesy of the Colonial Williamsburg Foundation, Department of Archaeological Research.

variety of alcoholic beverages available to patrons and the specific material culture of taverns. Archaeologists in Williamsburg have excavated several other taverns, including the King's Arms Tavern (Knight 1932), Shield's Tavern (Brown 1986; Brown et al. 1990), and Raleigh's Tavern (Bullock 1932). Gaming was a popular pastime at these taverns; for example, excavations at Shield's Tavern revealed a circular pit in the backyard area of the site that was probably once used as a cockfighting ring. The Williamsburg tavern assemblages have been compared with the assemblage from an eighteenth-century Williamsburg coffeehouse. Philip Levy et al. (2007) argued that, unlike the taverns in Williamsburg, the coffeehouse catered to an elite clientele. Archaeological remains, including evidence of a Chinese porcelain tea set, tea caddies, and fashionable folding fans, intimated the high status of coffeehouse patrons. The researchers also speculated that other finds, such as a vertebra and finger bone of a physician's human anatomy skeleton, showed that the coffeehouse provided an ethereal and educational atmosphere for the town's intellectual elite. Such activity, they claimed, contrasted with the more raucous entertainments, such as cockfighting, found in the town's taverns. Moreover, Levy et al. stressed the location of the coffeehouse within Williamsburg's landscape. Its close proximity to the Capitol building suggested to the researchers that the coffeehouse owner attempted to cater to the needs of a more elite clientele in this politically active city. Yet taverns were also located near the Capitol building; and competition among the town's many tavern owners may have led some, including the coffeehouse owner, to offer specialized activities such as human anatomy lectures to attract and maintain wealthy patrons.

Saloons have also been the focus of historical archaeological inquiry. Margaret Purser (1992: 109), for example, argued that saloons in Paradise Valley, Nevada, as with taverns in St. Mary's City, represented the public sphere of the town's built environment. Alcoholic beverages were indeed a requisite part of the vibrant public saloon culture that existed in the western United States, especially in gold-mining areas. The extraordinary

Figure 5–3. *A Midnight Modern Conversation* by William Hogarth (1732). Courtesy of the Colonial Williamsburg Foundation.

Figure 5–4. Punch-drinking scene from *Christmas in the Country*. Artist named Collings, engraved by Barlow, and published by Bentley and Company (London, 1791). Courtesy of the Colonial Williamsburg Foundation.

number of alcohol bottles recovered from the steamboat *Bertrand*, which sank on the Missouri River while on its way to deliver supplies to miners in the gold-mining region of Fort Benton, Montana, attests to the alcoholic demands of miners (Petsche 1974; Switzer 1974). Champagne and oysters were among the *Bertrand*'s cargo, highlighting the exuberance, extravagance, and flamboyance of the gold-rush mentality in the mid-nineteenth century. The discovery of poker chips at late-nineteenth- and early-twentieth-century saloon sites in Fairbanks, Alaska, is evidence of gambling among gold-rush miners on these rugged frontiers (Bowers and Gannon 1998). In Sacramento, California, Peter Schulz and Sherri Gust (1983: 44) examined faunal remains from nineteenth-century urban sites in order to determine the socioeconomic "status of the depositing population." Among the sites investigated were the city jail, two saloons, and a fine hotel. The presence of middle-value cuts of meat in faunal assemblages from the saloons showed that the socioeconomic rank of the two saloons fell, as expected, between the jail and the hotel. The saloon faunal assemblages also indicated greater use of carcass portions, which would have facilitated the preparation of roasts. According to Schulz and Gust, the evidence for roasts reflected the saloon owners' practice of providing free lunches to customers. Roasts were cheap and easy to prepare and thus made an ideal dish for free lunches. In contrast, the fine hotel offered patrons more expensive cuts of meat, such as T-bone cuts of steak from the short loin.

Kelly J. Dixon (2005) provided one of the most comprehensive studies of saloon life in the western United States. While Hollywood films, television shows, and popular writers have depicted nineteenth-century western boomtown saloons as brutal, violent, and debauched places, Dixon used archaeological evidence from Virginia City, Nevada, to dismantle these myths and show that rough-and-tumble saloons were not the norm. As with the study of taverns and coffeehouses in Williamsburg, Dixon embraced a comparative perspective on Virginia City saloons that showcased the variety of saloons available to saloon-goers in this frontier setting. Dixon was primarily interested, however, in capturing the spirit of the Boston Saloon, an upscale drinking establishment owned by an African American proprietor who largely catered to Virginia City's African American community. Using maps, census records, and other public documents, Dixon reconstructed the social geography of Virginia City and identified the location of African American households in this diverse urban setting. Dixon showed that African Americans did not concentrate in distinct and segregated African American neighborhoods. Instead, African Americans were integrated into the broader Virginia City community and lived side by side with European immigrants and Americans of European descent. Dixon's study thus raises important questions about why African Americans, who lived and worked side by side with whites, would seek or perhaps were forced to seek separation from the broader community in their leisure time at the Boston Saloon.

Dixon recovered items that one might expect to find at saloon sites. Glass and stoneware bottles used for storing alcohol, iron barrel hoops and copper-alloy faucets for whiskey kegs, clay tobacco pipes, and lead-glass decanter stoppers were prominent at the different saloon sites. Dixon also detailed the various forms of glassware found at western saloons, including tumblers, mugs, and goblets. Two of the saloons had a high frequency of fancy crystal stemware, which allowed Dixon to challenge popular depictions of the rough and gritty western saloon and discuss the more upscale nature of at least some of these establishments. Besides drinking, saloons offered a variety of other leisure entertainments. Dixon (2005: 112–13) recovered material evidence for gambling, which along with tobacco smoking and alcohol drinking was part of the "trinity of habits" that made boomtown saloons "havens for the expression of enjoyment." Yet perhaps the most interesting section of Dixon's analysis of saloon materials concerned the presence of artifacts associated with ethnic identity. Dixon identified the way in which saloon owners used material culture to signal their particular ethnicity in this frontier setting. For example, the heavy presence of German mineral water bottles at the Piper Saloon, owned by a German immigrant, may represent one of the ways in which the saloon owner celebrated his German heritage in this western boomtown.

Historians and anthropologists have contrasted the public use of alcohol by men at drinking establishments with the private drinking of women (Bjerén 1992; Murdock 1998; Tlusty 1997). Historical archaeological evidence has contributed to this dialogue. Donald Hardesty (1994: 138), for example, suggested that the high frequency of alcohol-related artifacts in domestic households in the mining West indicated that women "consumed alcoholic beverages at home instead of in public places." Yet alcohol use among women was not always confined to the privacy of their homes. Although drinking establishments catered predominantly to men, women were often present at these sites. Women have traditionally played a central role in the distribution of alcoholic beverages at male-oriented drinking establishments. Women serving drinks, wives of tavern owners, prostitutes, and hucksters were an integral part of tavern and saloon life (Powers 1998: 32–35; Tlusty 1997: 30–31). Historical archaeology is well positioned to shed light on the presence of women at male-oriented drinking establishments and increase our understanding of their particular roles within those contexts. The recovery of women's clothing items at saloons in western mining towns, for example, hints at the possibility that prostitutes added to the pleasures available to saloon-goers (Dixon 2005: 124–32; Spude 2005).

The study of brothels has also provided opportunities to explore the connection between women and alcohol and sociable drinking places. For example, a nineteenth-century privy from a brothel site in the Five Points section of New York contained fifty-eight glass tumblers and a variety of other goods associated with alcohol consumption (Yamin 1998). Alcohol-related materials "dominated" some nineteenth-century brothel sites in the western United States (Hardesty 1994: 138). And Catherine Holder Spude's (2005) study of late-nineteenth and early-twentieth-century brothel sites in the American West showed that the high frequency of liquor bottles at brothel sites mirrored that of contemporary saloon assemblages. Bottles have also been recovered from late-nineteenth-century brothel sites in Washington, D.C. According to Donna Seifert (1991: 99), whose team investigated the D.C. brothel sites, the evidence showed that "most" brothels served alcohol. The use of alcohol by women at brothels may illustrate ways in which women coped with the anxieties of prostitution. In addition, drinking reduced male inhibitions, and prostitutes may have used alcoholic drinks to loosen the wallets of brothel patrons. More fundamentally, clients were charged for their drinks, much to the satisfaction of the brothel owners.

A wide variety of material and ideological forces spurred the rise of centrally located and socially oriented drinking establishments. Historian W. Scott Haine (1996), for example, argued that cramped and poor housing conditions contributed to the popularity of café-going in nineteenth-century Paris. Haine also stressed the need for camaraderie, especially during an era when the industrial revolution in France was increasing the level of worker alienation. Cafés provided an escape from poor living and working conditions and a location for people with common plights to share their experiences. Archaeologists may be able to correlate the number of drinking establishments in a region with the living and working conditions of local residents. In addition, drinking establishments often possessed special amenities that were beyond the economic reach of most workers. Madelon Powers (1998), for example, argued that the popularity of the workingman's saloon in North America in the nineteenth and early twentieth centuries was due at least in part to the presence of pleasant amenities that were not available in the average home, such as mirrors and gas lighting. Archaeologists can identify the particular amenities that tavern and saloon owners used to entice local residents to patronize their establishments. Dixon (2005: 65–66), for example, recovered seashells from one saloon site in Virginia City, which suggested that saloon owners attempted to attract patrons with novelties such as aquariums. Moreover, it may be possible to link the impact of new inventions, such as punchbowls and billiard tables, to increasing levels of sociability in a community and therefore to the growth of tavern and saloon culture. Historical archaeologists can also investigate the purpose of different drinking establishments and show how their functions changed over time to meet the changing social climate of a region.

Alcohol-Related Material Culture and Social Relations

Anthropologist Mary Douglas argued that alcohol drinking acts as a marker of personal identity and as a way to distinguish boundaries of inclusion and exclusion. According to Douglas (1987a: 9), "the more that alcohol is used for signifying selection and exclusion the more might we expect its abuse to appear among the ranks of the excluded." Her observations about the inclusive and exclusive tensions exhibited in alcohol use are germane for understanding the way in which drinking has helped shape social relations, especially in the modern industrialized world. Indeed, historians and cultural anthropologists have investigated the relationship between alcohol use and the expression of social boundaries, including boundaries based on socioeconomic class. In these studies, working-class drinking is typically contrasted with middle-class temperance (Gusfield 1986; Pegram 1998; Powers 1998; Rorabaugh 1979). The public drinking of the working classes is also distinguished from the private drinking of elites (Barrows and Room 1991a; Powers 1998: 76–89). Moreover, researchers have explored the way in which social groups use specific types of alcoholic beverages to define class identity and strengthen group boundaries (Akyeampong 1996; Haine 1996; Smith 2001a). Historical archaeologists have also used the material culture of alcohol to view the ways in which alcohol consumption marks insider/outsider status and reinforces social boundaries.

In the preindustrial era, artisans, apprentices, and agricultural laborers routinely engaged in bouts of alcohol drinking throughout the day. In the nineteenth century, however, alcohol drinking confronted the disciplined labor structure of industrial capitalism. According to sociologist Joseph Gusfield (1987), industrial capitalism ushered in new concepts of time that institutionalized divisions between work and leisure. While regular drinking with fellow workers and tradesmen during the workday may have been acceptable in preindustrial settings, it was considered antithetical to the principles of industrial capitalism. Factory owners pursued various methods to foster a regimented workforce. The rise of temperance movements in the nineteenth century was spurred in part by factory owners who sought to improve the efficiency of their workforce through teetotalism (Gusfield 1986). Archaeological investigations into the lives of nineteenth- and early-twentieth-century workers at the Boott Cotton Mills in Lowell, Massachusetts, have revealed insights into the alcohol-related changes that accompanied industrial capitalism (Beaudry 1989, 1993; Beaudry et al. 1991; Beaudry and Mrozowski 1987; Bond 1988, 1989a, 1989b; Kelso 1993; Mrozowski et al. 1996). According to Beaudry (1989), mill owners practiced a system of moral policing that sought to restrict the drinking of mill workers. This corporate paternalism was meant to produce a structured, diligent workforce and reduce the likelihood of labor unrest. Yet archaeological evidence from the Boott Cotton Mill boardinghouses revealed that attempts to curb drinking were not entirely successful:

> Just as documents reveal that boardinghouse keepers did not always adhere strictly to company rules, the preliminary analysis of artifacts recovered from the fill of one of the Boott wells shows that there were many ways in which boardinghouse keepers and workers sought to personalize their surroundings and to exercise control over their own lives. The evidence for the consumption of alcoholic beverages (e.g., liquor, wine, and beer bottles, beer mugs, wine glasses) speaks of rather flagrant violation of one rule the corporation never relaxed.
> (Beaudry and Mrozowski 1987: 156)

Alcohol drinking sustained ethnic customs, strengthened worker solidarity, and provided a means of escape from the anomie of industrial work (Bond 1989b: 29). More importantly, according to Mary Beaudry and Stephen Mrozowski, alcohol use at the boardinghouses showed worker resistance to the dehumanizing effects of industrial labor and corporate attempts to control workers' leisure time. At the same time, however, alcohol drinking served the ideological needs of factory owners, who condemned alcohol use by the working classes and held it up as a banner to naturalize class distinctions, rationalize class boundaries, and validate their dominant position within the entrenched social hierarchy of industrial capitalism (Wurst 1991: 144–45).

Nor was illicit drinking confined to the domestic settings of industrial workers. Richard Veit and Paul W. Schopp (1999), for example, found caches of alcohol bottles in the workspaces of employees at the Lakehurst Shops, a late-nineteenth- and early-twentieth-century locomotive repair facility and roundhouse operated by the Central Railroad of New Jersey. Drinking by workers on the job violated company policy and, as with drinking in the domestic setting of the Boott Cotton Mill boardinghouses, challenged the efficacy of the industrial labor regimen. Yet antialcohol policies not only confronted preindustrial conditions of labor but also defied particular occupational customs. Sociologist William J. Sonnenstuhl (1996) explored the practice of on-the-job drinking in his study of the Sandhogs, members of the Tunnel and Construction Workers Union in New York City. Sandhogs represent one of many "intemperate occupational drinking cultures," which are characterized by all-male teams that regularly drink on the job. According to Sonnenstuhl (1996: 20–29), on-the-job drinking should be seen as an occupational ritual that marks occupational boundaries and builds solidarity among members of the work team (see also Gusfield 1987). The evidence from Lakehurst certainly suggests that shop workers for the Central Railroad of New Jersey qualify as an occupational drinking culture. Perhaps California aqueduct laborers represent another example. Thad M. Van Bueren (2002: 38) found that alcohol consumption was widespread among workers in the Alabama Gates camp, a temporary work camp for aqueduct laborers in southern California in the early twentieth century. Aqueduct workers drank in both domestic and industrial contexts at the site, suggesting the pursuit of occupational customs and preindustrial labor patterns of regular alcohol drinking by all-male work gangs. According to Van Bueren (2002: 39), levels of alcohol consumption were lowest in households with timekeeping devices, indicating that those households engaged in "behavior more consistent with capitalist expectations for efficiency and timeliness." Thus, the evidence for alcohol drinking at the Boott Cotton Mill boardinghouses, the Central Railroad of New Jersey shops, and the California aqueduct camps highlights some of the uneasy transitions that occurred at industrial workplaces in the nineteenth and twentieth centuries as North America shifted its economic gears.

Yet, while many employers attempted to restrict alcohol consumption among employees, some apparently overlooked drinking by their workers. For example, bottle glass and bottle label evidence from the Ben Schroeder Saddletree Factory in Madison, Indiana, indicated that supervisors were aware of beer drinking by workers at the site. Deborah Rotman and John Staicer (2002: 103) suggest that skilled workers and craftsmen at the family-owned Saddletree Factory had more freedoms than unskilled workers employed in the cold and impersonal industrial mills in places like Lowell. Similarly, Jed Levin (1985) found that employers at small-scale industrial/commercial sites in Manhattan, New York, in the late nineteenth and early twentieth centuries condoned alcohol use among workers despite an emerging capitalist work discipline that condemned drinking. According to Levin, the evidence for alcohol use among workers at the sites revealed inconsistencies in the early industrial labor regimen and showcased the impersonal forces that determined the rigidity of work discipline.

Covert alcohol drinking was not restricted to laborers in industrial work settings. Bente Bittmann and Gerda Alcaide (1984) identified alcohol-based resistance among late-nineteenth- and early-twentieth-century nitrate workers in northern Chile. According to Bittmann and Alcaide, bottle glass evidence indicated that nitrate workers regularly drank alcoholic beverages despite attempts by employers to curb alcohol use in the mining camps. Similarly, LouAnn Wurst (1999) examined alcohol use at a nineteenth-century domestic servant dwelling in Binghamton, New York, and found that, in contrast to the employer's house, the servant dwelling possessed an especially high frequency of liquor bottles. As with the Boott Cotton Mill boardinghouses, she claimed that the relatively high concentration of liquor bottles at the separate servant dwelling reflected the domestics' resistance to the employer's moralistic controls. In particular, Wurst (1999: 16–17) argued that the higher concentration of liquor bottles at the servant dwelling showed that "servants may have had more freedom in personal behavior than domestics who lived under the roof of their employer." Moreover, she believed that servant drinking helped define a working-class counterculture that rejected temperate values. Robert Fitts (1996: 64–65) explored antidrinking codes that prohibited alcohol use among enslaved domestic servants in New England who lived in the homes of their owners. Despite such prohibitions, enslaved servants in New England were able to circumvent such social controls by engaging in clandestine drinking at secret meeting places and taverns away from the view of their owners. William Kelso (1984: 190–91) also speculated that the presence of hand-blown glass bottles in the root cellars of enslaved peoples at the mid-eighteenth-century Kingsmill Plantation in Virginia reflected attempts by members of the estate's enslaved population to hide wine, which had been stolen from the home of the plantation owner (see also Samford 1996: 100). And Theresa Singleton (2006: 279) interpreted the presence of bottles at the enclosed El Padre slave village in Cuba as evidence of illicit alcohol use by enslaved peoples at the site.

Historical archaeological evidence of drinking from nineteenth-century households in Brooklyn, New York, has also shed light on the role of alcohol in demarcating social boundaries. According to Paul Reckner and Stephen Brighton (1999: 73), the absence of alcohol bottles from two of the households excavated in Brooklyn indicated that the residents "conformed to mainstream middle-class temperance rhetoric." A small number of alcohol bottles recovered from four other middle-class households, however, led them to conclude that the residents of those households did not conform to the ideal of total abstinence advocated by neighborhood reformers. Reckner and Brighton compared their findings from Brooklyn with evidence from nineteenth-century working-class households in the Five Points neighborhood of New York, a neighborhood composed primarily of Irish and German immigrants. They found that, although one household had a relatively low number of alcohol-related vessels, three others had higher concentrations than those observed at the middle-class households in Brooklyn. Reckner and Brighton incorporated two other assemblages into their study from nineteenth-century native-born and presumably middle-class tenements in Greenwich Mews, New York. The two Greenwich sites possessed alcohol-related vessels in numbers similar to those found at the immigrant working-class sites at Five Points. Reckner and Brighton (1999: 80) concluded that, "in the light of similar consumption patterns visible in both native-born and immigrant working-class assemblages, American reformers' emphasis on Irish and German intemperance appears unfounded." In fact, they believed that the discovery of a Staffordshire teacup bearing the image of Irish temperance advocate Theobald Mathew at one of the immigrant sites at Five Points even indicated Irish temperance reformers within that working-class community. Finally, Reckner and Brighton compared all of the New York assemblages with evidence from the Boott Cotton Mill boardinghouses in order to show the relatively low level of drinking at all the New York sites. They used this evidence to question the purity of middle-class temperance and challenge notions about excessive drinking among working-class immigrants. Reckner and Brighton argued that stereotypes about the drinking excesses of working-class immigrants, especially Irish, were created in an anti-immigrant and anti-Catholic context and used to validate the dominant position of native-born middle-class Americans in the existing social hierarchy.

Using evidence from the working-class Irish immigrant households at Five Points, Heather Griggs (1999: 94) contended that the significant drop in the percentage of wine and liquor bottles over time at the site reflected "the continuing effects that Catholic temperance societies, as well as the Mission Ladies, had on the Irish populace." Griggs (1999: 88–89) also praised Reckner and Brighton's work as an example of how archaeologists can challenge "sinister" assumptions and stereotypes about working class-immigrants:

A common manifestation of archaeological bias at the ethnic level is the examination of liquor and medicinal bottles from Irish sites. Presence of what may be deemed "a lot" of liquor or medicine bottles commonly creates a discussion of alcoholism among the Irish. While

archaeologists should conduct discussions about health and sickness among an immigrant group that had been through a devastating famine, who made long ocean voyages in squalid conditions, and who often settled in cramped and unsanitary neighborhoods, this has generally been neglected. Instead many archaeologists have consciously or unconsciously chosen to focus studies of certain items of material culture on a cultural stereotype passed down through historical images.
(Griggs 1999: 88–89)

Yet Griggs appears to have overstated the "common manifestation of archaeological bias," for it is not something that I have come across in my extensive survey of alcohol studies in historical archaeology. In fact, most historical archaeologists who have addressed alcohol-related themes embrace sophisticated concepts of social relations, which treat class and ethnicity as fluid and negotiated. Mrozowski et al. (1996), for example, make deliberate statements about drinking at the heavily Irish-populated Boott Cotton Mill boardinghouses because they recognize that class and ethnicity are not fixed. According to Mrozowski et al. (1996: 74), drinking was just one of many leisure activities in which mill workers engaged and there may have been many individuals who did not drink. Also, they explain that drinking activities leave behind "plentiful artifactual evidence, and thus become the focus of our investigation of leisure behavior."

In the late nineteenth and early twentieth centuries, the temperance movement in the United States was in full swing and reformers were confident they could curb alcohol drinking. Alice Ross (1993), for example, examined nineteenth-century cookbooks in order to show how temperance reformers demonized alcohol use and attempted to alter North American dietary habits. As with alcohol drinking, the rejection of alcoholic beverages expressed group affiliation. Gerard Thomas (cited in Peña and Denmon 2000: 92), for example, found a heavy concentration of soda mineral water bottles at a nineteenth-century boardinghouse in Buffalo, New York, which he believed reflected the impact of temperance ideals that helped "solidify social bonds between individuals." Lu Ann De Cunzo (1995) examined evidence of temperance reform at the site of the Magdalen Society asylum in Philadelphia, which largely housed former prostitutes. After 1810 temperance became a mainstay of the society. Although a small number of alcohol bottles were recovered from the asylum site, De Cunzo (1995: 78) believed that they were probably recycled for nonalcoholic purposes: for example, as containers to hold syrups, spring and soda waters, and medicinal concoctions. According to De Cunzo, the bottle evidence from the asylum reflected the pursuit of a temperate ideology.

Temperance was closely linked to middle-class notions of respectability, but bitters and other patent medicines with high alcohol contents were sometimes used to circumvent temperance reforms. For example, Kathleen Bond (1989a) contended that the large number of patent medicine bottles found at the nineteenth-century Boott Cotton Mill boardinghouses reflected surreptitious alcohol consumption. Similarly, Rebecca Yamin (1998) argued that the patent medicine bottles recovered from working-class Irish immigrant sites in the Five Points neighborhood in New York revealed attempts by residents to drink yet avoid the disdain of middle-class reformers and neighborhood temperance advocates. Masking alcohol use behind patent medicines was not limited to the working classes. Joan Geismar (1993: 68), for example, contended that, despite the low number of alcohol bottles found in the nineteenth-century privies of middle-class families in Greenwich Mews, the large number of patent medicines indicated high levels of alcohol use (see also Bonasera and Raymer 2001). The high frequency of bitters, however, may also represent gendered differences in alcohol drinking. In the nineteenth and twentieth centuries, some women were known to drink high-alcohol-content bitters and patent medicines alone in their homes to avoid the criticism of temperance reformers. These women, usually housewives, were sometimes referred to as "lace curtain alcoholics."

How did the choice of alcoholic beverages help define social boundaries? At nitrate mining camps in northern Chile, Bittmann and Alcaide (1984) recovered bottles for locally made alcoholic beverages in association with the workers' trash middens and bottles for imported alcoholic beverages in the trash middens of camp supervisors. They argued that the miners' consumption of locally made drinks contrasted with the consumption of expensive imported drinks by the employers and managers. The choice of alcoholic beverages therefore facilitated the construction of class boundaries between workers and supervisors. Charles Ewen (1986) examined the relationship between alcohol drinking and class hierarchy at an early-nineteenth-century fur-trading camp in Wisconsin. Using documentary evidence, he found that lower-rank traders consumed alcohol from common kegs while higher-ranked traders consumed bottled forms of expensive alcohol. The presence of bottle glass in some areas of the fur-trade camp therefore allowed Ewen to identify the structures of higher-status occupants.

The consumption of high-quality alcoholic beverages, however, is not always an indication of wealth. In the seventeenth century, the fish trade to Europe gave Newfoundland fishermen direct access to expensive French wine and brandy. According to Peter Pope (1997: 52–53), British officials and large landowners in Newfoundland disapproved of the fishermen's access to such elite drinks and tried to prevent them from enjoying commodities that they considered above the fishermen's socioeconomic position. The dynamic realities of the fish-for-alcohol trade, however, meant that attempts to restrict the fishermen's access to these premium drinks were unsuccessful.

Historical archaeologists have inferred elite status from particular alcohol-related artifacts. For example, Robert Marx (1967, 1968) was surprised to recover only a few wine glasses during underwater excavations at Port Royal, Jamaica. He hypothesized that the excavations must have been conducted in a poor section of Port Royal, where residents used less expensive drinking vessels. Noël Hume (1968) challenged Marx's interpretation, however, and argued that the discovery of so few fine drinking glasses should not be surprising, since it was likely that the people of Port Royal dumped their trash in a central location in the town. Moreover, Noël Hume (1968: 18) deduced from the various excavations at Port Royal that the glassware recovered was, "with a few notable exceptions, what one would expect to find on a site occupied by a reasonably affluent society at the close of the seventeenth century." Elite status is also evident in discussions about ceramic and porcelain punchbowls. According to Yentsch (1990), British colonists in the Chesapeake in the late seventeenth century incorporated punchbowls into their foodways. The use of punchbowls represented the colonists' adoption of the fashionable drinking habits of metropolitan elites. Madeira wine, from the Portuguese island of Madeira, was a main ingredient of punch, which may help explain why Portuguese tin-glazed punchbowls were prominent ancillary items in the Portuguese wine trade to New England (Hancock 1998; Pendery 1999: 63). Interestingly, the dregs of wine were sometimes used as an ingredient in the tin glazes found on Iberian majolica (Lister and Lister 1974: 26). Glass and ceramic punchbowls appear to have undergone morphological changes over time. Seventeenth-century punchbowls were smaller than ones produced in the Georgian period, which sometimes held as much as two gallons (Connell 1957). Commemorative punchbowls with elaborate motifs and whimsical inscriptions also became more prevalent during the eighteenth century (Gollannek 2007). Perhaps the growing availability of Madeira wine and distilled spirits in the

Figure 5–5. Polychrome tin-glazed (delft) punchbowl from England, ca.1755 bearing the inscription "One Bowle More & then." Courtesy of the Colonial Williamsburg Foundation.

eighteenth century, as well as the growing availability of spices and other ingredients used to make punch, led to the increasing size and decoration of punchbowls.

Glass and crystal alcohol decanters were also an elite item associated with alcohol consumption. Investigations at eighteenth-century households in Charleston, South Carolina, led Martha Zierden (1999: 81) to conclude

Figure 5–6. Engraved Madeira wine decanter (ca. 1760) from Wetherburn's Tavern, Williamsburg, Virginia. Courtesy of the Colonial Williamsburg Foundation, Department of Archaeological Research.

that crystal decanters were part of a formal dining pattern that allowed elites to display their wealth. Finely engraved Madeira decanters have also been recovered from the eighteenth-century Wetherburn's Tavern site in Williamsburg and Thomas Jefferson's home at Monticello (Kelso 1982; Noël Hume 1969a). Possessing a wide variety of drinking vessels was itself a sign of wealth (Scott 1991: 46). Archaeologists have interpreted bottle size as an indicator of socioeconomic standing. For example, according to Mrozowski et al. (1996: 73), most liquor bottles recovered from the Boott Cotton Mill boardinghouses "were small, suggesting that workers could only afford small amounts at a time." Smaller bottles were also easier to conceal, however, and may have been necessary for workers who wished to hide their drinking in the strict antialcohol environment of the corporate-run boardinghouses.

In contrast to the public nature of working-class taverns and saloons, elite sociability tended to be a private affair. Historians Susanna Barrows and Robin Room (1991a) argued that researchers often lack evidence of elite drinking patterns because elites tended to drink and socialize in the privacy of their homes. Maurie McInnis (1999: 45) identified a wide range of alcohol-related glass and ceramic items in the early-nineteenth-century probate inventories of wealthy residents in Charleston. According to McInnis, these items helped Charleston's elite display gentility and thus affirm their standing among peers. Also, Robert Leath (1999: 57) argued that Chinese porcelain drinking mugs were popular among elites in eighteenth-century Charleston, who used them to pursue the art of upper-class sociability. For example, the eighteenth-century probate inventory of Peter Manigault, a Charleston lawyer and planter, listed fifteen Chinese porcelain punchbowls. According to Leath (1999: 52), "Manigault's inventory reflects the primacy placed by colonial Charlestonians on their more sociable town residences as well as the vast number of wares required to maintain a stylish, eighteenth-century Charleston household." By the end of the eighteenth century, the desire to perform elite drinking rituals and display fashionable ceramics and glassware (such as imported tin-glazed punchbowls and stylish crystal wine glasses) was so widespread that it could be found among even the small planters in the Carolina Backcountry (Groover 1994: 51).

Similar displays of wealth and private upper-class sociability are evident in the Caribbean. For example, glass bottles dominated the artifact assemblage of a late-eighteenth- and early-nineteenth-century planter's residence in the Bahamas. According to Paul Farnsworth (1996: 17), the archaeologist who investigated the site, the artifact assemblage resembled "more a tavern than a permanent residence." David Watters and Desmond Nicholson (1982: 226) made similar observations about Highland House in Barbuda, the eighteenth-century estate of the wealthy and politically powerful Codrington family. Alcohol-based sociability was also present among relatively wealthy British colonists in Bridgetown, Barbados, in the mid-seventeenth century. A comparative look at ceramic and glass vessels suggests that British colonists in the densely populated bustling port of Bridgetown, unlike their British colonial counterparts in the Chesapeake, fully embraced the sociable art of drinking and engaged in fashionable drinking performances similar to those practiced by contemporary elites in England. The widespread availability of alcohol, the frequency of transient visitors, and the desire to emulate elite forms of alcohol-based hospitality increased the Barbadians' special fascination with sociable drinking and elevated it to a reverential level. Sociable drinking became a popular pastime in Bridgetown, and the wealth generated by sugar production, as well as the influence of Dutch traders, made sociable drinking performances possible (Smith 2001b). The presence of alcohol bottles and fashionable drinking vessels at urban domestic dwellings and wealthy planter households in the

Figure 5–7. Blue and white porcelain wine cups from a mid-seventeenth-century domestic site in Bridgetown, Barbados. Photo: author's collection.

Caribbean highlights the same preoccupation with alcohol-based gentility and sociability found among urban elites and planters in South Carolina.

Private alcohol-based sociability was not limited to wealthy residents in plantation societies. New England merchants also used alcohol to express ideals of elite gentility. For example, at the late-seventeenth- and early-eighteenth-century Turner's House site in Salem, Massachusetts, Lorinda Goodwin (1999: 134) recovered evidence of alcohol-based gentility. According to Goodwin, the Turners were an important merchant family in Salem and "understood the value of alcoholic entertainment." She interpreted the large number of alcohol-related artifacts recovered from the site as evidence of the "mannerly" behavior of wealthy New England merchants. The high percentage of punchbowls, fancy drinking cups, and wine glasses led to similar conclusions at merchant sites in Newbury, Massachusetts (Beaudry 1995), and Newport, Rhode Island (Mrozowski 1984: 43). Alcohol-based sociability was one of the ways in which New England merchants helped authenticate their dominant station in society.

Historical archaeologists have also studied patterns of alcohol consumption to explore social relations and boundary maintenance between African and European Americans. For example, John Solomon Otto (1984) compared planter and slave assemblages at the late-eighteenth- and nineteenth-century Cannon's Point Plantation in Georgia in an attempt to understand how race and legal status shaped the material conditions of life for free and enslaved. With regard to alcohol consumption, Otto wrote:

> Assuming there was a correlation between the hue of the olive-green bottles and their contents, the higher frequencies of the black bottle fragments in the slave refuse suggested the slaves drank more brewed beverages; conversely, the higher frequencies of medium-green fragments at the overseer and planter sites suggested that plantation whites drank more wine.
>
> (Otto 1984: 76)

In addition, Otto (1984: 80, 115–16) accepted Noël Hume's claim that square case bottles held gin and used the evidence to argue that the overseer and planter drank more gin than did the enslaved peoples on the estate. According to Otto (1984: 168), the cheaper brewed beverages associated with Cannon's Point enslaved population and the expensive wine and gin associated with the overseer and planter represented substantive differences in the material conditions between free and enslaved and thus provide insights into the way in which social relations and legal status shape the archaeological record. Jean Howson (1990: 87–88), however, challenged Otto's emphasis on status markers when comparing slave, overseer, and planter assemblages. She argued that Otto's static interpretation of "white dominance" in racial and legal status overlooked the way in which domination operated in the plantation complex. According to Howson, the bottles found at the Cannon's Point slave quarters reflect not status differences and the subordination of enslaved peoples but simply the private and communal activities of enslaved peoples on the estate. Similarly, Charles Cheek and Amy Friedlander (1990: 54) compared materials from late-nineteenth- and early-twentieth-century African American and European American households in Washington, D.C., and argued that the absence of wine glasses in African American households reflected disinterest in the European American middle-class "social customs" of wine drinking. Yet perhaps the absence of wine glasses in African American households in D.C. represents broader African American social strategies aimed at disrupting racist ideologies that exploited African American consumers and imposed false barriers to African American consumer choices (Mullins 1999). More importantly, the absence of wine glasses in African American households in D.C. provides an opportunity for historical archaeologists to enter into discussions about the emergence of African American temperance reform and the tradition of teetotalism that emerged in African American communities in North America in the nineteenth century (Fahey 1997; Herd 1991).

Alcohol Use and the Survival of Old World Cultural Traditions

The massive movement of peoples to new locations is one of the defining features of the modern world, and historical archaeologists have investigated the survival of Old World cultural traditions in New World settings, including traditions surrounding the use of alcoholic beverages. Alcohol drinking is a conservative social behavior loaded with symbolic meaning. The type of alcoholic beverages consumed, levels of alcohol consumption, preparation of drinks, drunken comportment, and context of drinking performance convey powerful messages that distinguish social groups, including ethnic groups in pluralistic societies. In the diverse settings of the modern world, alcoholic beverages often became markers of ethnic identity that expressed and defined boundaries between self and other. Indeed, alcohol drinking was deeply ingrained in the social fabric of the Old World societies that served as departure points for migrants headed for the New World either by coercion or by free will. The immigrants' desire to re-create traditional Old World drinking customs gave rise to distinct drinking patterns in the New World. It also led to experimentation with local plant resources and attempts to produce alcoholic beverages that would serve as substitutes for the drinks left behind. The rise of brew houses in the Chesapeake and the Carolinas, for example, illustrates the seventeenth-century British and German colonists' demand for familiar alcoholic drinks (Cotter 1958: 102–9; King 1990; Thomas 1994). Such endeavors allowed New World colonists to retain Old World drinking habits and sustain important social, sacred, and symbolic links to their homelands overseas.

In Spain, wine traditionally played a central role in dietary habits and was common at most meals. The Spanish imbued wine with classical symbolism, nationalistic pride, and sacred attributes in Catholic religious rites, which elevated the meaning of wine drinking in Spanish foodways. The insufficient imports of Spanish wine in the Spanish colonies stimulated the emergence of *bodegas* in Mexico and Peru and no doubt strengthened the Spanish colonists' appetite for colonial imitations (Rice and Smith 1989; Skowronek 1992: 112). Prudence Rice and Greg Smith, for example, argued that the difficulty in obtaining wine from Spain led to the rise of Spanish colonial wine making in the Moquegua Valley (see also Avery 1997). The Moquegua Valley *bodegas* fed the demand for wine in the Spanish New World colonies and were so important that they dominated the economy of that region. Donna Ruhl (1997: 44) wrote that the inadequacies of Spanish trade and the high cost of imported goods in La Florida led to "agricultural experimentation," including failed attempts at viticulture. The secular and sacred need for wine in the Spanish colonies probably explains why Iberian storage jars, frequently used for the transport of wine, were some of the most common European ceramic forms found at the convent at San Luis Mission in Apalachee, Florida, and the Santo Domingo monastery in La Antigua, Guatemala (Carruthers 2003; McEwan 1991: 50). Julia Costello (1992: 63–64) examined the purchasing patterns of Spanish colonial missions, using early-nineteenth-century shipping records from American and Spanish traders. A comparison of purchases revealed that religious items, including sacramental wine, were typically purchased from Spanish traders. Yet, while Spanish colonists and Spanish Creoles may have preferred wine, Indian peasants in Spanish colonies often maintained their own traditions of alcohol use. Bernard Fontana (1968: 53), for example, argued that the limited number of glass alcohol bottles at eighteenth- and early-nineteenth-century sites in Sonora, Mexico, reflected the Indians' traditional practice of drinking locally made alcoholic beverages, such as *pulque*, from leather and wooden containers.

As with Spanish colonists in Americas, Italian immigrants in the United States also imbued wine with social and sacred meaning. During Prohibition, some Italian immigrant families in Battle Creek, Michigan, planted small vineyards near their houses to grow grapes for wine. According to Michael Nassaney and Carol Nickolai (1999: 81), the practice ensured that, despite Prohibition, the Italian families would be able to celebrate traditional Italian feast days and "create more familiar and culturally consistent surroundings" in their New World setting. William Adams (1977: 49) speculated that the high frequency of wine bottles recovered at the Weiss Ranch site in Silcott, Washington, was due to the fact that the owners of the ranch "were German immigrants who may have brought with them Old World drinking habits." Irish immigrants in North America also maintained Old World drinking patterns. Yamin (1998: 79), for example, found glass and stoneware bottles used for storing beer, ale, and whiskey in the households of Irish tenants in the Five Points neighborhood of New York, which demonstrate the sense of ethnic pride in traditional Irish drinks felt by the Irish immigrants who lived at the sites. Other materials, including decorated clay tobacco pipes and a temperance cup bearing the image of Irish temperance reformer Theobald Mathew, support claims about the pervasiveness of Irish nationalism among Irish residents in Five Points (Reckner and Brighton 1999). Old World traditions of alcohol drinking were also indicated by alcohol-related artifacts discovered in Jewish immigrant households at Five Points, according to Yamin:

> There was plenty of wine at the Goldberg table, perhaps for the traditional blessings that were part of the Jewish Friday night supper. Drunk from matching tumblers and firing glasses, it reminded the family of its Jewish roots and loosened the tongues of the otherwise shy boarders.
> (Yamin 1998: 76)

Edward Staski (1983) used archaeological evidence to examine how cultural traditions shaped Irish American and Jewish American drinking patterns in New York. Staski embraced sociological studies that compared Irish American and Jewish American drinking patterns but found that household tensions had a greater influence on the level of alcohol consumption than ethnic identity. He argued that individual households characterized by social heterogeneity, in which, for example, a husband and wife held substantially unequal social positions, experienced high rates of alcohol consumption because of the stresses that accompanied interpersonal conflict.

At seventeenth- and early-eighteenth-century sites in New Amsterdam, Meta Janowitz (1993) examined the role of alcohol in Dutch colonial foodways. Janowitz described a number of Dutch ceramic forms specifically designed for the storage and consumption of alcoholic beverages. Traditions of alcohol use also shaped material culture in the English colonies. For example, Yentsch (1990: 44–45) noted that the long history of alcohol use in England ensured that English colonists in North America would quickly adopt new trends in punch drinking. According to Yentsch, the colonists' familiarity with alcoholic beverages helped accelerate the spread of punch drinking and its related ceramic equipment. French colonists in the New World also sought familiar alcoholic beverages. For example, French-manufactured glass bottles that once contained French wine and brandy figured prominently in the eighteenth-century households of French Creoles in New Orleans, Louisiana (Dawdy 2000: 116). John Walthall (1991) examined French colonial drinking at Fort Michilimackinac, Michigan, and at French colonial sites in Illinois. Walthall (1991: 101) believed that the small number of porcelain and faience drinking vessels recovered from eighteenth-century French colonial sites in Michigan and Illinois "reflect the lack of development of formal traditions of beverage consumption among the eighteenth-century French." More recent discoveries of fashionable drinking vessels at French colonial sites in Acadia, Nouvelle France, Old Mobile, and French Guyane, however, appear to refute such claims (Bernier 2003; Croteau 2004; Faulkner 1992; Faulkner and Faulkner 1987; Gums 2002; Moussette 1994, 1996; Shulsky 2002; Waselkov and Walthall 2002). Perhaps the paucity of porcelain and faience drinking vessels at sites in Michigan and Illinois reflects the peripheral nature of these settlements in the French colonial world and their distance from the well-stocked marketplaces of major French colonial ports.

Eastern European immigrants pursued traditional drinking patterns in the Americas too. Despite restrictions on alcohol use at northern Michigan logging camps in the early twentieth century, bottle glass evidence indicated that Slovenian workers were allowed to enjoy their tradition of beer drinking (Franzen 1992: 84). Bottle glass evidence also showed that imported Russian vodka was one of the principal alcoholic drinks consumed by Russian fur traders in eighteenth-century Alaska (Crowell 1997: 181).

Chinese immigrants in North America also attempted to maintain traditional drinking customs. Staski (1993: 141–43) found that imported Chinese wines and spirits were widely consumed among Chinese immigrants in late-nineteenth-century El Paso, Texas. Evidence from early-twentieth-century sites in El Paso, however, showed that Chinese immigrants were increasingly consuming American-made alcoholic drinks. According to Staski, the increasing use of American alcoholic beverages illustrated changes in Chinese consumer choices and the "assimilation" of the overseas Chinese to American drinking patterns. Similarly, Michael Diehl et al. (1998) found evidence of alcohol use at late-nineteenth-century Chinese expatriate sites in Tucson, Arizona. Among the artifacts were Chinese stoneware liquor bottles (*tsao tsun*) and other alcohol-related vessels. According to the researchers,

Most of the recovered alcoholic beverage bottles held contents brewed in Europe and the United States. These beverages probably served as a replacement for Chinese liquors, which were probably more expensive, and consumed only on important occasions . . . Foodstuffs and beverages manufactured in China helped recall memories of meals eaten in China.

(Diehl et al. 1998: 30–31)

More recent studies of overseas Chinese communities have tried to avoid the essentializing pitfalls of acculturation studies. In Oakland, California, for example, Adrian Praetzellis and Mary Praetzellis (2004: 255) investigated the lives of Chinese laundry workers and uncovered extensive evidence of overseas Chinese leisure activities, including the consumption of imported Chinese wine and liquor. They identified similar types of alcohol at the boardinghouse sites of overseas Chinese miners in Sacramento, California. These alcoholic beverages not only served recreational purposes for Chinese immigrants but also played a key role in overseas Chinese funerary rites, and participants sometimes adapted American alcoholic beverages for these purposes (Akin 1992: 60). The presence of imported Chinese alcoholic beverages at Chinese laundry-worker sites in Oakland and Chinese miner sites in Sacramento provides insights into the consumer activities of Chinese immigrants, the political-economic links emerging between China and California, and the market forces that helped spur the success of Chinese merchants in the western United States in the nineteenth and early twentieth centuries (Praetzellis 1999; Praetzellis and Praetzellis 1997, 2001).

Historical archaeologists have also examined the survival of West African drinking traditions in the Americas. Leland Ferguson (1991, 1992), for example, investigated the production of earthenware vessels, known to historical archaeologists as *colono* ware, by enslaved peoples in South Carolina. According to Ferguson (1992: 103), some of the larger *colono*-ware jars recovered from slave cabins in South Carolina may have once been used for brewing beer. He argued that similar jars served similar purposes in West Africa and that the presence of such jars in South Carolina suggests the survival of West African beer-brewing traditions in the New World. In one of the more provocative interviews by Ferguson (1992: 103–6), the initial response of Roy Seiber, an art historian familiar with West African crafts, to small *colono* bowls was that they would have been appropriate in West Africa for the consumption of palm wine, a traditional alcoholic beverage produced in many areas along the West African coast (see also Smith 2004b). Otto (1984) discovered a high concentration of bowls at the quarters of enslaved peoples at Cannon's Point Plantation and argued that bowls reflected the maintenance of West African eating habits in the Americas. Yet, if such bowls were traditionally used for palm wine consumption in West Africa as Seiber indicated, then the heavy concentration of bowls at Cannon's Point may reflect not only West African eating behaviors, as Otto argued, but also the pursuit of West African drinking practices.

Enslaved Africans and Creoles in the New World also had access to European and American alcoholic beverages. For example, Barbara Heath (1997, 1998) challenged the popular belief that poverty, plantation rationing, and planter paternalism limited the consumer choices of enslaved Africans and Afro-Creoles in eighteenth-century Virginia. Using archaeological evidence and store accounts, she showed that enslaved peoples were active consumers who created their own distinct material world. The consumer choices of enslaved peoples in Virginia, according to Heath, included purchases of alcoholic beverages (see also Martin 1997; Samford 2007: 143).

Alcohol has a transformative quality, and its ability to alter consciousness has led to the rise of alcohol-based rituals surrounding death and spirituality. Many cultures recognize links between alcohol and death and have often used alcoholic beverages to facilitate communication with ancestral and spiritual worlds (Akyeampong 1996; Leacock 1964; McAllister 2005; Smith 2005: 95–117). Indeed, alcoholic beverages played a central role in the spiritual beliefs of enslaved Africans and Afro-Creoles in the Americas, especially in burial practices, and these traditions have deep roots in West Africa (Jamieson 1995; Smith 2004b, 2005: 95–117).

Historical archaeologists have explored the connections between alcohol and the survival of West African burial customs among enslaved peoples in the Americas. For example, archaeological investigations at the eighteenth-century Harney slave cemetery in Montserrat may have revealed evidence of the ritual use of alcohol in the funerary rites of enslaved peoples (Petersen and Watters 1988; Watters 1987, 1994; Watters and Petersen 1991). According to David Watters (1994: 64), a Turlington Balsam of Life bottle recovered from the cemetery may have once contained rum and been a grave good buried with one of the deceased interred at the site. Although a number of historical documents refer to the placement of bottles filled with alcoholic beverages in the graves of deceased slaves, the Harney cemetery represents the strongest archaeological evidence to date of such practices. In the 1970s Jerome S. Handler and Frederick W. Lange (1978) excavated more than one hundred burials at the Newton Plantation slave cemetery in Barbados. Although they discussed documentary evidence that enslaved peoples placed bottles of alcohol in the graves of their deceased comrades, they recovered no bottles with any of the burials at Newton. Glass bottle fragments were also recovered from a burial at an unmarked seventeenth- to nineteenth-century Afro-Barbadian cemetery in Bridgetown, Barbados. The fragmentary nature of the glass, however, suggested that it entered the grave accidentally and not as grave goods (Crain et al. 2004; Farmer et al. 2005; Farmer et al. 2007). Nor were any whole bottles recovered from the graves of the more than four hundred burials excavated at the New York African Burial Ground site in New York (Perry et al. 2006). Despite documentary sources that claim enslaved peoples placed alcohol bottles in the graves of their deceased friends and family, the paucity of alcohol bottles recovered from the burials of enslaved peoples indicates that the demand for bottles among the living outweighed the need for bottles in funerary rites. Bottles were prized for practical purposes, and enslaved peoples probably modified West and Central African burial traditions to meet local conditions. Thus, enslaved peoples may have simply sprinkled alcohol into the graves of deceased rather than relinquish useful bottles (Smith 2004b, 2005: 95–117).

The relationship between alcohol and burial traditions has also been investigated in the Pacific. David Burley (1995), for example, studied the placement of beer bottles and cans on graves in the Pacific Island of Tonga. He accepted the emic perspective of islanders that aesthetic decoration alone inspired the use of beer bottles and cans on graves. Burley summarized possible symbolic interpretations of the beer bottles and cans but dismissed the etic interpretations of anthropologists, arguing that, in terms of social metaphor, Tongans did not connect the beer containers and their alcoholic contents in funerary decoration. The purpose of Burley's study was to provide a cautionary tale to western researchers who, in their attempts to "recover the mind," incorrectly infer symbolic connections where none exist.

Alcohol and Health

Alcohol is linked to health in a number of folk traditions. In medieval France, for example, brandy was marketed as a preventative against the plague, and Dutch physician Franciscus Sylvius invented gin in the sixteenth century to combat the illnesses faced by Dutch sailors on their long-distance overseas voyages (Berlin 1996: 3; Unwin 1991: 179). In fact, in the sixteenth and early seventeenth centuries, apothecaries and physicians were the primary producers and distributors of distilled spirits. Beliefs about alcohol's medicinal qualities, founded upon Galenic principles of health, no doubt helped spur the rise of alcohol making in the harsh new disease environments on the colonial frontiers (Laudan 2000).

Historical archaeologists have used alcohol-related material culture to investigate issues of health in the modern world. Ivor Noël Hume (1982: 102), for example, stressed the medicinal aspects of distilling in his discussion of the alembic head found at a seventeenth-century site at Martin's Hundred, Virginia. Audrey Horning (1995: 165) argued that one of the main reasons colonists established a brewery in Jamestown, Virginia, was to avoid the illnesses associated with having to drink Jamestown's "notoriously brackish water." Peter Pope (1997: 55–56) found a high frequency of alcohol bottles at seventeenth-century sites in Newfoundland and suggested that alcohol drinking by colonists there was driven in part by conventional wisdom that considered the consumption of alcoholic beverages, especially distilled spirits, a proper way to warm the body. According to Pope, the colonists' perception of alcohol as a hot fluid led them to use alcoholic beverages as a prophylactic against illness and a counter to Newfoundland's cold and wet climate. Caroline Carley (1981) found liquor bottles associated with a physician's quarter at an early-nineteenth-century Hudson Bay Company fort in Washington, which may have been used to treat the illnesses of those garrisoned at the fort. Mary Maniery (2002: 75) suggested that whiskey bottles recovered from early twentieth-century "dry" work-camp sites in California were used for medicinal purposes. And Praetzellis and Praetzellis (2004: 255) stressed the medicinal value of alcohol at sites associated with overseas Chinese workers in California. Yet some archaeological evidence linking health and alcohol is less obvious. Iain Walker (1976), for example, identified alternative uses for white clay tobacco pipes, including evidence that the pipes were occasionally ground up and mixed with wine as a curative for le flux de sang. Ethnobotanical evidence for alcohol production at historic-period sites may also represent the production of alcoholic beverages for medicinal rather than convivial purposes (Holt 1991: 52–53).

Patent medicines show a clear link between alcohol and health. In the nineteenth and early twentieth centuries, medicines with high alcohol contents became popular home remedies. Michael Torbenson et al. (2000) conducted biochemical tests on an undisturbed bottle of Lash's Bitters from the early twentieth century, which revealed that the alcohol content was nearly

20%. Further research identified some varieties of bitters with alcohol contents as high as 43%. Olive Jones (1981) studied "essence of peppermint" bottles, a popular patent medicine that contained peppermint oil and high concentrations of alcohol. The numerous patent medicine bottles recovered from the halfway house stations of lifesavers in Cape Cod, Massachusetts, may have been used to treat illnesses (Lenik 1972). Similarly, Laurie Wilkie (1997: 85) described patent medicine bottles from an African American site in Alabama, which may have been used by midwives to treat women during childbirth. She also argued that the presence of whiskey bottles at African American sites might represent the production of homemade bitters for medicinal purposes (see also Wilkie 2003).

Excavations at the Wayman African Methodist Episcopal (AME) Church site in Bloomington, Illinois, revealed more evidence concerning the therapeutic role of high-alcohol-content patent medicines in the African American community in the mid-nineteenth and early twentieth centuries. According to Melanie Cabak et al. (1995), providing health care to the congregation was one of the main functions of the Wayman AME Church, and glass medicine bottles represented about 6% of the total artifact assemblage from the site. Other health-related finds at the site, however, showed that patent medicines were not as widely used as prescription medicines for treating parishioners. Although the researchers dismissed patent medicines as possessing "little medicinal value," they noted that patent medicines were used to treat the congregations for a number of specific ailments (Cabak et al. 1995: 66).

The detrimental effects of alcohol are also evident in the archaeological record. Jerome Handler et al. (1986) found evidence of lead toxicity in the human skeletal remains of enslaved peoples buried at Newton Plantation, Barbados, between the seventeenth and nineteenth centuries. According to Handler et al., enslaved peoples in Barbados were frequently exposed to lead, but the particular cause of lead toxicity in this enslaved population may have been the consumption of rum, which was tainted by lead during the distilling process.

Alcoholism has also been a focus in historical archaeological inquiry. For example, Edward Staski (1984), using modern material culture evidence from Tucson, Arizona, set out to investigate how the frequency of bottles at archaeological sites might enhance our understanding of alcohol addiction. Staski compared the drinking patterns of Anglo-Americans and Mexican Americans but found no significant difference in levels of alcohol consumption in particular households based on income or ethnicity. Instead,

Staski believed that individual choice (or perhaps more accurately addiction), rather than cultural factors, determined excessive drinking. Based on the evidence from Tucson, Staski (1984: 41–42) claimed that "treatment programs that focus on the individual are more useful than social reform movements when it comes to treating alcohol-related problems." Treatment of alcoholism is also evident in the archaeological record. For example, James Garman and Paul Russo (1999: 128) argued that the temperance policy of the nineteenth-century Smithfield Town Farm, a poorhouse in Smithfield, Rhode Island, explains the small number of ceramic drinking mugs associated with "lower forms of alcohol consumption" recovered from the site.

Alcohol, Anxiety, and Archaeology

In a seminal work in alcohol studies, anthropologist Donald Horton (1943) systematically investigated cross-cultural drinking patterns and attempted to explain the universal function of drinking. Underlying Horton's argument was the basic premise that unpredictable circumstances increase levels of alcohol consumption, and he doggedly wrote that "*the primary function of alcoholic beverages in all societies is the reduction of anxiety*" (Horton 1943: 223; emphasis in the original). While there are numerous causes of individual anxiety, Horton focused on the level of the social group. He argued, for example, that the unstable subsistence base of hunters and gatherers led to anxieties that were eased by excessive drinking. Since Horton's initial study, anthropologists and historians have identified the anxieties that cause excessive drinking in a number of different cultural and historical settings.

Historical archaeologists have also explored the relationship between anxiety and excessive drinking. For example, Susan Kent (1983) linked anxiety and excessive alcohol use at historic-period Navajo Indian sites in the Southwest United States. According to Kent (1983: 56), the Navajo's increasing interactions with European Americans led to a rapid shift from a "traditional" to a "semi-traditional" society, which created anxieties and cultural stress. Based on archaeological finds from one site in New Mexico, Kent wrote:

The numerous alcoholic beverage bottles found at the site—wine, whiskey, and beer—may be a reflection of a group of people caught between two cultures and belonging to neither. Alcohol often provides

a temporary escape from the painful alienation caused by a decreasing faith in the traditional culture and an increasing confusion concerning another, nontraditional, culture.
(Kent 1983: 61–62)

Perhaps many of the alcohol-related materials found on historic-period indigenous sites throughout the Americas tell us less about trade relations between Native Americans and Europeans and more about the way in which Native Americans coped with the frustrations of routine colonial assaults on traditional indigenous social structures and efforts by Native Americans "to regain a psychological stronghold in a world gone seemingly astray" (Mancall 1995: 84).

Other archaeological examples of anxiety-based drinking are less explicit. Evidence for excessive alcohol use is especially strong at military sites and may reflect the anxieties caused by the unpredictable nature of warfare and beliefs about the courage-promoting effects of drinking (Carstairs 1979). For example, the high concentration of bottle glass at Fort Moultrie in South Carolina led Stanley South (1977: 178) to conclude that "soldiers drank a lot." David Colin Crass and Deborah Wallsmith (1992: 8–10) made similar observations about U.S. soldiers stationed at forts in New Mexico in the 1850s. Joseph Balicki (2000: 143) noted that alcohol bottles were among the most common finds at Fort C. F. Smith, a Union garrison on the banks of the Potomac River during the American Civil War. Archaeological evidence from latrines at Johnson Island Prison in Ohio, which housed Confederate prisoners of war, revealed an unequal distribution of liquor bottles in the latrines. According to David Bush (2000: 74), the archaeologist who investigated the site, liquor bottles were concentrated in the latrines of groups of prisoners who were willing to take an oath of allegiance to the federal government. These Confederate soldiers received "special treatment," including access to alcoholic beverages.

Archaeologists frequently lump alcoholic beverages under the functional heading of "indulgences." At Fort Snelling, Minnesota, Robert Clouse (1999: 103–4) found that alcohol use was concentrated in certain areas inside the fort. Commanders apparently set aside areas of the fort for alcohol consumption as a way for soldiers to "escape from the rigidity and rigors of military life." According to Clouse, this pattern of separate indulgence areas continues to operate on U.S. military bases today and may provide soldiers with "an escape mechanism from the military structure of servility and inequality."

The rank and marital status of soldiers shaped patterns of alcohol use at military sites. For example, bottle glass evidence from the nineteenth-century site of Fort Independence in Boston led Joyce Clements (1993: 57) to conclude that single commissioned officers drank more than and differently from their married and noncommissioned counterparts. At the mid-nineteenth century site of Fort Fillmore in New Mexico, however, Staski (1990) found little variation in bottle-glass assemblages between officers' quarters and enlisted men's barracks. The study of glassware from eighteenth-century British military sites has also helped historical archaeologists sort out the way in which rank influenced drinking patterns (Smith 1983; Jones and Smith 1985).

Loneliness, hard work, and unpredictable natural environments increased anxieties and fueled the widespread use of alcohol by colonists at the frontier margins of the Atlantic World. Transient lifestyles compounded levels of anxiety and may help explain evidence of drinking at sites associated with rootless social groups. For example, Daniel Finamore (1994) investigated how former pirates who became transient logwood cutters in the jungles of Belize embraced a lifestyle of communal binge drinking. The logwood cutters would travel upriver to cut wood, return downriver when they had enough to sell, collect their pay, buy liquor, and drink themselves blind. When the logwood cutters ran out of money, they returned upriver to cut more wood to buy more liquor and start the process all over again. The paucity of liquor bottles at upriver logwood cutter sites, according to Finamore, is the result of this pattern of downriver binge drinking. Communal binge drinking also figured prominently among the rootless fur trappers on the early frontiers in the western United States (Rorabaugh 1979: 155–61). Noël Hume (1968) argued that the large number of wine glasses recovered from Port Royal confirmed documentary reports about heavy drinking and the debauched lifestyles of Port Royal inhabitants, many of whom were transient seamen. John Franzen (1992: 84) also noted archaeological evidence of heavy alcohol consumption among workers at northern Michigan logging camps in the early twentieth century. And Thad M. Van Bueren (2002: 38) found evidence that alcohol consumption was widespread among workers at temporary work camps in southern California in the same period.

Perhaps anxiety and transience explain the plethora of alcohol bottles recovered from gold-rush era saloon sites in Alaska and Nevada (Bowers and Gannon 1998; Dixon 2005; Purser 1992). Similarly, Julian Toulouse (1970) examined embossed bottles from nineteenth-century western mining towns, which revealed the wide variety of alcoholic beverages available to western miners. Loneliness and anxiety might also explain the numerous whiskey bottles found at Truro halfway house sites associated with lifesavers and rescuers who lived along the isolated shores of Cape Cod (Lenik 1972). In Mexico, according to Anthony Andrews (1981: 5), "large heaps of discarded potsherds and rum bottles" dominate seasonal work and hunting camps in the Yucatán. And a liquor store at Fort Garry, a nineteenth-century Hudson Bay Company post in Manitoba, catered to the alcoholic needs of anxious settlers in this frontier setting (Monks 1992: 45).

There is some evidence that temperance reform penetrated the rootless frontier society. For example, according to George Teague (1980), the growth of temperance among western miners at the late-nineteenth- and early-twentieth-century Reward mining site is evident in the decreasing number of alcoholic beverage bottles at the site between 1880 and 1920. Teague argued that the shift reflected the influence of temperance reform on the Reward miners. Franzen (1992: 84) noted that Finns at northern Michigan logging camps formed temperance organizations in order to strengthen class and ethnic solidarity. Yet the anxiety, boredom, and loneliness encountered on remote and rootless frontiers could also test the resolve of teetotalers. Stacy C. Kozakavich (2006), for example, used archaeological evidence from Kirilovka Village in Saskatchewan, Canada, to investigate the Doukhobors, an ascetic Christian religious sect that migrated from Russia and settled in remote areas of western Canada in the late nineteenth and early twentieth century. Although temperance was a mainstay of Doukhobor philosophy, alcohol bottles figured prominently in the privies and domestic spaces of some Doukhobor residents at Kirilovka Village.

Yet anxiety-driven alcohol use is not limited to the rootless soldiers, transient laborers, and religious exiles on the frontier. The presence of alcohol bottles at the sites of enslaved peoples may also be seen as an avenue of temporary escape from the many anxieties associated with a precarious existence within the confines of a coerced labor system (Smith 2004b, 2005: 118–67). The anomie and alienation felt by wageworkers in emerging industrial societies may also help explain the need for alcohol at corporate-run boardinghouses and the homes of working-class wage earners (Beaudry 1989; Bond 1989b; LeeDecker et al. 1987: 255; Mrozowski et al. 1996). Perhaps, too, the bitters and patent medicines in the bottles recovered from middle-class households in New York neighborhoods provided women with occasional opportunities to escape the rigid confines of an ideology of feminine domesticity. And anxiety may explain the heavy drinking sometimes attributed to archaeological field technicians, who live transient life-styles and suffer the tribulations of unpredictable employment (McGuire and Walker 1999: 173).

Conclusion

Alcoholic beverages have penetrated all societies in the modern world, and it would be difficult to find an archaeological site completely devoid of their presence. Every bottle, can, mug, and cup recovered during an archaeo-logical excavation has the potential to initiate discussions about alcohol use at the site. Even the absence of alcohol-related materials raises questions about the beliefs and behaviors of the site's occupants. For example, the absence of alcohol bottles at the southwest Michigan home of James and Ellen White, founders of the Seventh-Day Adventist Church, is consistent with the temperate philosophy of their faith (Nassaney et al. 2001). Few, if any, of the historical archaeological studies mentioned above specifically set out to examine alcohol drinking, yet these studies have increased our understanding of many alcohol-related themes, especially the role of alco-hol in foodways, alcohol's ability to enhance sociability, the use of alcohol in the construction of social boundaries, the survival and pursuit of tradi-tional drinking patterns, beliefs about alcohol's medicinal properties, and the conditions that spur drinking.

Although this survey is only a small sample of the better-known histori-cal archaeological works, it highlights some of the unique strengths of the historical archaeological study of alcohol. There are, however, many aspects that are beyond the scope of most historical archaeological research. For example, while archaeological methods can address individual and site-specific processes, they are simply not in a good position to investigate general epidemiological issues, such as alcoholism. Human soft tissues, which show the effects of excessive drinking and might provide conclusive evidence of alcoholism, seldom survive in the archaeological record. Bottle recycling practices also undermine attempts to obtain an accurate assess-ment of the levels of alcohol consumption at particular sites. However, the study of lead toxicity through bone chemistry analysis may be one indirect measure of excessive drinking (Handler et al. 1986). Our dearth of knowl-edge about the original contents of glass bottles from the seventeenth and eighteenth centuries is also a shortcoming. Although Noël Hume (1974) and Jones (1993) speculated about the original contents of glass bottles, the widespread reuse of bottles for various alcoholic and nonalcoholic liquids prevents a clear understanding of how different types of alcoholic beverages moved through communities. Such information could provide valuable insights into trade patterns and the ways in which alcohol consumption strengthened social boundaries.

One of the most disturbing discoveries in the historical archaeology of alcohol drinking is that Victorian ideals of abstinence have penetrated the scholarship of researchers and shaped the direction of historical archaeological inquiry. For example, some of the studies at working-class and Irish immigrant sites attempt to downplay levels of alcohol use within those communities (Griggs 1999; Reckner and Brighton 1999). Underlying the dismissal of alcohol-related evidence and the need to qualify statements about immigrant working-class drinking are Victorian middle-class notions of respectability that demonize alcohol use. Why not interpret alcohol use among working-class immigrants as the persistence of cultural traditions, resistance to middle-class values, or the escapist response to poor living and working conditions? Beaudry (1989), Bond (1989b: 29), and Mrozowski et al. (1996: 71–74), for example, clearly recognized the resistance ideology behind worker drinking at the Boott Cotton Mill boardinghouses. Fitts (2002: 11) noted that alcohol bottles recovered from a nineteenth-century Italian immigrant household in New York underscored the residents' rejection of middle-class temperance ideals. And Orser (2007: 123–24) raised the possibility that the Staffordshire teacup bearing the image of Theobald Mathew recovered at Five Points represents not the embrace of temperance ideals by Irish immigrants at the site but perhaps their "rejection of the image of Irish men and women as drunkards in need of salvation from the good priest." The ongoing emphasis on temperance values in historical archaeological discussions of alcohol use is motivated by modern beliefs that continue to view alcohol consumption as simply aberrant social behavior.

Archaeological methods have been much more successful at exploring alcohol-related themes surrounding the seemingly divergent escapist and integrative functions of alcohol drinking. The archaeologists' ability to link material culture to the residents of particular sites provides a good foundation for exploring the way in which alcohol drinking has been used to escape temporarily from the anxieties of everyday life. Certainly some social groups experienced greater degrees of anxiety than others, and site comparisons reveal different alcoholic responses to stress. As noted above, drinking appears to have been especially prevalent at military sites and sites occupied by transient social groups, individuals who often lived anxious lives on unpredictable frontiers. Yet alcohol drinking also has an integrative function—it acts as a social lubricant that breaks down barriers to social interaction and enhances sociability. The structures and material culture used for alcohol consumption encourage social interaction and therefore allow us to view sociality and sociability in different historical and regional contexts. While escape and integration are outwardly opposed, they are really two sides of the same coin. Sociability is a form of escape, and alcoholic escape is often performed within the context of sociability.

Yet what does a comprehensive historical archaeology of alcohol and drinking look like? Archaeological investigations at Mapps Cave, a cavern and sinkhole complex in St. Philip, Barbados, have shed new light on the production of alcoholic beverages by enslaved peoples, the transfer of West African drinking traditions to the New World, and the social and spiritual meanings that enslaved peoples gave to alcohol use. The evidence from Mapps Cave therefore contributes to the broader field of alcohol studies by providing historical archaeological insights into the escapist and integrative role of alcohol drinking in Barbados.

6

Mapps Cave

The Archaeology of Alcohol, Marronage, and Slave Revolt in Barbados

Historical archaeologists have encountered alcohol-related material culture on the sites of enslaved peoples throughout the Americas, yet historical archaeological evidence has contributed little to our understanding of the role of alcohol in slave societies. What did enslaved peoples drink? Where did they drink? And how did the coercive structures of the slave labor system shape the meaning of alcohol for enslaved peoples? In my book *Caribbean Rum: A Social and Economic History* (Smith 2005), I explored the history of alcohol drinking in the Caribbean and highlighted alcohol's social and symbolic role in the lives of enslaved peoples. That study embraced a historical anthropological perspective and used alcohol as a prism through which to view the material and ideological forces shaping the lives of people in the Caribbean. The historical archaeological study of alcohol and drinking at Mapps Cave, a cavern and sinkhole complex in St. Philip, Barbados, used by enslaved peoples in the seventeenth to nineteenth centuries, is a natural outcome of that earlier scholarly work. Alcohol-related materials represented a significant proportion of the Mapps Cave artifact assemblage and indicated that alcohol drinking was one of the primary activities that occurred at the site. What were the social and symbolic meanings that enslaved peoples at Mapps Cave gave to alcohol use, especially within the context of the 1816 slave uprising, the largest slave revolt in Barbadian history? Mapps Cave is located on Bayleys sugar plantation, home to many of the enslaved peoples involved in the 1816 revolt. Drawing on the work of alcohol studies researchers, this chapter argues that Mapps Cave, a liminal space on the plantation landscape, provided enslaved peoples from Bayleys and surrounding sugar estates with a temporary refuge from the rigors of plantation life and that the use of alcohol at Mapps Cave enhanced those feelings of escape.

Archaeological Investigations at Mapps Cave

In the early 1970s Jerome S. Handler and Frederick W. Lange collected oral histories, conducted archaeological excavations, and scoured archives and other repositories for documentary records in order to gather information on slavery and plantation life in Barbados. The massive program they initiated was one of the pioneering projects in the development of African Diaspora studies in historical archaeology. After testing a number of sites, the researchers settled in for a substantial excavation of a seventeenth- through nineteenth-century slave cemetery at Newton Plantation in the parish of Christ Church. The findings from the Newton excavations were published in a landmark volume, *Plantation Slavery in Barbados: An Archaeological and Historical Investigation* (Handler and Lange 1978).

One site that Handler and Lange tested was the subject of a separate article (Lange and Handler 1980). The site was Mapps Cave, located in the southeastern corner of Barbados. The cave lies between the great houses of Mapps Plantation and Bayleys Plantation. Following the lead of an informant, who indicated that the cave had once been used to quarter slaves, Handler and Lange and their field assistant, Robert Riordan, conducted archaeological tests at Mapps Cave in 1972. Their article on the testing of the site focused entirely on the prehistoric Amerindian occupation, although brief mention was made of historic period "trash" found scattered throughout the cavern site. A 1998 study of the assemblage of white clay tobacco pipe stems from the site led L. Daniel Mouer and me to conclude that the historic occupation of Mapps Cave covered a long period and that stratified occupational deposits at the site were probably intact (Mouer and Smith 2001). Mouer and I also reviewed original field and laboratory records from the 1972 excavation, notes pertaining to subsequent artifact analyses, and Handler, Lange, and Riordan's correspondence about the site (Handler 1998). This was sufficient to convince us that the site warranted further study, and in 1998 we conducted additional archaeological tests at Mapps Cave. In 2003 I returned to Mapps Cave to carry out further analysis of archaeological and architectural remains at the site.

The goal of the 1998 and 2003 research was to determine the periods of occupation and the integrity of the deposits and, if possible, to confirm evidence that enslaved peoples used Mapps Cave. Work by Handler and his colleagues, both in the early 1970s and in another research project conducted in the 1980s, demonstrated that, while it is not difficult to locate sites of slave quarters in Barbados, finding such sites with substantial strati-

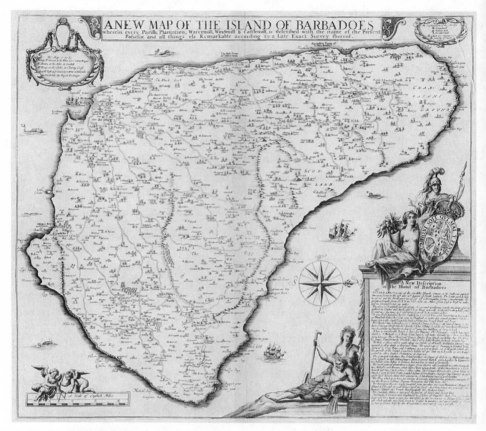

Figure 6–1. *A New Map of the Island of Barbadoes* by Richard Ford (London, ca. 1674). Courtesy of the John Carter Brown Library at Brown University.

graphic integrity is a challenge (Handler 1989). Cultivation of the island has been intensive for the past 350 years, and most sites of slave dwellings have been deeply plowed, often to bedrock. Moreover, many such sites were originally placed on rocky soil of marginal agricultural value, suggesting that little was left behind in the way of subsurface remains to begin with and that the thin deposits have largely been eroded away over time. While deep deposits with well-defined stratigraphic sequences are present in Barbados in the urban contexts of Bridgetown and Holetown, it has been difficult to find slave-village sites with good integrity in the Barbadian countryside (Crain et al. 2004; Farmer et al. 2005; Farmer et al. 2007; Smith 2001b, 2004a; Smith and Watson 2007, forthcoming; Stoner 2003).

Caves are common on limestone islands like Barbados, yet Mapps Cave (33 m long, 15 m wide, and 7 m high) represents an unusual geologic for-

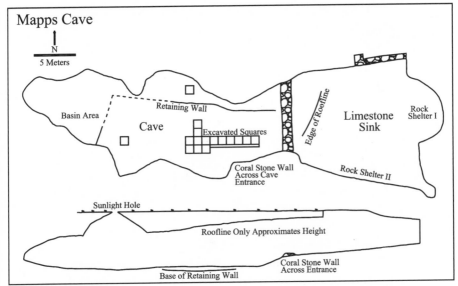

Figure 6–2. Plan and profile of Mapps Cave, Barbados. Original drawing (1972) courtesy of Robert Riordan and Jerome S. Handler. Plan and profile updated, modified, and drawn by Meredith Mahoney (2006).

mation on the Barbadian landscape. It is located less than 3 km from the island's rugged Atlantic coast. Today the area around the site is used for growing sugarcane and provision crops. The rapid pace of economic development in Barbados in recent years has also led to considerable residential construction within a kilometer of the site.

In 1998 and 2003 the units from the 1972 excavation (a 9 × 1 m trench as well as six 1 × 1 m units perpendicular to the trench) were reopened. In reexcavating, the walls of the trench were expanded by 20 cm in order to observe and record the stratigraphy. In addition, controlled surface collections were conducted in two rock shelters located in the sinkhole just outside the entrance to the cave. One new 1 × 1 m unit was excavated in a part of the cave that had not been tested in 1972. Finally, measured drawings of masonry walls in the cave and sinkhole were made.

The cave entrance and two rock shelters sit in a limestone sink roughly 15 m square and between 3 and 5 m below the normal ground surface (figure 6–2). The sink lies east of the cave and may have been covered by a limestone roof at one time; that is, it was probably once part of the cavern proper. Upon descending into the sink it is obvious that the site was used extensively during the historic period. Shards of eighteenth- and nineteenth-century ceramic and bottle glass are liberally scattered about the ground surface.

The Sink and Rock Shelters

Testing began with the systematic surface collection of the two rock shelters. Rock Shelter I is located in the eastern wall of the limestone sink. The entrance to the rock shelter is 8 m wide, with a clearly pronounced opening. The shelter reaches 5 m deep and is between 2 and 3 m high. Several natural tunnels are located in the back wall of the shelter, and eighteenth- and nineteenth-century artifacts are present in these passages. Rock Shelter II is located on the south side of the limestone sink. It is an extension of the south side of the interior cave wall. This shelter opening was less pronounced, making a gradual ascent from the sink floor to the ground surface above. Rock Shelter II stretches 15 m long, almost the entire length of the south wall of the sink. It is 2 m deep at the base. Grids were established within the two rock shelters, and artifacts were collected from the surface in 2–m squares. The remainder of the sink was not surface collected because the trunk and roots of a large bearded fig tree dominate the sink and hindered attempts to recover archaeological remains.

Among the artifacts recovered from the rock shelters were numerous pieces of wheel-thrown, unglazed, red earthenware pottery. These redwares represent a variety of forms, including thinly potted bowls and thick storage jars. Some of the redwares were the remains of early historic-period sugar molds and molasses drip jars associated with the substantial Barbados sugar industry (Handler 1963a, 1963b; Handler and Lange 1978; Loftfield 1991, 1992, 2001). Also, some of these redwares were fragments of traditional slave-made jugs, known around the Caribbean as monkeys, and of the cooking pot form known as *conarees*. Other unglazed red earthenwares included architectural forms, such as pantiles, flat roofing tiles, and bricks. The shelter collections also included numerous redwares with lead glaze. Many of the lead-glazed redwares are local products, but some are clearly imports, primarily English wares, such as Buckley lead-glazed and Staffordshire slipware. Creamware and pearlware vessel fragments were the most common refined European pottery types found at the site, though there were also fragments of white salt-glazed stoneware, dry-bodied Staffordshire stoneware, Westerwald and English stoneware, and a few shards of English delftware. Other artifacts included hand-blown black glass bottle fragments, white clay tobacco pipe stems and bowls, shell buttons, and a small blue tubular glass bead. The surface artifacts indicate that the main historic occupation of the rock shelters was in the late eighteenth and early nineteenth centuries, although a few seventeenth- and early-eighteenth-century artifacts were recovered as well. These include large-bore white clay tobacco pipe stems, fragments of an incised Westerwald jug, and a few shards that appear to be from a small West-of-England baluster jar found elsewhere on British colonial sites in the Americas only in the first half of the seventeenth century (McLearen and Mouer 1993; Outlaw 2002).

Two important architectural features were also identified in the limestone sink. The first is a cut coral-stone masonry retaining wall on the north side of the sinkhole. This wall stands 1.5 m high and is connected with the north corner of Rock Shelter I. We recorded this wall in detail. The other architectural feature is a collapsed set of cut coral-stone stairs, on the north side of the sink, built into the masonry retaining wall just mentioned. The stairs were constructed to facilitate the descent from the ground surface to the sinkhole and cave below.

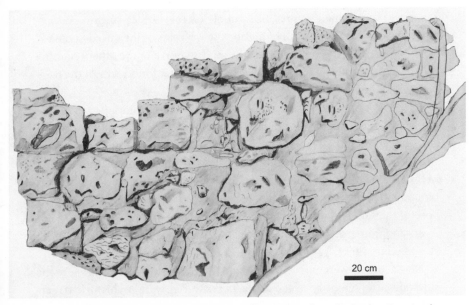

Figure 6–3. Profile view of coral-stone retaining wall at Mapps Cave, Barbados. Drawing by Meredith Mahoney (2006).

Inside the Cave

The cavern is a long, narrow feature with a high vaulted roof that rises into a dome near the back. The top of this dome has been artificially pierced, apparently to allow sunlight into the dark recesses of the cave. The walls and roof of the cave are stained with soot. The floor is covered with husks of almonds dropped by the hundreds of fruit bats that inhabit niches in the cave's roof. To enter the cave one must step over the remains of another cut coral-stone masonry wall. The wall is presently rather low, but many large coral-stone blocks lie scattered near it. The wall today is much lower than it was in 1972; at that time investigators were told that students from the nearby Mapps College had knocked the wall down. Based on this information it is likely that this coral-stone wall nearly closed the mouth of the cave, at least sufficiently to block out wind and rain.

Upon entering the cave the next thing one is likely to notice is that the floor, which is relatively raised and level, is bounded on the north side by another coral-stone wall that runs roughly parallel to the north wall of the cave. This appears to be a retaining wall. The floor's surface is 50 cm lower on the north side of this wall, suggesting that dirt was added on the south side of the wall to make a raised and level floor surface. While excavation has not yet confirmed its presence, rubble on the surface suggests yet another masonry retaining wall bounding the west side of the raised floor. It is worth noting that the soil west of this wall, and north of the other retaining wall, is of a completely different character than that found within the floor defined by these walls.

The 1972 excavation trench and adjoining units inside the cave were reopened. The backfill was completely removed down to bedrock, which lay between 10 and 60 cm below the surface. The bedrock and strata slope steeply from the south to the north. The stratigraphy is complex and shows well-defined episodes of deposition. Some of the features seen in the stratigraphy include natural deposits, such as a thin layer of roof fall, and purposeful human activity, such as the prepared floor. There were nine major layers and numerous smaller features, including two pits that had not been identified in the 1972 study.

New artifacts were uncovered during the expansion and cleaning of the sidewalls. The majority of the artifacts recovered were prehistoric Amerindian materials of the Suazoid type. Suazoid is a late Amerindian phase found throughout the Lesser Antilles and is likely the material culture of the Island Carib peoples. Among the Suazoid materials were pottery fragments, several adze/axes made of conch shell (*Strombus gigas*), and a small greenstone celt that had been brought to Barbados from the South American mainland or from one of the nearby volcanic islands during the pre-Columbian era. One of the more interesting finds was the presence of what appears to be unfired Suazoid pottery, including one piece with a finger impression. Lange and Handler (1980: 8) speculated that the Suazoid peoples used Mapps Cave as a "specialized activity area." They argued that, because evidence of Suazoid occupation is generally limited to terraces in front of caves and rock overhangs, the Suazoid materials within the cave itself are anomalies. The production of pottery may have been the specialized activity that the Suazoid engaged in at the site. Peter Drewett (1991: 17) also speculated that the Suazoid might have used Mapps Cave as a place to trap birds and gather forest foods.

Relatively few Amerindian pieces were found on the surface within the cave. Instead the floor was littered with a variety of historic-period ceramics dating from perhaps as early as the second quarter of the seventeenth century to very recent times. The vast majority of materials, like those from the sinkhole rock shelters, have manufacture dates from the third quarter of the eighteenth century to the 1830s or so. Clusters or concentrations of historic-period artifacts were found in some of the natural niches along the wall. One niche, for example, contained a number of flat roof tiles, pantiles, and fragments of what was probably a coal pot, the traditional ceramic stove of the Caribbean. The walls surrounding several niches are stained with soot, suggesting that these may have once served as cooking areas.

Historic-period artifacts were also recovered from some of the upper layers of stratigraphy during the expansion and cleaning of the excavation-unit sidewalls. These artifacts include hand-blown black bottle glass, iron nails, locally made and imported ceramics, and roof tiles. Fragments of red earthenware pottery of various forms were by far the most common historic-period artifacts recovered at the site. A clear break in occupation exists between the prehistoric occupations in the lower strata and the historic period in the upper layers, though a few pieces of Suazoid material were found in layers clearly deposited in the historic period, including two conch shell adze/axes and the greenstone celt.

A 1 × 1 m excavation unit was opened in the far north-central portion of the cave, north of the retaining wall. The excavation unit was situated halfway between the cut coral-stone retaining wall and the natural cave wall, and it was opened to determine the depth of the soil in that area of the cave and to identify any stratigraphy or evidence of cultural material. The soil in this area was extremely dark rich organic fill mixed with some clay. The rather uniform deposit was fairly deep. We reached bedrock at about 120 cm below the cave floor surface. There was no visible stratigraphy, simply a dark, organically rich fill. No Amerindian artifacts were recovered from this fill. Most of the recovered cultural material included very small fragments of red earthenware ceramic. At the very bottom of the excavation unit, lying on top of the bedrock, was a large brick. This same fill material covers the major part of the north and west portions of the cave. Obviously, this deep fill was deposited entirely in the historic period, and it indicates that the cave had at least two separate tiers at the height of its use and occupation.

Marronage at Mapps Cave in the Seventeenth Century

The presence of seventeenth-century ceramics and large-bore white clay tobacco pipe stems at Mapps Cave raises the possibility that runaway slaves used the cave in the early years of British colonial settlement of Barbados. The British landed in Barbados in 1627 and found the island uninhabited. Amerindians, known to archaeologists as Suazoid, lived in Barbados until sometime in the early sixteenth century, when Spanish slave raids forced the indigenous peoples of the island to flee to the safety of kin in other parts of the Caribbean. Early British colonists grew tobacco and cotton on small farms, which were located primarily along the southern and western coasts. Indentured servants from Europe were the main source of labor in the early years of settlement, though enslaved Africans became an increasingly important source of labor in the late 1630s (Sheridan 1974: 247). The southeastern portion of the island, demarcated as St. Philip Parish in 1639, was very sparsely populated during the first few decades after settlement. The rise of sugar production in the 1640s, however, substantially increased the number of enslaved Africans in Barbados and led to the development of sugarcane-growing estates in some of the more remote interior parts of the island. Yet, despite the expansion of sugar production and the increasing population density of the island, early maps of Barbados show that the area around Mapps Cave remained relatively undeveloped. This windswept corner of the island was known as the Thickets and was veiled by a nearly impenetrable tangle of thick forest and scrub vegetation until the second half of the seventeenth century, when a handful of large sugar estates, including Mapps and Bayleys, were erected in the area.

Caves and remote bush in St. Philip combined to make an environment suitable for runaway slaves. In the late 1640s Richard Ligon (1673: 105), an English colonist familiar with slave life in Barbados, wrote that fugitive slaves on the island "harbour themselves in Woods and Caves, living upon pillage for many months together." According to Ligon,

> These Caves are very frequent in the Island, and of several dimensions, some small, others extreamly large and Capacious: The runaway Negres, often shelter themselves in these Coverts, for a long time, and in the night range abroad the Countrey, and steale Pigs, Plantins, Potatoes, and Pullin, and bring it there; and feast all day, upon what they stole the night before.
>
> (Ligon 1673: 98)

Some caves were large enough to hold hundreds of people, and in many cases a thick natural curtain of vines obscured cave entrances from the view of would-be slave catchers. As a result, whites employed trained Liam hounds to flush out fugitive slaves who were hold up in caves in the out-of-the-way hills, gullies, and dense forests of Barbados. Ligon's map of Barbados, for example, illustrates two fugitive slaves being chased and fired upon by a man on horseback in these rugged and unsettled parts of the island (figure 6–4). Nearly a decade later, in 1657, the Barbados Council and Assembly continued to receive complaints from frustrated planters about rebellious runaways "lurkeing in woods and secrett places" (cited in Gragg 2003: 159 and Handler 1997: 188). Although the small size and high population density of Barbados made it impossible for runaway slaves in the island to establish permanent maroon communities like those in Jamaica, Brazil, and Suriname, Handler (1997) has uncovered compelling documentary evidence for various forms of marronage in Barbados, including the use of caves as temporary hiding places for runaways.

While the seventeenth-century remains at Mapps Cave are few, at least some artifacts indicate that people occupied the cave before the establishment of plantations in the area. Did runaway slaves leave these artifacts? In the early years of settlement, some British colonists were known to dwell in caves. For example, James Drax, an Englishman who arrived with the first party of English colonists in 1627, was reported to have "sheltered in a cave in the rocks" with a half-dozen or so other Englishmen during the early years of settlement (Father Antoine Biet in 1654, cited in Handler 1967: 69). Drax later became one of the wealthiest sugar planters in Barbados

Figure 6–4. Section of *A Topographicall Description . . . of Barbados* illustrating two runaway slaves. Frontispiece of Richard Ligon, *A True and Exact History of the Island of Barbadoes*, 2nd ed. (London, 1673). Courtesy of the John Carter Brown Library at Brown University.

and built a magnificent great house; but in the early days of settlement, caves offered Drax and some of his comrades an alternative to the timber and stone houses being erected in the island at that time. Yet, while some colonists may have exploited the caves of Barbados for shelter, instances of cave-dwelling English colonists were no doubt rare and probably occurred only during the first few years of colonization and only near primary settlements located along the southern and western coasts. In contrast, Mapps Cave, located in what was the isolated eastern fringe of the island in the early to mid-seventeenth century, probably served as a temporary hideout for individuals and small groups of runaway slaves seeking a short-term flight from bondage, otherwise known as petite marronage.

Terry Weik (1997) outlined the archaeology of marronage in the New World and identified the key contributions that maroon archaeology has made to our understanding of African cultural continuities as well as high-lighted the resistance, resiliency, and adaptability of enslaved peoples in the Americas. A survey of maroon sites supports claims that Mapps Cave probably once served as a temporary refuge for enslaved Africans and Afro-Creoles in Barbados. Its remote location, for example, is consistent with maroon settlement sites investigated by archaeologists in many other areas of the New World, including Palmares in Brazil, El Maniel de José Leta in the Dominican Republic, El Cobre in Cuba, the Great Dismal Swamp in Virginia and North Carolina, and the maroon communities of Jamaica (Agorsah 1993; Funari 1995; García Arévelo 1986; La Rosa Corzo 2003; Nichols 1988; Orser 1993, 1994, 1996: 41–55; Orser and Funari 2001; Sayers 2005; Sayers et al. 2007). Moreover, the particular use of caves by fugitive slaves is known archaeologically from sites in Cuba and possibly parts of the Dominican Republic (García Arévelo 1986: 50–53).

Archaeological investigations indicate that sites of marronage typically contain few European-manufactured materials, even sites associated with long-term or grand marronage. In Brazil, for example, Charles E. Orser Jr. and Pedro P. A. Funari conducted archaeological investigations at Palmares, site of one of the largest and most organized maroon communities in the Americas. They found that, despite its nearly 100–year existence and sizable population, European-manufactured materials at the site were scarce (Funari 1995; Orser 1993, 1994, 1996: 41–55; Orser and Funari 2001). Similarly, at El Maniel de José Leta, Manuel A. García Arévelo (1986) found only a handful of European-manufactured objects. The near absence of European-manufactured items has often made it difficult for archaeologists to locate maroon settlements, such as those in the Great Dismal Swamp (Sayers 2005: 62–73; Sayers et al. 2007). Even at Accompong and Nanny Town, two major maroon communities in Jamaica excavated by E. Kofi Agorsah in the 1980s and 1990s, relatively few European-manufactured materials were recovered from the sites (Agorsah 1993). The paucity of European-manufactured materials at maroon sites reflects the fact that maroon communities, though part of the broader social, political, and economic milieu of the Atlantic World, generally lived outside the reach of state powers and at the margins of internal marketing networks. Thus, maroons rarely had ready access to the durable sorts of European-manufactured material goods that typically survive in the historical archaeological record, such as ceramics, glass, and iron. Moreover, the need for mobility and the constant threat of capture may have also reduced the feasibility of maroons' possessing an extensive and cumbersome material world. Though maroons in some areas produced pottery and tobacco pipes, and perhaps even engaged in iron smelting, the evidence clearly indicates that the demands of marronage restricted the material world of runaways. This pattern would have been especially true for sites of petite marronage, such as Mapps Cave.

While European-manufactured goods are rare at maroon sites, runaways appear to have frequently recycled prehistoric Amerindian pottery and tools that they found and used those objects to help them survive their flight. For example, Amerindian pottery and/or lithics made up sizable portions of the artifact assemblages from Palmares, El Maniel de José Leta, the Great Dismal Swamp, and the Accompong and Nanny Town sites. García Arévelo (1986: 51) speculated that the prehistoric Amerindian stone pestles recovered from El Maniel de José Leta were found fortuitously at the site by maroons, who then recycled and reused the pestles to grind foods collected in the surrounding forests or to break up the bones of wild hogs hunted by the fugitives who lived at the site.

The fragments of Westerwald stoneware, West-of-England baluster jar, and large-bore white clay tobacco pipe stems at Mapps Cave provide compelling evidence that the site was used by fugitive slaves in the early years of British settlement of Barbados, when the area around Mapps Cave would have been suitably remote for marronage. As with other maroon sites investigated by archaeologists in the New World, only a handful of European-manufactured objects were present at Mapps Cave. Those artifacts date to the seventeenth century, the period when marronage at the site would have been most feasible. Moreover, the discovery of Suazoid materials in historic-period contexts (especially the conch-shell tools and the greenstone celt) hint at the possibility that, if runaways used the site, they reused and recycled items produced by the prehistoric Suazoid peoples to help them survive their flight. The conch shell tools and the greenstone celt, for example, would have been well suited for hunting and processing the meat of the numerous wild hogs that roamed these outlying areas of Barbados during the early years of British colonization. In addition, the runaways who sought shelter in the cave may have imbued the Amerindian objects they found scattered about the site with magical properties and used them as talismans or in the production of charms to help aid their escape (Russell 1997: 72–74). The presence of European materials manufactured in the seventeenth century, as well as the Suazoid objects, offers persuasive evidence that runaways used Mapps Cave as a temporary hideout.

The expansion of sugar production in the mid-seventeenth century led to the development of sugar estates in the southeastern part of Barbados, which would have precluded the use of Mapps Cave as a temporary refuge for runaway slaves. While Ligon's map of Barbados in the late 1640s shows a lack of development in the southeastern portion of the island, Richard Ford's map of Barbados, published ca. 1674, shows several large sugar estates in St. Philip Parish in the vicinity of Mapps Cave, including Mapps and Bayleys. Mapps Cave itself was located on plantation lands, and the great house at Bayleys Plantation was built within a kilometer of the site. Yet, while the development of sugar estates in St. Philip precluded the use of Mapps Cave as a hideout for runaways, the site continued to provide a sanctuary for enslaved peoples from the surrounding plantations, and alcohol use at the site enhanced that escape.

Evidence for Alcohol Use at Mapps Cave

While only a few seventeenth-century artifacts were recovered from Mapps Cave, the site contained an extensive array of late-eighteenth- and early-nineteenth-century materials. The artifacts recovered from Mapps Cave show that a number of activities occurred at the site during that period and support the oral traditions of local informants that the site was once used to quarter enslaved peoples from nearby sugar estates. A letter written by a plantation manager from an adjacent estate dated September 20, 1816, also hints that the cave may have once served as a dwelling for enslaved peoples whose homes had been destroyed by Barbados militiamen and imperial forces during the 1816 slave uprising (Fitzherbert ca. 1750–1850). The artifact assemblage included materials that provide insight into personal adornment, foodways, sociability, craft production, and other aspects of domestic life. Yet, while Mapps Cave may have been used to house enslaved peoples at some point in its history, the materials recovered suggest that it typically served a more specialized function. In particular, the artifact assemblage contained a large number of alcohol-related materials, which indicate that alcohol drinking was one of the primary activities that occurred at the site.

The most obvious examples of alcohol-related materials recovered from Mapps Cave are fragments of hand-blown black glass bottles. The 230 shards

Figure 6–5. *Slaves in Barbados*. In John A. Waller, *A Voyage in the West Indies* (London, 1820). Courtesy of the John Carter Brown Library at Brown University.

of black glass bottles represent more than 12% of the entire historic-period artifact assemblage from the site. This figure is high when compared with the amount of bottle glass recovered from seven slave village sites surveyed by Handler and his colleagues in Barbados in the late 1980s (Handler 1989). Glass bottle fragments represented an average of only about 4% of the artifacts recovered from those seven sites, one-third the amount found at Mapps Cave. Stoneware bottles were also present at Mapps Cave. Although archaeological analysis cannot confirm that the glass and stoneware bottles recovered from Mapps Cave were used exclusively for alcoholic beverages, the historical and social context of slave life in Barbados suggests that they often served alcoholic purposes. Rum making was central to the Barbadian economy throughout the slavery period, and rum was readily available to enslaved peoples, especially those who lived on sugar estates. Rum was doled out as part of weekly rations, as a prophylactic against colds, and as part of a rewards system. Enslaved peoples also made a variety of fermented alcoholic beverages out of local plant resources. Moreover, enslaved peoples, like other social groups in Barbados, had few reservations about alcohol drinking (Smith 2001a, 2004b, 2005: 95–117).

Plantation accounts and travelers' reports attest that enslaved peoples throughout the Caribbean used glass and stoneware bottles to store and consume alcoholic beverages. In 1740, for example, Jamaican sugar planter Charles Leslie (1740: 35) indicated that the enslaved peoples on his estate received "bottles" of rum for killing the numerous rats that damaged sugarcane crops. Leslie (1740: 325–26) described the funerary practices of enslaved peoples of Jamaica, which entailed burying "a Bottle of Rum at the Feet" of their deceased comrades. Historical archaeologists have also interpreted the presence of glass and stoneware bottle fragments at the dwelling sites of enslaved peoples in the Caribbean and North America as evidence of alcohol drinking. In Jamaica, for example, Douglas Armstrong (1990: 135) argued that the large number of glass and stoneware bottle shards recovered from an area of the slave village at Drax Hall Plantation indicated that one structure at the site was probably the remains of a "village bar or liquor shop." Theresa Singleton (2006: 279) contended that bottle glass recovered from the El Padre slave village in Cuba was evidence that enslaved peoples at the site were engaged in illicit alcohol consumption. John Solomon Otto (1984: 76) found numerous hand-blown glass bottle fragments in the artifact assemblage of slave domestic dwellings at the late-eighteenth- and nineteenth-century Cannon's Point Plantation in Georgia and used the evidence to elucidate the drinking patterns of enslaved peoples on the estate. Similarly, Paul Farnsworth (2000, 2001: 25–26) argued that the glass bottle fragments recovered from the dwelling sites of enslaved peoples at Clifton Plantation in the Bahamas reflected the slaves' pursuit of traditional West African beer drinking practices.

However, glass and stoneware bottles were not the only containers used for storing and consuming alcoholic beverages. In Barbados, coconut shells, calabash gourds, and sugarcane stalks were sometimes used in lieu of bottles for holding alcohol. In 1814 Benjamin Browne (1926: 84), an American privateer captured by the British and imprisoned in Barbados, reported that enslaved people on the island drank rum from coconut shells that had been drained of their milk. The practice of drinking rum from coconut shells, Browne was told by his fellow inmates, was called "sucking the monkey." It may have been a way for enslaved peoples in Barbados to conceal their public rum drinking from the watchful eyes of island whites, who believed that the coconut shells contained only plain coconut milk. In the late 1820s F. W. N. Bayley (cited in Handler and Lange 1978: 55), a visitor to Barbados, noted that enslaved peoples on the island used the calabash for a variety of purposes, including "as a bottle to contain rum." The practice was evidently widespread among enslaved peoples throughout the Caribbean. According to an anonymous eighteenth-century writer in Jamaica,

> When [slaves] travel, they have different ways of carrying their rum; the most common utensil is a calabash bottle, stopt with the stem on which the Indian corn grows. A cane is sometimes used for this purpose, to fit it for which they clear it of the membranes at the joints and cork the upper end: a large cane will hold a considerable quantity, and serves the double purpose of a bottle and a walking stick.
>
> (Anonymous 1797: 16)

Unfortunately, organic materials, such as coconut shells, calabash gourds, and modified sugarcane stalks, decompose quickly in the ground, even in the relatively dry and stable environment of Mapps Cave. As a result, these organic items rarely survive in the archaeological record and leave little for archaeologists interested in the drinking habits of enslaved peoples in the Caribbean to ponder other than the durable alcohol-related materials. While glass and stoneware bottles found at Mapps Cave were probably used for storing and consuming a variety of liquids, they often, if not primarily, served as containers for alcoholic beverages. The ubiquity of glass and stoneware bottle fragments at Mapps Cave, relative to the slave village sites surveyed by Handler, suggests that alcohol drinking was one of the main activities that occurred at the site.

Were enslaved peoples at Mapps Cave also producing alcoholic beverages? The accounts of early explorers, slave traders, and missionaries in West and Central Africa attest to the popularity of indigenous-produced alcoholic beverages prior to the expansion of the transatlantic slave trade in the mid-seventeenth century. Like ethnographic field notes, these reports detailed the production of alcoholic beverages from honey, plantains, and various species of millets. Palm wine, produced from the raphia variety of palm, appears to have been one of the most common alcoholic beverages found along the West and Central African coasts. The production of fermented alcoholic beverages was well known in most of the West and Central African societies that made up the enslaved populations of Barbados. In particular, palm-wine drinking was widespread among the Akan from the Gold Coast and the Igbo from the Bight of Biafra, two West African ethnic groups that assuredly had a greater cultural impact in Barbados than other African ethnic groups. Akan slaves were most common in the British Atlantic slave trade in the seventeenth century, and their early arrival in Barbados meant that they had a profound socializing impact on later slave arrivals from other West and Central African societies (Handler and Lange 1978: 20–29; Herskovits 1966: 96–98; Mintz and Price 1992: 42–51). The majority of enslaved peoples brought to Barbados in the eighteenth century were Igbo from the Bight of Biafra. Between 1740 and 1810 the Igbo represented as much as 40% of all slave arrivals in Barbados, a higher percentage than any other African ethnic group in this period (Chambers 1997: 77; Handler and Lange 1978: 20–29).

The production of fermented alcoholic drinks was widespread in Akan and Igbo societies before the arrival of Europeans along the African coasts. As early as the eleventh century, Al-Bakri of Cordoba (cited in Pan 1975: 20–21) referred to "intoxicating drinks" served at the burial of the king of the ancient kingdom of Ghana. Oral traditions collected in the late nineteenth century intimate a long history of palm-wine use in the Gold Coast, dating back to the Asante's initial migration into the region in the early sixteenth century (Akyeampong 1996: 27). Palm wine was also available in Igbo lands prior to the seventeenth century. Trader James Welsh (1589: 297) wrote that in the Bight of Biafra "there are great store of palme trees, out of which they gather great store of wine." The process of making palm wine was simple. John Barbot (1746: 203), a slave trader well acquainted with life on the West African coasts, described the production of palm wine on the Gold Coast. According to Barbot, a palm tapper made a small hole near the base of the palm tree, inserted a reed tube into the hole, and collected the sap that drained from the tube in a large earthenware pot or calabash. In a few days, the sucrose-rich sap fermented to produce an alcoholic drink similar in strength to wine or a strong beer.

The Akan and Igbo, as well as enslaved peoples from the many other African ethnic groups that labored on Barbadian plantations, brought their knowledge of alcohol production to Barbados and sought to re-create the traditional fermented alcoholic drinks that they had left behind in Africa. However, they adapted their alcohol-production techniques to fit their new Caribbean environment. Lacking the proper palm trees for the extraction of palm sap, the enslaved peoples of Barbados turned to another source for fermentable sucrose: sugarcane juice. Sugar production was the dominant industry throughout the slavery period in Barbados, and sugarcane juice and molasses were readily available for fermentation, especially for enslaved peoples who lived on sugar estates.

As early as the 1640s, Ligon described the production of fermented sugarcane-based alcoholic beverages in Barbados. Ligon (1673: 32) called the drink "punch" and said that it was "made of water and sugar put together, which in ten dayes standing will be very strong, and fit for labourers." He appears to have confused punch, a drink usually consisting of distilled spirits and spices, with a fermented sugarcane-based alcoholic drink (Smith 2005: 12). Fermented sugarcane-based alcoholic drinks made by enslaved peoples were typically called *cowow* and "cool drink" in Barbados. Griffith Hughes (1750: 34), the rector of St. Lucy's parish church in Barbados, described *cowow* as "a drink made with the scummings of boiled cane juice, mixed with water, and fermented; and then drank." According to Hughes, *cowow* was generally associated with the "poorer Sort." Hans Sloane, a physician who traveled to Barbados, described the production of cool drink:

> To make cool Drink, Take three Gallons of fair water, more than a Pint of Molossus, mix them together in a Jar; it works in twelve hours time sufficiently, put to it a little more Molossus, an immediately Bottle it, in six hours time 'tis ready to drink.
> (Sloane 1707–25, 1: xxix)

Yet the production of fermented sugarcane-based alcoholic drinks was not restricted to Barbados. Indeed, enslaved peoples throughout the Caribbean were known to ferment sugarcane juice, molasses, and the frothy "scum" skimmed from the boiling sugar cauldrons to produce alcoholic drinks. Fermented sugarcane-based alcoholic drinks were called *guarapo* in the Spanish Caribbean, and enslaved peoples on sugar estates produced them as early as the 1510s (Las Casas 1971: 258; Layfield 1906: 98). Fermented sugarcane juice was called *grappe* in the French Caribbean and was considered the "ordinary" drink of enslaved peoples who worked on sugar plantations (Labat 1724, 1: 134). Various terms were used for fermented sugarcane-based alcoholic drinks in Jamaica, but "cool drink" appears to have been the most common. In the late eighteenth century, for example, an anonymous (1797: 15) writer in Jamaica wrote that water was the common drink among enslaved peoples, "but they prefer *cool drink*, a fermented liquor made with chaw-stick, lignum vitae, brown sugar, and water."

While we know the names of these fermented drinks, we know much less about the process used to make them. In particular, what sorts of vessels were used to ferment these drinks? In Barbados, as well as other parts of the Caribbean, enslaved peoples probably used large earthenware jars to ferment alcoholic beverages. Sloane, for example, mentioned the use of a "Jar" in the production of cool drink. "Jars" were also used in the production of other fermented alcoholic drinks in Barbados, including *perino*, an alcoholic beverage made from cassava, and *mobbie*, an alcoholic beverage made from several varieties of sweet potatoes. Presumably these "jars" were made of earthenware. This was certainly the case in other parts of the Caribbean. In Martinique, for example, Father Jean-Baptiste Labat (1724, 1: 133–36) noted that enslaved peoples and Carib Indians on the island fermented a number of alcoholic drinks in earthenware vessels. Moreover, in 1625 English Dominican monk Thomas Gage (1677: 323) reported that the Indians of Guatemala made drinks that they "confection in such great Jarrs as come from *Spain*; wherein they put some little quantity of water, and fill up the Jar with some Melasso's, or juice of the Sugar Cane." The practice of fermenting sugarcane juice in large earthenware jars was probably similar to that described by Ross Jamieson (2000: 96, 184–85) in Cuenca, Ecuador, where Andean women used *botijas* to brew *chicha* beer.

In Barbados, the most suitable earthenware vessels for the fermentation of alcoholic drinks were *conarees:* wide-mouthed, lead-glazed, kiln-fired, wheel-thrown, lidded cylindrical pots that were made by enslaved peoples at potteries in Barbados as early as the mid-seventeenth century (Handler 1963a, 1963b; Handler and Lange 1978: 141–43). Some *conarees* had a capacity of several gallons. Thomas Loftfield (2001: 232) has stressed the use of *conarees* as stew pots, especially for the production and consumption of the protein-rich stew known as "pepper pot," a national dish that has a long history in Barbados. Yet the size of these jars would have also made them well suited for the fermentation of alcoholic beverages. Leland Ferguson (1992: 103), for example, studied *colono* vessels recovered from slave sites in South Carolina and hinted that enslaved peoples in South Carolina may occasionally have used large *colono* jars to produce fermented alcoholic drinks. Moreover, Ferguson suggested that smaller *colono* bowls may have been used in the consumption of fermented drinks. In addition, Paul Farnsworth (2000, 2001: 27) recovered shards of large ceramic vessels from slave cabins at Clifton Plantation in the Bahamas and intimated that such vessels may have been used by enslaved peoples there to brew beer from sorghum and maize grown on provision grounds on the estate. In Barbados, *conarees* may have served similar purposes.

Glazed and unglazed red earthenware ceramics represented about 62% of the Mapps Cave artifact assemblage. Many of the red earthenware vessels were local products, including *conarees* and small bowls. Many of the other earthenware ceramics were imported utilitarian vessels, including molasses drip jars (large, unglazed globular vessels used in sugar-plantation purging houses to catch the molasses that drained from sugar molds). The presence of molasses drip jars, an industrial ceramic used in sugar making, in Mapps

Cave is unusual. Enslaved peoples at Mapps Cave may have used molasses drip jars for a variety of purposes, especially as storage containers for food and drink. As with *conarees*, however, these large earthenware jars would have been well suited for the production of fermented alcoholic drinks. Thus, the presence of *conarees* and molasses drip jars at Mapps Cave, when combined with the evidence for alcohol consumption at the site, suggests that enslaved peoples at Mapps Cave were engaged in the production of alcoholic beverages, such as *cowow* and cool drink, fermented sugarcane-based alcoholic beverages known to have been made and consumed by enslaved peoples in Barbados and throughout the Caribbean.

Alcoholic Marronage and the 1816 Slave Uprising

The ubiquity of glass and stoneware bottles at Mapps Cave indicates that alcohol drinking was one of the principal activities that occurred at the site. The fragments of *conarees* and molasses drip jars also hint that enslaved peoples at Mapps Cave may have been producing fermented alcoholic beverages. Yet why did alcohol figure so prominently at Mapps Cave?

Anthropologists and historians have investigated the spaces in which alcohol is communally consumed and identified numerous reasons for the emergence of distinct drinking places. For example, American folklorist Madelon Powers (1998) argued that the workingman's saloon gained popularity in the late nineteenth century because laborers, especially newly arrived immigrants from Europe, sought camaraderie and companionship among ethnic and occupational peers. Powers also stressed the lure of "creature comforts," such as gas lighting, pool tables, and fancy toilet facilities, which were not available in the average workingman's home. Other researchers have stressed push factors to explain the popularity of drinking places. W. Scott Haine (1996: 37–38), for example, points out that one of the factors that led working-class men and women in nineteenth-century Paris to frequent cafés was that they provided a temporary refuge from the city's cramped and poor housing conditions. Using court records from Augsburg, historian Beverly Ann Tlusty (1997: 26) attributed the rise of male tavern going in sixteenth-century Germany in part to men's desire to escape their "nagging and shrewish" wives, who drove their husbands from the home.

Perhaps similar pull and push factors were operating at Mapps Cave. The cool, dry cave environment may have offered a pleasant respite from the heat of the Barbadian sun. As an unusual geologic feature on the plantation landscape, however, Mapps Cave may also have involved other factors. Mapps Cave was a unique underground setting that created distance from the harsh realities of plantation labor. In a society driven by a coerced labor system, Mapps Cave provided a subterranean shield from the panoptic gaze of plantation whites. It was a liminal space where enslaved peoples could escape the rigors of plantation life, albeit temporarily, and alcohol drinking at the site enhanced that sense of escape.

In his study of Afro-Brazilian religious cults, anthropologist Seth Leacock (1964) argued that alcohol drinking had two primary functions among cult members. First, according to Leacock, alcohol drinking fostered sociability and thus helped integrate cult members into the community. Perhaps alcohol drinking at Mapps Cave served a similar function. Social integration would have been a key component of life for enslaved peoples on Barbadian sugar plantations. Alcohol drinking at Mapps Cave may have acted as a social lubricant that helped reinforce social bonds among comrades on Bayleys Plantation and surrounding sugar estates. The need for social integration would have been especially important in a community, such as Bayleys, that saw a regular influx of newly arrived Africans. Second, Leacock believed that the physiological effects of alcohol drinking helped make spiritual conversion (possession trances in the case of Afro-Brazilian religious groups) more convincing. Similarly, the physiological effects of alcohol drinking may have strengthened the effectiveness of status change among those who frequented Mapps Cave. Although part of the plantation landscape, Mapps Cave was separate from the public sphere of estate labor and the private sphere of household domesticity. The site thus was a sanctuary that provided a sense of escape from the hardships of the physical world, and alcohol drinking at the site would have helped make the sense of escape more convincing. Moreover, the knowledge that Mapps Cave once served as a shelter for fugitive slaves, as well as a haunt of Carib Indians, the first to challenge British colonialism in the region, may have added to the meaning of the site as a temporary refuge.

As a temporary sanctuary for enslaved peoples, did Mapps Cave inspire revolutionary sentiment? On the night of Easter Sunday 1816, whites in Barbados awoke to the largest slave uprising in the island's history. The rebels set fire to sugarcane fields, looted storehouses, and battled scores of local militiamen and British military forces, including the imperial troops of the First West India Regiment, who were sent to quell the rebellion. The revolt was a major blow to proponents of slavery. It struck fear in the hearts of white Barbadians, fanned abolitionist flames in Britain, and helped convince Britain's Parliament that slavery must end. The writing was on the wall, and within two decades enslaved peoples in the British Caribbean had won their emancipation.

The slave revolt began in St. Philip but quickly spread to surrounding parishes in the central and southern parts of the island. Smaller skirmishes between rebels and militia forces were also reported in the northern and western parishes. Arson was a key weapon of the rebels, who burned a quarter of the island's sugarcane crop for that year. One white militiaman and two black soldiers of the First West India Regiment were killed in the fighting, and many more were wounded. The number of rebel casualties is not certain, but estimates two days after the initial outbreak of the revolt indicate that somewhere around 50 rebels had been killed. By September 1816, 144 rebels and conspirators had been executed, and many others were imprisoned or were awaiting transport off the island. Official hearings held after the uprising revealed that most of the revolt's alleged leaders were from plantations in St. Philip. Of the 22 principal slaves suspected of organizing the revolt, 6 were from Bayleys Plantation, including Bussa, the head ranger on the estate, who is celebrated by many in Barbados today as the leader of the revolt (Beckles 1998; Handler and Hughes 2001). In fact, the event is popularly referred to in Barbados as "Bussa's Rebellion."

The revolt was planned and organized at a number of locations in southeastern Barbados, especially at the home of an enslaved head driver named Jackey who lived at Simmons Plantation in St. Philip. The final planning and organizational meeting before the revolt also occurred in St. Philip, at a dance held on Good Friday evening, April 12, at the River Plantation (Beckles 1998: 25–35). Oral traditions, however, indicate that Mapps Cave also played a key role in the planning and organization of the 1816 revolt. While archaeological evidence cannot confirm that conspirators met at Mapps Cave to plan and organize the revolt, the liminal location of Mapps Cave fits well with what is known historically about the locations used to plan and organize other slave uprisings in the Caribbean. For example, the final planning and organizational meeting of rebels that preceded the 1791 St. Domingue slave uprising occurred deep in the forest of Bois Caïman, far away from the watchful eyes of whites or those who might betray the rebellion (Geggus 1991, 1992a, 1992b).

If Mapps Cave served as a scene for the planning and organization of the 1816 revolt, did the use of alcohol at the site contribute to the revolutionary fervor of rebels? Drawing on numerous ethnographic accounts of alcohol drinking, anthropologists Craig MacAndrew and Robert Edgerton (1969) explored cross-cultural differences in drunken comportment and attempted to explain the appeal and primary function of alcohol drinking. According to MacAndrew and Edgerton, one of the factors that makes alcohol drinking so appealing is that drunkenness removes individual accountability, albeit temporarily, and helps circumvent certain social controls:

> The state of drunkenness is a state of societally sanctioned freedom from the otherwise enforceable demands that persons comply with the conventional proprieties. For a while—but just for a while—the rules (or, more accurately, *some* of the rules) are set aside, and the drunkard finds himself, if not beyond good and evil, at least partially removed from the accountability nexus in which he normally operates. In a word, drunkenness in these societies takes on the flavor of *"time-out"* from many of the otherwise imperative demands of everyday life.
> (MacAndrew and Edgerton 1969: 89–90)

Thus, while drunken comportment remains within the boundaries of acceptable social behavior, alcohol can help the drinker stretch those boundaries and do so without serious repercussions.

Planters in the British Caribbean were ambivalent about the alcohol drinking of the enslaved peoples who labored on their estates. On the one hand, they feared slave drinking as liberating, a fomenter of insurrections that threatened the social order. On the other hand, they saw it as a tool of domination: a way to placate frustrations and soothe social tensions between planters and slaves by allowing enslaved peoples to drink and regularly blow off steam. Although planters doled out considerable amounts of rum to enslaved workers, they implemented laws and informal rules that sought to discourage drunkenness. Like marronage, drunkenness was a form of escape that stole productive labor. Both forms of escape removed the planters' resources and were thus considered acts of theft. When drunkenness interfered with work, it was rarely tolerated and, like marronage, was severely punished. Enslaved peoples prone to frequent bouts of intoxication were sometimes forced to wear iron collars and masks or were chained to their beds. In 1778 and 1779 the annual slave lists from York Plantation in Jamaica identified Juba and Thomas as excessive drinkers (Gale-Morant Papers 1731–1925). Their excessive drinking was noted under the heading "conditions," a column usually reserved for information about a slave's illnesses and injuries. Like old age or a debilitating disease, their drunkenness inhibited their work performance and was thus considered by the planter to be a form of theft of productive labor. They remained heavy drinkers over the years, which suggests that their drinking had not become intolerable, but the potential danger was conspicuous enough to make it noteworthy as a disability.

Indeed, the high level of slave accountability was most evident in work situations, the fundamental and least negotiable relationship between slaves and planters. Dr. Collins, a physician in St. Vincent, wrote:

> [Slaves] who have been dancing, or drinking, or otherwise engaged on some nocturnal excursion, either on the business of love, or depredation, will be found at the hospital the next morning. They may be detected by the lateness of the hour at which they come there, and the soundness of their sleep, much greater than indisposition would admit. You will order them to their work, and wink at their transgressions, unless too frequently repeated.
> (Collins 1811: 224)

Although planters may have winked at a few transgressions, they rarely tolerated frequent drunkenness, especially if it challenged their authority or reduced plantation productivity. Slavery, more than anything else, shaped patterns of drunken comportment in the Caribbean. Slaves were an investment in productive labor to the planters, who wanted sobriety from their slaves. In order to identify particularly hard-working and temperate slaves, planters even constructed elaborate stereotypes of African ethnic groups that included references to their drinking habits (Smith 2005: 126–28). A temperate workforce was a more efficient workforce, and in 1812 a committee of British West Indian planters recommended a reward system for slaves who adhered to principles of sobriety (cited in Handler and Lange 1978: 78).

Although planters in Barbados often frowned upon and sometimes severely punished bouts of drunkenness among the enslaved peoples that labored on their estates, at times drunkenness was tolerated, and even encouraged, among the planter class. These were rituals of rebellion, liminal periods when the planter class sanctioned the temporary reversal of social roles. The underlying principle behind rituals of rebellion is that social inequities produce tensions within society that regularly need to be released (Gluckman 1954; Turner 1969: 96–97). Collins (1811: 224) confirmed the tension-releasing function of alcohol drinking when he wrote that to "wink at" or turn a blind eye to a few hangovers reduced the inclination of enslaved peoples to run away. In Barbados and other parts of the Caribbean, rituals of rebellion, such as weekend dances and annual celebrations, acted as pressure valves. They provided regular opportunities for enslaved peoples temporarily to reverse social roles and release social pressures. The occasional release of tension, in turn, helped dilute rebellious impulses and thus strengthen the existing social order. The physiological effects of alcohol drinking on these occasions helped make the reversal of roles and the change in status all the more convincing.

The tension-releasing function of alcohol was familiar to newly arrived African slaves in the Caribbean. Rituals of rebellion, such as the Akan *odwira* festival and the Igbo yam festival, have a long history in West and Central Africa and were revived in a modified form in the slave societies of the Caribbean. Bacchanalian celebrations occurred at Easter, Crop-Over, Christmas, and New Year. Like the role of the Asantehene (king of the Asante) at the Akan *odwira* festival, the Caribbean planter encouraged rituals of rebellion and often dispensed alcohol at these events. For example, Dominican sugar planter Thomas Atwood (1791: 260) wrote that, for the enslaved peoples on his estate, the Christmas holiday was a time of "dancing, singing, and making merry." Atwood added: "This they are able to do, by having also given them at this time . . . rum." Plantation accounts from Barbados frequently mention the sizable distribution of rum to enslaved peoples for such celebrations.

It was only on these sanctioned occasions that alcohol provided a shield for enslaved peoples safely to stretch the limits of what the planter class considered acceptable behavior. According to an anonymous (1797: 23) writer in Jamaica, "The negroes ideas of pleasure [at the Christmas holiday] are rude and indistinct: They seem chiefly to consist in throwing off restraint and spending two or three days in rambling and drinking." During a New Year's celebration, Jamaica sugar planter Edward Long wrote:

> The masquerader, carrying a wooden sword in his hand, is followed with a numerous croud of drunken women, who refresh him frequently with a sup of aniseed-water, whilst he dances at every door, bellowing out *John Connu!* with great vehemence; so that, what with the liquor and the exercise, most of them are thrown into dangerous fevers; and some examples have happened of their dying.
> (Long 1774, 2: 424)

It is generally thought that Akan slaves were the originators of the Jonkonnu (John Canoe) character and greatly influenced the nature of these ceremonies in the British Caribbean (Burton 1997: 66–67).

Planters indulged the release of social pressures during these times, but the events did not always go according to expectations. The risk of slave revolt increased during holiday celebrations, when sizable allotments of rum were dispersed, social conventions were relaxed, plantation work was halted, and large numbers of enslaved peoples had greater opportunity to roam and assemble. Thus, it is not surprising that the 1816 slave uprising in Barbados took place on Easter. Similarly, in Jamaica, Tacky's Rebellion in 1760 occurred at Easter and the Jamaican slave revolt of 1831–32 occurred at Christmas. The lack of wide-scale involvement in many of these revolts suggests that inhibitions continued to exist despite the relaxation of rules and the shield that drunken comportment provided during these liminal periods. The increase in slave revolts on these occasions, however, indicates that some enslaved peoples decided to take advantage of the more relaxed conventions and sanctioned freedoms in order to turn their short "time-out" into an actual reversal of the social order.

Leaders of slave revolts often evoked African cultural traditions in order to mobilize and strengthen the resolve of rebels. Among the traditions used to excite slave rebellion was the powerful symbol of alcohol. Alcohol was a key to spiritual and physical escape (especially in Akan and Igbo societies), and this is evident in the use of alcohol in slave uprisings and in the ritualistic manipulation of white victims. Alcohol was also necessary for integrating ancestral spirits into revolts and receiving ancestral guidance. For example, Jamaican maroons, after defeating British troops during an uprising in 1795, "returned to their town to recruit their spirits by the aid of rum" (Dallas 1803, 1: 191). The pouring of alcohol libations underscores the way in which alcohol helped unite the slaves' physical and spiritual world. Individuals and groups poured libations and made alcohol offerings to seek favor from ancestral spirits and deities. They performed these acts to protect the community from evil, propitiate angry spirits, and accelerate an individual's recovery from illness. Libations and offerings therefore created a path to a spiritual world that secured community needs. Archaeological evidence has helped confirm the practice of these spiritual activities. Drawing on palynological evidence from the dwelling sites of enslaved peoples in colonial Virginia, Patricia Samford (2007: 160–61) found evidence that some enslaved peoples, influenced by Igbo religious practices, poured alcohol libations on shrines located in the subfloor pits of their houses.

Oath drinks were an important feature of slave uprisings. The oath drinks held before slave uprisings and conspiracies in the British Caribbean reveal the transfer of Igbo- and Akan-styled oaths (Smith 2004b, 2005: 163–65).

As in Africa, oath drinks strengthened alliances and reaffirmed individual obligations to the community. During the organizational stages of the 1736 slave conspiracy in Antigua, the participants consumed oath drinks that consisted of rum, dirt from the graves of deceased slaves, and cock's blood (Craton 1982: 122). During the Jamaica slave conspiracy of 1765, enslaved peoples consumed oath drinks consisting of rum, gunpowder, grave dirt, and blood (Williams 1932: 163). And the consumption of rum and gunpowder oath drinks preceded the slave uprising in St. Croix in 1848 (Hall 1992: 223). Even after emancipation, the oath drink continued to be an important facet of black resistance. During the peasant uprising at Morant Bay in Jamaica in 1865, captured police officers were forced to consume oath drinks of rum and gunpowder in order to show loyalty to the rebels (Heuman 1994: 6).

The combination of rum and other powerful ingredients in these oath drinks highlights the manipulation of the lowest common denominator of shared beliefs of diverse African ethnic groups in the British Caribbean, especially the Akan and Igbo. For example, the enduring and important role of ancestors in daily life and the need for ancestral assistance in the uprisings is evident in the use of grave dirt (Gaspar 1985: 245). Gunpowder, the basis for power in Africa and the Caribbean, was probably a means of intensifying the violent purpose of the oath. Blood was another powerful fluid associated with ancestors and warfare. On the Gold Coast, blood was offered to gods and ancestors in order to secure favors. In Akan society, for example, blood was usually reserved for war gods. Blood was not only an important offering to ancestors and war gods but also a powerful symbol of military conquest, which may explain why alcohol and the blood-red color symbolism were often combined in oaths and uprisings. Ethnographies from the Gold Coast reveal that Akan war gods preferred the red color of rum, underscoring the war gods' particular desire for blood (Akyeampong 1996: 28).

The use of rum in oath drinks also reflects shared beliefs about the spiritual power of alcohol and the loyalty-building role of oaths. Alcohol and blood were sacred fluids in both Akan and Igbo societies, and the widespread use of these ingredients in oath drinks suggests that Akan- and Igbo-styled oath-taking practices were particularly strong in the British Caribbean. Historian David Barry Gaspar (1985: 245) argued that the oath drinks consumed during the 1736 Antigua slave conspiracy "were deeply rooted in Akan religious tradition." Yet there is some evidence that the mixture of ingredients in the oaths had an especially strong Igbo influence.

Although oath drinks were common on the precolonial Gold Coast, and blood was a symbol of warfare, the Akan did not integrate blood into their oath drinks. According to historian Robin Law (1999), Igboland was one of the few places in West Africa that clearly used blood in oath drinks. In addition, Law argued:

> Despite the reputation of Igbo slaves in the Americas for docility (or more precisely for expressing their dissatisfaction through suicide rather than rebellion), it seems quite likely that it was the Igbo form of blood-oath which was utilized in some recorded slave insurrections.
> (Law 1999: 15)

In fact, some documentary sources indicate a strong Igbo component in the oath drinks consumed prior to the Antigua slave revolt (Gaspar 1985: 244).

While the use of blood may have been characteristic of Igbo oath drinks, the use of alcohol, a substance for contacting spirits and receiving ancestral guidance, probably represents a braiding of Akan, Igbo, and other West and Central African ethnic traditions. The widespread use of oath drinks in British Caribbean slave revolts reveals that slaves sought to mobilize all potential allies, including ancestral spirits, through the powerful symbolism of alcohol.

The power attributed to alcohol is also evident in the ritualistic treatment of white victims in British Caribbean slave uprisings. For example, during Tacky's Rebellion in Jamaica in 1760, slave rebels, after killing white servants at Ballard's Valley Plantation, drank the blood of their victims mixed with rum (Edwards 1819, 2: 78). During a slave revolt at a plantation in St. Anne's Parish, Jamaica, rebels cut off the head of the plantation owner and "made use of it as a punch-bowl" (Long 1774, 2: 447). According to reports of the 1701 slave uprising in Antigua, rebels cut off the head of a white victim "and washed it with rum and triumphed over it" (Craton 1982: 118). While archaeological evidence is not in a position to confirm that those involved in the Barbados slave revolt of 1816 consumed oath drinks at Mapps Cave or used alcohol in ritual displays of violence, documentary reports indicate that at least some rebels in St. Philip celebrated their conquest in the hours immediately following the revolt by ransacking the homes of planters and drinking "bottles of liquor" stolen from planters' residences (Handler and Hughes 2001: 274).

Conclusion

Theresa Singleton (2006), in her recent overview of African Diaspora archaeology, argued that in order for archaeologists to properly interpret their findings they must be familiar with the colonial contexts of slavery. By drawing on anthropological studies of alcohol and exploring the history of slave drinking and slave revolt in the British Caribbean, this study has sought to interpret the presence of alcohol-related materials at Mapps Cave. Without developing such a context, we are simply left with an unusual geologic formation littered with broken shards of bottle glass. The evidence suggests that Mapps Cave, a secretive and liminal space on the plantation landscape, provided enslaved peoples from Bayleys sugar plantation and surrounding sugar estates with a place to escape from the panoptic gaze of the planter class and circumvent, at least temporarily, a means of social control. Its links to marronage, and perhaps Carib Indians, may have enhanced the meaning of Mapps Cave as a site of resistance for enslaved peoples from St. Philip. Without opportunities for petite marronage after the expansion of sugar production in the seventeenth century, alcohol drinking at the site provided a momentary means of escape that helped ease social pressures. The release of social pressures that alcohol drinking bestowed upon enslaved peoples was, in some respects, a hindrance to collective action and outright revolt.

Yet, as alcohol studies research has shown, there are often two sides to the same coin when it comes to alcohol use. While drinking may have reduced aggressive impulses and impeded revolutionary action, alcohol use at Mapps Cave may have offered fertile ground for the overthrow of the existing social order. Just as taverns in eighteenth-century Boston and cafés in eighteenth-century Paris were nurseries for radical sentiment and hotbeds for the expression of radical thought, Mapps Cave may have provided enslaved peoples from Bayleys and surrounding sugar estates with a place to foment revolutionary ideas. It was a parliament of the people, and alcohol drinking at the site would have broken down social barriers and loosened the tongues of participants, which in turn would have helped facilitate sedition among those who frequented the site. Over the years, Mapps Cave may have nurtured those revolutionary ideals and thus strengthened the resolve of rebels at the outbreak of the 1816 revolt.

7

Conclusion

In his influential book *Sweetness and Power: The Place of Sugar in Modern History*, the celebrated anthropologist Sidney W. Mintz (1985) investigated the social and symbolic meaning of sugar and used it as a prism through which to view the political-economic processes that connected societies in disparate regions of the emerging Atlantic World. His commodity-based approach has set the model for historical anthropologists seeking to explicate the forces that have shaped life in the modern era. Soon after its release, Kathleen Deagan, in her thoughtful commentary on "questions that count" in historical archaeology, foresaw the potential value of this work for historical archaeologists. Deagan (1988:9), recognizing the need for historical archaeologists to grapple with broad issues of colonialism, capitalism, and slavery, wrote that one could "conceive of archaeological studies along the lines of Mintz's study of sugar, tracing material mechanisms by which economic and class structures are reinforced and maintained." Yet, despite Deagan's foresight, historical archaeology has been slow to appreciate the work of Mintz and to embrace commodity-based studies. Inspired by Mintz, as well as the work of colleagues in history and anthropology engaged in alcohol studies research in particular, this book has attempted to highlight the contributions that historical archaeology has made to our understanding of alcohol in the modern world, especially in terms of its impact on the American experience.

The historical archaeological study of alcohol does indeed provide a fresh prism through which to view the complicated social, political, and economic processes that have shaped life in the modern era. Archaeological investigations of breweries, wineries, and distilleries show that the alcohol business has followed a series of intricate steps that inform us about technological changes in modern world. Simple glass bottle fragments and the rusty bits of iron from wooden casks reveal how the almost insatiable appetite for alcoholic beverages has helped spur long-distance trade and foster complex relationships between peoples spread throughout an increasingly connected colonial and postcolonial world. Historical archaeological studies of alcohol drinking have helped shed new light on sociability, class struggles, the changing structure of work regimens, and advances in medical science. They provide original insights into the conservative nature of alcohol-based cultural traditions and illuminate the various conditions in modern society that motivate individual and group alcohol consumption. And historical archaeological research on alcohol and drinking has presented new opportunities to investigate the construction and negotiation of social boundaries based on class, race, gender, ethnicity, and religion.

While historical archaeological research has made valuable contributions to our understanding of alcohol in the modern era, the theoretical models advanced in social history and cultural anthropology compel historical archaeologists to develop more nuanced and sophisticated approaches to alcohol and alcohol drinking. There is a tendency in historical archaeology to subsume alcohol-related material culture under the heading of foodways or to treat alcohol-related materials as simply an expression of dietary habits. Doing so, however, obfuscates the uniquely meaningful character of alcohol drinking. While alcohol has certainly played an important role in the dietary habits of peoples throughout the modern world, the decision to quench one's thirst with alcohol, rather than milk, water, soda, or coffee, raises profound questions about the meaning of particular drinks as well as the material and ideological forces driving alcohol use. Moreover, because the choice of alcoholic beverage is deeply ingrained in the fabric of cultural tradition, identifying the emergence of new drinking patterns provides important opportunities to explore the dynamics of cultural change.

The uniquely meaningful character of alcohol is magnified by the fact that alcohol drinking is an art. Societies throughout the world have devised complex rules to govern where, when, how much, and with whom one can drink. Learning the art of social drinking and the rules that govern drinking events is a long process fraught with many stumbles and gaffes. The young man in present-day North America who orders a cosmopolitan on his date with a young woman, the seventeenth-century Chesapeake tobacco farmer who forgets to toast the king's health at the tavern, the parishioner who brings beer to the church picnic, and the archaeology field technician who fails to buy a round of drinks for his comrades at the corner bar after work are just a few examples of the *faux pas* encountered down that long road toward learning proper drinking etiquette. Moreover, the accoutrements used to generate the appropriate atmosphere for social and sociable drinking, such as ceramic punch bowls, brass corkscrews, electric mixers, crystal decanters, and silver ladles, require more nuanced and specialized knowledge than those reserved for nonalcoholic drinks. Perhaps the only real exception is tea drinking and the array of accoutrements associated with the tea ceremony. In fact, historical archaeological research has generated a sizable body of scholarly literature concerning the accoutrements of tea drinking. It has, however, provided little insight into the production, distribution, and consumption of this important commodity and its impact on the modern world.

Specialized knowledge and skill are also necessary for understanding the nuanced meaning of the spaces that societies have designated for the social and sociable consumption of alcoholic beverages. Perhaps many readers can relate to the experience of entering the "wrong" bar. Rarely do societies set aside space for other beverages, though the recent surge in coffee shops in the United States is certainly an exception. Indeed, the coffee phenomenon is noteworthy for its dissimilarities with alcohol. Coffee, a highly caffeinated drink, is germane for a society, such as the present-day United States, which is fascinated with productivity and the fast pace of the high-tech information age. The lack of sociability at present-day coffee shops in North America may be signaling an increasing emphasis on public individualism or antisociability, which is most pronounced at coffee shops that also feature wireless Internet, computer stations, and books. Whoever in the future chooses to write the historical archaeology of coffee and coffee consumption will no doubt find many divergences from the study of alcohol and alcohol drinking. The historical archaeological emphasis on alcohol's role in dietary habits, therefore, overlooks the learned and regulated nature of alcohol drinking and dilutes the important social meanings that control the consumption of this powerful liquid.

There is also a trend in historical archaeology to treat alcohol-related material culture as representative of "indulgences." This category too is misleading, however, because it simplifies the complexities of alcohol drinking in the modern world. While glass alcohol bottles, ceramic drinking mugs, and crystal wine glasses may often reflect indulgent behavior and attempts to secure personal gratification, uncritical assumptions about pleasure ignore the complicated processes that compel people to seek alcoholic escape. For example, it is unlikely that the men and women who drank alcoholic beverages at Mapps Cave were seeking solely to indulge themselves. The notion of indulgence implies a sense of agency that, in the slave societies of the Caribbean, clearly had to be negotiated within a broader framework of labor and racism. Instead Mapps Cave should be seen a place where enslaved peoples used alcohol to socialize, solve problems, carry on familiar alcohol-based traditions, and, perhaps most importantly, temporarily escape from the challenges of everyday life on sugar plantations in Barbados. At Mapps Cave, alcohol—a fluid loaded with social and sacred meanings, many of which derive from a blending of West and Central African cultural traditions—facilitated those activities.

Nor is alcohol use the inevitable outcome of the need to escape. There are plenty of people who find other, perhaps more constructive, ways to mollify the challenges of daily life. Religion, for example, serves as an alternative to drink, which may explain the strong religious overtones found in Alcoholics Anonymous and the fervent church participation in global temperance movements (Antze 1987; Blocker 1985; Bordin 1981; Epstein 1981; Murdock 1998; Tyrrell 1979, 1991). Moreover, the church has often served many of the same functions as taverns, rum shops, and saloons, especially as a social support network and as a place for peers to share common plights and experiences. The emphasis on "indulgences" seems to underscore the convivial nature of drinking, which is a distraction that waters down our understanding of the two interconnected functions of alcohol use that could reveal provocative insights into the social priorities that have helped shape life in the modern world: escape and integration.

In 1943 Donald Horton, a pioneer in the anthropological study of alcohol, stressed that alcohol drinking provides an escape from anxiety. More than two decades later, Craig MacAndrew and Robert Edgerton (1969) also attributed the motivation for drunken comportment to people's desire to remove themselves temporarily from the rigid rules of everyday life. Clearly, historical archaeologists, with their contextual insights drawn from the dialectic interplay of documentary and archaeological evidence, possess a keen awareness of the ways in which social inequities based on race, class, and gender have fostered alcoholic escape in different historical and regional settings. While historical archaeological research can provide insights into alcohol's escapist function, it can also cultivate our understanding of alcohol's role in integrating community members. The drinking places investigated by historical archaeologists showcase the way in which alcohol generates an appropriate atmosphere for sociability.

While the escapist and integrative functions of drinking are seemingly opposed, they are actually two sides of the same coin. Seventeenth-century taverns in the Chesapeake, saloons in nineteenth-century western boomtowns, and caves in early Barbados served as sanctuaries for people seeking temporary respites from the challenges of everyday life. Alcohol drinking at these sites removed barriers to social interaction among members of these respective communities. Drinking together as a group helped promote discourse, which itself enhanced the sense of escape. Indeed, the study of alcohol reveals that drinking often possesses a dual character. Alcohol is an elixir of life and the cause of illness. It is a sacred fluid with links to the spiritual world and a profane fluid that promotes a secular life. And it is a means to escape from the world and means of integrating members into the social realities in which they live.

While historical archaeological research has helped expand our knowledge of the escapist and integrative aspects of drinking, it has also helped expose alcohol's role as a resistance tool of the counterculture. Different social groups, especially young male peer groups, have used alcohol drinking to construct value systems that reinforce mutual responsibility, solidarity, and identity, often in opposition to the power of dominant "mainstream" society. Alcohol drinking by workers has confronted the demands of employers. Alcohol drinking by college students has confronted the concerns of college administrators. Alcohol drinking by working-class immigrants has confronted the temperance values of middle-class Americans. And alcohol drinking by Native Americans and Australian Aborigine has confronted the controls of colonial officials. Historical archaeological investigations into the lives of industrial wage workers, western gold miners, Belizean logwood cutters, soldiers, and other groups of young, rootless, and transient men highlight not only the escapist and integrative functions of alcohol but also the way in which alcohol helped construct a counterculture value system that confronted the moralistic standards of "upright" society.

Drawing on the political-economic model of Mintz, I have examined alcohol production, distribution, and consumption to showcase historical archaeology's contributions to our understanding of the modern world. As historical archaeology becomes increasingly international in scope, I suspect that there will come a day when historical archaeologists employ commodity-based models similar to those outlined by Mintz to illuminate the production, distribution, and consumption of other commodities. It is easily imaginable that historical archaeologists could pursue similar studies focused on tobacco, cotton, rice, flowerpots, cannonballs, sugar molds, and countless other agricultural and industrial commodities that have helped define the lives of people in the modern era. For those interested in alcoholic beverages, the industrial expansion of sake distilling in Japan and the colonial underpinnings of arrack distilling in South Asia are potential avenues of archaeological inquiry that have yet to be explored. The markets and trade networks that arose from Russian vodka, Irish whiskey, and Indian Ocean rum also hold promise in future historical archaeological research on alcohol. Investigations into the European alcohol trade with the Pacific and East Africa will also shed new light on the way in which colonial powers used indigenous patterns of alcohol consumption to construct racist ideologies and bolster colonial agendas. And historical archaeological investigations in the Atlantic Islands may someday hold out comparative evidence that will enhance our understanding of the forces shaping alcohol and drinking in the modern Atlantic World.

References

Adams, William Hampton
1977   *Silcott, Washington: Ethnoarchaeology of a Rural American Community.* Reports of Investigations no. 54. Pullman: Laboratory of Anthropology, Washington State University.
2002   "Recycling Bottles as Building Materials in the Pacific Islands." *Historical Archaeology* 36(2): 50–57.
2003   "Dating Historical Sites: The Importance of Understanding Time Lag in the Acquisition, Curation, Use, and Disposal of Artifacts." *Historical Archaeology* 37(2): 38–64.

Agnew, Aileen B.
1995   "Women and Property in Early Nineteenth-Century Portsmouth, New Hampshire." *Historical Archaeology* 29(1): 62–74.

Agorsah, E. Kofi
1993   "Archaeology and Resistance History in the Caribbean." *African Archaeological Review* 11: 175–95.

Akin, Marjorie Kleiger
1992   "The Noncurrency Functions of Chinese *Wen* in America." *Historical Archaeology* 26(2): 58–65.

Akyeampong, Emmanuel
1996   *Drink, Power, and Cultural Change: A Social History of Alcohol in Ghana, c. 1800 to Recent Times.* Portsmouth, N.H.: Heinemann.

Allchin, F. R.
1979   "India: The Ancient Home of Distillation?" *Man* 14(1): 55–63.

Allen, Jim
1973   "The Archaeology of Nineteenth-Century British Imperialism: An Australian Case Study." *World Archaeology* 5(1): 44–60.

Ambler, Charles
2003   "Alcohol and the Slave Trade in West Africa." In *Drugs, Labor, and Colonial Expansion*, ed. W. R. Jankowiak and D. Bradburd, 73–87. Tucson: University of Arizona Press.

Andrews, Anthony P.
1981   "Historical Archaeology in Yucatan: A Preliminary Framework." *Historical Archaeology* 15(1): 1–18.

Anonymous
1797   *Characteristic Traits of the Creolian and African Negroes in Jamaica, &c. &c. Columbian Magazine* (Kingston, Jamaica, April–October 1797). Reprinted 1976, ed. B. Higman. Jamaica: Caldwell Press.

Antze, Paul

1987 "Symbolic Action in Alcoholics Anonymous." In *Constructive Drinking: Perspectives on Drink from Anthropology*, ed. M. Douglas, 149–81. Cambridge: Cambridge University Press.

Armstrong, Douglas V.

1990 *The Old Village and the Great House: An Archaeological and Historical Examination of Drax Hall Plantation, St. Ann's Bay, Jamaica.* Urbana: University of Illinois Press.

Arnold, J. Barto III

1996 "The Texas Historical Commission's Underwater Archaeological Survey of 1995 and the Preliminary Report on the *Belle*, La Salle's Shipwreck of 1686." *Historical Archaeology* 30(4): 66–87.

Arthur, Paul

1986 "Roman Amphorae from Canterbury." *Britannia* 17: 139–258.

Ashurst, Denis

1970 "Excavations at Gawber Glasshouse, Near Barnsley, Yorkshire." *Post-Medieval Archaeology* 4: 92–140.

1987 "Excavations at the Seventeenth – Eighteenth Century Glasshouse at Bolsterstone and the Eighteenth Century Bolsterstone Pothouse, Stocksbridge, Yorkshire." *Post-Medieval Archaeology* 21: 147–226.

Atwood, Thomas

1791 *The History of the Island of Dominica.* London.

Avery, George

1997 "Pots as Packaging: The Spanish Olive Jar and Andalusian Transatlantic Commercial Activity, Sixteenth–Eighteenth Centuries." Ph.D. diss., University of Florida.

Babor, Thomas F., ed.

1986 *Alcohol and Culture: Comparative Perspectives from Europe and America.* New York: New York Academy of Sciences.

Bacon, Margaret K., Herbert Barry III, and Irvin L. Child

1965 "A Cross-Cultural Study of Drinking." *Quarterly Journal of Studies on Alcohol*, supplement 3: 29–48.

Badler, Virginia R., Patrick E. McGovern, and Rudolph H. Michel

1990 "Drink and Be Merry!: Infrared Spectroscopy and Ancient Near Eastern Wine." In *Organic Contents of Ancient Vessels: Materials Analysis and Archaeological Investigation*, ed. W. Biers and P. McGovern, vol. 7, 25–36. Philadelphia: MASCA Research Papers in Science and Archaeology.

Baker, Vernon G.

1980 "Glass Wine Bottles." In *Burr's Hill: A Seventeenth-Century Wampanoag Burial Ground in Warren, Rhode Island*, ed. S. Gibson, 58–66. Providence: Haffenreffer Museum of Anthropology.

Balicki, Joseph

2000 "Defending the Capital: The Civil War Garrison at Fort C. F. Smith." In *Archaeological Perspectives on the American Civil War*, ed. C. Geier and S. Potter, 125–47. Gainesville: University Press of Florida.

Barbot, John
1746 *A Description of the Coasts of North and South Guinea.* London.

Barka, Norman F.
1993 *Archaeological Survey of Sites and Buildings, St. Maarten, Netherlands Antilles I.* St. Maarten Archaeological Research Series no. 3. Williamsburg, Va.: Department of Anthropology, College of William and Mary.

Barrows, Susanna, and Robin Room
1991a "Introduction." In *Drinking: Behavior and Belief in Modern History,* ed. S. Barrows and R. Room, 1–28. Berkeley: University of California Press.

Barrows, Susanna, and Robin Room, eds.
1991b *Drinking: Behavior and Belief in Modern History.* Berkeley: University of California Press.

Barry, Herbert
1976 "Cross-Cultural Evidence That Dependency Conflict Motivates Drunkenness." In *Cross-Cultural Approaches to the Study of Alcohol: An Interdisciplinary Perspective,* ed. M. Everett, J. Waddell, and D. Heath, 249–63. The Hague: Mouton.

Bass, George F., Cemal Pulak, Dominique Collon, and James Weinstein
1989 "The Bronze Age Shipwreck at Ulu Burun: 1986 Campaign." *American Journal of Archaeology* 93(1): 1–29.

Beaudry, Mary C.
1981 "Pot-Shot, Jug-Bitten, Cup-Shaken: Object Language and Double Meanings." Paper presented at the 80th annual meeting of the American Anthropological Association, Los Angeles.

1989 "The Lowell Boott Mills Complex and Its Housing: Material Expressions of Corporate Ideology." *Historical Archaeology* 23(1): 19–32.

1993 "Public Aesthetics Versus Personal Experience: Worker Health and Well-Being in Nineteenth-Century Lowell, Massachusetts." *Historical Archaeology* 27(2): 90–105.

1995 "Scratching the Surface: Seven Seasons at the Spencer-Pierce-Little Farm, Newbury, Massachusetts." *Northeast Historical Archaeology* 24: 19–50.

Beaudry, Mary C., Lauren J. Cook, and Stephen A. Mrozowski
1991 "Artifacts and Active Voices: Material Culture as Social Discourse." In *The Archaeology of Inequality,* ed. R. H. McGuire and R. Paynter, 150–91. Oxford: Blackwell.

Beaudry, Mary C., Janet Long, Henry M. Miller, Fraser D. Neiman, and Garry Wheeler Stone
1983 "A Vessel Typology for Early Chesapeake Ceramics: The Potomac Typological System." *Historical Archaeology* 17(1): 18–43.

Beaudry, Mary C., and Stephen A. Mrozowski, eds.
1987 *Interdisciplinary Investigations of the Boott Mills, Lowell, Massachusetts, vol. 1: Life at the Boarding Houses: A Preliminary Report.* Cultural Resources Management Study 18. U.S. Department of Interior, National Park Service, North Atlantic Regional Office, Boston.

Becker, Marshall J.

1978 "A Witch-Bottle Excavated in Chester County, Pennsylvania: Archaeological Evidence for Witchcraft in the Mid-Eighteenth Century." *Pennsylvania Archaeologist* 48(1–2): 1–11.

1980 "An American Witch Bottle." *Archaeology* 33(2): 19–23.

Beckles, Hilary

1998 *Bussa: The 1816 Barbados Revolution.* Rewriting History Series no. 2. Bridgetown, Barbados: Department of History, University of the West Indies, Cave Hill, Barbados, and the Barbados Museum and Historical Society.

Bennett, Judith M.

1996 *Ale, Beer, and Brewsters in England: Women's Work in a Changing World, 1300–1600.* Oxford: Oxford University Press.

Berlin, Michael

1996 *The Worshipful Company of Distillers: A Short History.* West Sussex: Phillimore.

Bernier, Maggy

2003 *Caractérisation typologique, microscopique et chimique des faïences du XVIIIe siècle du site Saint-Ignace de Loyola en Guyane française.* Cahiers d'Archéologie du CELAT no. 14. Québec: Université Laval.

Bickerton, L. M.

1984 *English Drinking Glasses, 1675–1825.* Aylesbury: Shire Publications.

Bittmann, Bente, and Gerda Alcaide

1984 "Historical Archaeology in Abandoned Nitrate 'Oficinas' in Northern Chile: A Preliminary Report." *Historical Archaeology* 18(1): 52–75.

Bjerén, Gunilla

1992 "Drinking and Masculinity in Everyday Swedish Culture." In *Alcohol, Gender, and Culture,* ed. D. Gefou-Madianou, 157–66. London: Routledge.

Blitz, John H.

1978 "Moonshining and Archaeology." *Journal of Alabama Archaeology* 24(2): 92–101.

Blocker, Jack S.

1985 *"Give to the Winds thy Fears": The Women's Temperance Crusade, 1873–1874.* Westport, Conn.: Greenwood Press.

Blocker, Jack S., and Cheryl Krasnick Warsh, eds.

1997 *The Changing Face of Drink: Substance, Imagery, and Behaviour.* Ottawa: Les Publications Histoire Sociale/Social History.

Boiten, Adriaan, and Saskia van Vuuren

1982 "European Ceramics." In *The Ceramic Load of the "Witte Leeuw," 1613,* ed. C. L. Van der Pijl-Ketel, 246–49. Amsterdam: Rijksmuseum.

Bonasera, Michael C., and Leslie Raymer

2001 "Good for What Ails You: Medicinal Use at Five Points." *Historical Archaeology* 35(3): 49–64.

Bond, Kathleen H.

1988 "Alcohol Use in the Boott Mills Boardinghouses: Tension between Workers and Management—A Documentary and Archaeological Study." M.A. thesis, Boston University.

1989a "The Medicine, Alcohol, and Soda Vessels from the Boott Mills." In *Interdisciplinary Investigations of the Boott Mills, Lowell, Massachusetts, vol. 3: The Boarding House System as a Way of Life*, ed. M. Beaudry and S. Mrozowski, 121–40. Cultural Resources Management Study 21. U.S. Department of Interior, National Park Service, North Atlantic Regional Office, Boston.

1989b "'That we may purify our corporation by discharging the offenders': The Documentary Record of Social Control in the Boott Boardinghouses." In *Interdisciplinary Investigations of the Boott Mills, Lowell, Massachusetts, vol. 3: The Boarding House System as a Way of Life*, ed. M. Beaudry and S. Mrozowski, 23–36. Cultural Resources Management Study 21. U.S. Department of Interior, National Park Service, North Atlantic Regional Office, Boston.

Bordin, Ruth Birgitta Anderson

1981 *Women and Temperance: The Quest for Power and Liberty, 1873–1900*. Philadelphia: Temple University Press.

Bowers, Peter M., and Brian L. Gannon

1998 *Historical Development of the Chena River Waterfront, Fairbanks, Alaska: An Archaeological Perspective*. Fairbanks: Alaska Department of Transportation and Public Facilities, Northern Region and the Federal Highway Administration.

Bragdon, Kathleen J.

1988 "Occupational Differences Reflected in Material Culture." In *Documentary Archaeology in the New World*, ed. M. Beaudry, 223–49. Cambridge: Cambridge University Press.

Braidwood, Robert J.

1953 "Symposium: Did Man Once Live by Beer Alone?" With responses from Jonathan D. Sauer, Hans Helbaek, Paul C. Mangelsdorf, Hugh C. Cutler, Carleton S. Coon, Ralph Linton, Julian Steward, and A. Leo Oppenheim. *American Anthropologist* 55(4): 515–26.

Braudel, Fernand

1981 *Civilization and Capitalism: Fifteenth–Eighteenth Century, vol. 3: The Structures of Everyday Life: The Limits of the Possible*. Trans. S. Reynolds. New York: Harper and Row.

Breen, Eleanor E.

2004 "Whiskey on the Rocks: Excavating and Interpreting the Archaeological Remains of George Washington's Distillery." Paper presented at the 37th annual meeting of the Society for Historical Archaeology, St. Louis.

Breen, Eleanor E., and Esther C. White

2006 "'A Pretty Considerable Distillery': Excavating George Washington's Whiskey Distillery." *Quarterly Bulletin: The Archaeological Society of Virginia* 61(4): 209–20.

Bretherton, George

1997 "The Battle between Carnival and Lent: Temperance and Repeal in Ireland, 1829–1845." In *The Changing Face of Drink: Substance, Imagery, and Behaviour*, ed. J. S. Blocker and C. K Warsh, 65–94. Ottawa: Les Publications Histoire Sociale/ Social History.

Brown, Gregory J.
1986   *Block 9 in the Eighteenth Century: The Social and Architectural Context of the Shield's Tavern Property.* Report of the Colonial Williamsburg Foundation, Department of Archaeological Research, Williamsburg, Va.
Brown, Gregory J., Thomas F. Higgins III, David F. Muraca, S. Kathleen Pepper, and Roni H. Polk
1990   *Archaeological Investigations of the Shield's Tavern Site Williamsburg, Virginia.* Report of the Colonial Williamsburg Foundation, Department of Archaeological Research, Williamsburg, Va.
Brown, Margaret Kimball
1971   "Glass from Fort Michilimackinac: A Classification for Eighteenth-Century Glass." *Michigan Archaeologist* 17(3–4): 97–215.
Brown, Marley R., III
1973   "Ceramics from Plymouth, 1621–1800: The Documentary Record." In *Ceramics in America*, ed. I. M. G. Quimby, 41–74. Charlottesville: University Press of Virginia.
1980   "European Ceramics." In *Burr's Hill: A Seventeenth-Century Wampanoag Burial Ground in Warren, Rhode Island*, ed. S. Gibson, 50–57. Providence: Haffenreffer Museum of Anthropology.
Browne, Benjamin F.
1926   *The Yarn of a Yankee Privateer.* Ed. N. Hawthorne. New York: Funk and Wagnalls.
Bruman, Henry J.
2000   *Alcohol in Ancient Mexico.* Salt Lake City: University of Utah Press.
Bullock, Helen
1932   "The Raleigh Tavern." Typescript of the Colonial Williamsburg Foundation, Williamsburg, Va.
Burley, David V.
1995   "Contexts of Meaning: Beer Bottles and Cans in Contemporary Burial Practices in the Polynesian Kingdom of Tonga." *Historical Archaeology* 29(1): 75–83.
Burton, Richard D. E.
1997   *Afro-Creole: Power, Opposition, and Play in the Caribbean.* Ithaca, N.Y.: Cornell University Press.
Busch, Jane
1981   "An Introduction to the Tin Can." *Historical Archaeology* 15(1): 95–104.
1987   "Second Time Around: A Look at Bottle Reuse." *Historical Archaeology* 21(1): 67–80.
Bush, David R.
2000   "Interpreting the Latrines of the Johnson's Island Civil War Military Prison." *Historical Archaeology* 34(1): 62–78.
Bushnell, Amy
1981   *The King's Coffer: Proprietors of the Spanish Florida Treasury, 1565–1702.* Gainesville: University Press of Florida.

Cabak, Melanie A., Mark D. Groover, and Scott J. Wagers
1995 "Health Care and the Wayman A.M.E. Church." *Historical Archaeology* 29(2): 55–76.

Carley, Caroline D.
1981 "Historical and Archaeological Evidence of Nineteenth Century Fever Epidemics and Medicine at Hudson's Bay Company's Fort Vancouver." *Historical Archaeology* 15(1): 19–35.

Carruthers, Clive
2003 "Spanish *Botijas* or Olive Jars from the Santo Domingo Monastery, La Antigua Guatemala." *Historical Archaeology* 37(4): 40–55.

Carstairs, G. M.
1979 "Daru and Bhang: Cultural Factors in the Choice of Intoxicants." In *Beliefs, Behaviors, and Alcoholic Beverages: A Cross-Cultural Survey*, ed. M. Marshall, 297–312. Ann Arbor: University of Michigan Press.

Chambers, Douglas B.
1997 "'My own nation': Igbo Exiles in the Diaspora." In *Routes to Slavery: Direction, Ethnicity, and Mortality in the Transatlantic Slave Trade*, ed. D. Eltis and D. Richardson, 72–97. London: Frank Cass.

Cheek, Charles D., and Amy Friedlander
1990 "Pottery and Pig's Feet: Space, Ethnicity, and Neighborhood in Washington, D.C., 1880–1940." *Historical Archaeology* 24(1): 34–60.

Clark, Peter
1988 "The 'Mother Gin' Controversy in the Early Eighteenth Century." *Transactions of the Royal Historical Society* 38: 63–84.

Clement, Christopher Ohm
1997 "Settlement Patterning on the British Caribbean Island of Tobago." *Historical Archaeology* 31(2): 93–106.

Clements, Joyce M.
1993 "The Cultural Creation of the Feminine Gender: An Example from Nineteenth-Century Military Households at Fort Independence, Boston." *Historical Archaeology* 27(4): 39–64.

Clouse, Robert Alan
1999 "Interpreting Archaeological Data through Correspondence Analysis." *Historical Archaeology* 33(2): 90–107.

Collins, Dr.
1811 *Practical Rules for the Management and Medical Treatment of Negro Slaves, in the Sugar Colonies*. London.

Connell, Neville
1957 "Punch Drinking and Its Accessories." *Journal of the Barbados Museum and Historical Society* 25(1): 1–17.

Costello, Julia G.
1992 "Purchasing Patterns of the California Missions in ca. 1805." *Historical Archaeology* 26(1): 59–66.

Cotter, John L.

1958 *Archaeological Excavations at Jamestown, Virginia.* Archaeological Research Series no. 4. Washington, D.C.: National Park Service.

Courtney, Yolanda

2000 "Pub Tokens: Material Culture and Regional Marketing Patterns in Victorian England and Wales." *International Journal of Historical Archaeology* 4(2): 159–90.

Crain, Christopher, Kevin Farmer, Frederick H. Smith, and Karl Watson

2004 "Human Skeletal Remains from an Unmarked African Burial Ground in the Pierhead Section of Bridgetown, Barbados." *Journal of the Barbados Museum and Historical Society* 50: 66–83.

Crane, Brian D.

2000 "Filth, Garbage, and Rubbish: Refuse Disposal, Sanitary Reform, and Nineteenth-Century Yard Deposits in Washington, D.C." *Historical Archaeology* 34(1): 20–38.

Crass, David Colin, and Deborah L. Wallsmith

1992 "Where's the Beef?: Food Supply at an Antebellum Frontier Post." *Historical Archaeology* 26(2): 3–23.

Craton, Michael

1982 *Testing the Chains: Resistance to Slavery in the British West Indies.* Ithaca, N.Y.: Cornell University Press.

Craton, Michael, and James Walvin

1970 *A Jamaican Plantation: The History of Worthy Park 1670–1970.* Toronto: University of Toronto Press.

Croteau, Nathalie

2004 "L'habitation de Loyola: Un rare exemple de prospérité en Guyane Français." *Journal of Caribbean Archaeology,* Special Publication 1: 68–80.

Crowell, Aron L.

1997 *Archaeology and the Capitalist World System: A Study from Russian America.* New York: Kluwer Academic/Plenum.

Dallas, Robert Charles

1803 *The History of the Maroons, from Their Origin to the Establishment of their Chief Tribe at Sierra Leone.* 2 vols. London.

Davies, Peter

2006 "Mapping Commodities at Casselden Place, Melbourne." *International Journal of Historical Archaeology* 10(4): 343–55.

Dawdy, Shannon Lee

2000 "Understanding Cultural Change through the Vernacular: Creolization in Louisiana." *Historical Archaeology* 34(3): 107–23.

Deagan, Kathleen A.

1972 "Fig Springs: The Mid-Seventeenth Century in North-Central Florida." *Historical Archaeology* 6: 23–46.

1973 "*Mestizaje* in Colonial St. Augustine." *Ethnohistory* 20(1): 55–65.

1983 *Spanish St. Augustine: The Archaeology of a Colonial Creole Community.* New York: Academic Press.

1985 "The Archaeology of Sixteenth Century St. Augustine." *Florida Anthropologist* 38(1–2): 6–33.

1987 *Artifacts of the Spanish Colonies of Florida and the Caribbean, 1500–1800, vol. 1: Ceramics, Glassware, and Beads.* Washington, D.C.: Smithsonian Institution Press.

1988 "Neither History Nor Prehistory: The Questions That Count in Historical Archaeology." *Historical Archaeology* 22(1): 7–12.

1992 "La Isabela, Foothold in the New World." *National Geographic* 181(1): 40–53.

1996 "Colonial Transformation: Euro-American Cultural Genesis in the Early Spanish-American Colonies." *Journal of Anthropological Research* 52(2): 135–60.

Deagan, Kathleen A., and José María Cruxent

2002 *La Isabela: America's First European Town.* New Haven: Yale University Press.

De Cunzo, Lu Ann

1995 "Reform, Respite, Ritual: An Archaeology of Institutions: The Magdalen Society of Philadelphia, 1800–1850." *Historical Archaeology* 29(3): 1–168.

Deetz, James F.

1973 "Ceramics From Plymouth, 1620–1835: The Archaeological Evidence." In *Ceramics in America*, ed. I. M. G. Quimby, 15–40. Charlottesville: University Press of Virginia.

1977 *In Small Things Forgotten: The Archaeology of Early American Life.* Garden City, N.Y.: Anchor Press.

1993 *Flowerdew Hundred: The Archaeology of a Virginia Plantation, 1619–1864.* Charlottesville: University Press of Virginia.

deFrance, Susan D.

1996 "Iberian Foodways in the Moquegua and Torata Valleys of Southern Peru." *Historical Archaeology* 30(3): 20–48.

de Garine, Igor, and Valerie de Garine, eds.

2001 *Drinking: Anthropological Approaches.* New York: Berghahn Press.

Delle, James A., and Patrick Heaton

2003 "The Hector Backbone: A Quiescent Landscape of Conflict." *Historical Archaeology* 37(3): 93–110.

Devlin, Sean, and Frederick H. Smith

2007 *Archaeological Investigations at St. Nicholas Abbey Sugar Plantation, St. Peter, Barbados: The 2007 Field Season.* Report on file at the Department of Anthropology, College of William and Mary, Williamsburg, Va.

Diehl, Michael, Jennifer A. Waters, and J. Homer Thiel

1998 "Acculturation and the Composition of the Diet of Tucson's Overseas Chinese Gardeners at the Turn of the Century." *Historical Archaeology* 32(4): 19–33.

Dietler, Michael

1990 "Driven by Drink: The Role of Drinking in the Political Economy and the Case of Early Iron Age France." *Journal of Anthropological Archaeology* 9: 352–406.

1995 "The Cup of Gyptis: Rethinking the Colonial Encounter in Early Iron Age Western Europe and the Relevance of World-Systems Models." *Journal of European Archaeology* 3(2): 89–111.

2006 "Alcohol: Anthropological/Archaeological Perspectives." *Annual Review of Anthropology* 35: 229–49.

DiVirgilio, Justin

2003 "Still-Crazy after All These Years: The Rum Distillery at Quackenbush Square." Paper presented at the 36th annual meeting of the Society for Industrial Archaeology, Providence.

Dixon, Kelly J.

2005 *Boomtown Saloons: Archaeology and History in Virginia City*. Reno: University of Nevada Press.

Douglas, Mary

1987a "A Distinctive Anthropological Perspective." In *Constructive Drinking: Perspectives on Drink from Anthropology*, ed. M. Douglas, 3–15. Cambridge: Cambridge University Press.

Douglas, Mary, ed.

1987b *Constructive Drinking: Perspectives on Drink from Anthropology*. Cambridge: Cambridge University Press.

Drake, St. Clair

1987–90 *Black Folk Here and There: An Essay in History and Anthropology*. 2 vols. Los Angeles: Center for Afro-American Studies, University of California.

Dressel, Heinrich

1899 *Corpus Inscriptionum Latinarum*. Vol. 15. Berlin: Societas Regia Scentiarum.

Drewett, Peter L.

1991 *Prehistoric Barbados*. London: Institute of Archaeology, University College London.

Dubell, Gregory Robert

2002 "Brewing Social Consciousness: An Investigation Into Newport, Rhode Island's Pre-Revolutionary Brewery and Its Ties to Illicit Trade." Senior honors thesis, Salve Regina University, Newport.

Dudek, Martin G., Lawrence Kaplan, and Marie Mansfield King

1998 "Botanical Remains from a Seventeenth-Century Privy at the Cross Street Back Lot Site." *Historical Archaeology* 32(3): 63–71.

Dumbrell, Roger

1983 *Understanding Antique Wine Bottles*. Woodbridge, U.K.: Antique Collectors Club/ Baron Publishing.

Eckholm, Erik and James F. Deetz

1971 "Wellfleet Tavern." *Natural History* 80(7): 49–56.

Edwards, Andrew C.

2001 *Digging the Dug: Archaeology at Peyton Randolph*. Report of the Colonial Williamsburg Foundation, Department of Archaeological Research, Williamsburg, Va.

Edwards, Andrew C., Linda K. Derry, and Roy A. Jackson

1988 *A View from the Top: Archaeological Investigations of Peyton Randolph's Urban Plantation*. Report of the Colonial Williamsburg Foundation, Department of Archaeological Research, Williamsburg, Va.

Edwards, Bryan
1819   *The History, Civil and Commercial, of the British West Indies.* 5th ed. 5 vols. London.

Eltis, David, and Lawrence Jennings
1988   "Trade between Western Africa and the Atlantic World in the Pre-Colonial Era." *American Historical Review* 93(4): 936–60.

Epstein, Barbara Leslie
1981   *The Politics of Domesticity: Women, Evangelism, and Temperance in Nineteenth-Century America.* Middletown, Conn.: Wesleyan University Press.

Everett, Michael W., Jack O. Waddell, and Dwight B. Heath, eds.
1976   *Cross-Cultural Approaches to the Study of Alcohol: An Interdisciplinary Perspective.* The Hague: Mouton Publishers.

Ewen, Charles R.
1986   "Fur Trade Archaeology: A Study of Frontier Hierarchies." *Historical Archaeology* 20(1): 15–27.

2001   "Historical Archaeology in the Colonial Spanish Caribbean." In *Island Lives: Historical Archaeologies of the Caribbean,* ed. P. Farnsworth, 3–20. Tuscaloosa: University of Alabama Press.

Ewing, John, and Beatrice Rouse, eds.
1978   *Drinking: Alcohol in American Society—Issues and Current Research.* Chicago: Nelson Hall.

Fahey, David M.
1997   "Blacks, Good Templars, and Universal Membership." In *The Changing Face of Drink: Substance, Imagery, and Behaviour,* ed. J. S. Blocker and C. K. Warsh, 133–61. Ottawa: Les Publications Histoire Sociale/Social History.

Fairbanks, Charles H.
1952   "Creek and Pre-Creek." In *Archaeology of Eastern United States,* ed. J. Griffin, 285–300. Chicago: University of Chicago Press.

1973   "The Cultural Significance of Spanish Ceramics." In *Ceramics in America,* ed. I.M.G. Quimby, 141–74. Charlottesville: University Press of Virginia.

1978   "The Ethno-Archaeology of the Florida Seminole." In *Tacachale: Essays on the Indians of Florida and Southeastern Georgia during the Historic Period,* ed. J. Milanich and S. Proctor, 163–93. Gainesville: University Press of Florida.

Farmer, Kevin, Frederick H. Smith, and Karl Watson
2007   "The Urban Context of Slavery: An Archaeological Perspective from Two Afro-Barbadian Slave Cemeteries in Bridgetown, Barbados." In *Proceedings of the 21st International Congress for Caribbean Archaeology,* 477–85. Trinidad and Tobago: IACA.

Farmer, Kevin, Frederick H. Smith, Karl Watson, and Jennifer Yamazaki
2005   "The Health and Lifestyles of Bridgetown's Enslaved Population: An Archaeological and Physical Anthropological Analysis of Dentition from the Fontabelle and Pierhead Slave Burial Grounds in Bridgetown, Barbados." *Journal of the Barbados Museum and Historical Society* 51: 151–65.

Farnsworth, Kenneth B.
1996   *A Short History of the Gravel Springs Distillery and Bottling Works*. Kampsville Studies in Archeology and History no. 2. Kampsville, Ill.: Center for American Archeology.

Farnsworth, Paul
1992   "Missions, Indians, and Cultural Continuity." *Historical Archaeology* 26(1): 22–36.
1996   "The Influence of Trade on Bahamian Slave Culture." *Historical Archaeology* 30(4): 1–23.
2000   "Identity through Beer." *Anthropology News: The Newsletter of the American Anthropological Association* 41(2): 18.
2001   "Beer Brewing and Consumption in the Maintenance of African Identity by the Enslaved People of the Bahamas, 1783–1834." *Culture and Agriculture* 23(2): 19–30.

Faulkner, Alaric
1992   "Gentility on the Frontiers of Acadia, 1635–1674: An Archaeological Perspective." In *New England/New France, 1600–1850*, ed. P. Benes, 82–100. The Dublin Seminar for New England Folklife Annual Proceedings 1989. Boston: Boston University Press.

Faulkner, Alaric, and Gretchen Fearon Faulkner
1987   *The French at Pentagoet, 1635–1674: An Archaeological Portrait of the Acadian Frontier*. Augusta: Maine Historic Preservation Commission.

Ferguson, Leland
1991   "Struggling with Pots in Colonial South Carolina." In *The Archaeology of Inequality*, ed. R. H. McGuire and R. Paynter, 28–39. Oxford: Blackwell.
1992   *Uncommon Ground: Archaeology and Early African America, 1650–1800*. Washington, D.C.: Smithsonian Institution Press.

Finamore, Daniel
1994   "Sailors and Slaves on the Woodcutting Frontier: Archaeology of British Bay Settlement, Belize." Ph.D. diss., Boston University.

Fitts, Robert K.
1996   "The Landscapes of Northern Bondage." *Historical Archaeology* 30(2): 54–73.
2002   "Becoming American: The Archaeology of an Italian Immigrant." *Historical Archaeology* 36(2): 1–17.

Fitzherbert, William
ca. 1750–1850   William Fitzherbert Papers, Letters, and Correspondences Relating to Turners Hall. Barbados Department of Archives, Black Rock, Barbados.

Fontana, Bernard L.
1968   "Bottles and History: The Case of Magdalena de Kino, Sonora, Mexico." *Historical Archaeology* 2: 45–55.

Ford, Richard
ca. 1674   *A New Map of the Island of Barbadoes*. London.

Franklin, Maria
1997   "Out of Sight, Out of Mind: The Archaeology of an Enslaved Virginian House-
       hold, ca. 1740–1778." Ph.D. diss., University of California, Berkeley.

Franzen, John G.
1992   "Northern Michigan Logging Camps: Material Culture and Worker Adaptation
       on the Industrial Frontier." *Historical Archaeology* 26(2): 74–98.

Friedlander, Amy
1991   "House and Barn: The Wealth of Farmers, 1795–1815." *Historical Archaeology*
       25(2): 15–29.

Fulford, Michael
1987   "Economic Interdependence among Urban Communities of the Roman Mediter-
       ranean." *World Archaeology* 19(1): 58–75.

Funari, Pedro Paulo A.
1995   "The Archaeology of Palmares and Its Contribution to the Understanding of the
       History of African-American Culture." *Historical Archaeology in Latin America*
       7: 1–41.

Gage, Thomas
1677   *A New Survey of the West Indies: Or, The English American His Travel by Sea and
       Land: Containing a Journal of Three Thousand and Three Hundred Miles within the
       Main Land of America.* 3rd ed. London.

Gaimster, David
1997a *German Stoneware 1200–1900: Archaeology and Cultural History.* London: British
       Museum Press.
1997b "Rhenish Stoneware from Shipwrecks: The Study of Ceramic Function and
       Lifespan." In *Artefacts from Shipwrecks: Dated Assemblages from the Late Mid-
       dle Ages to the Industrial Revolution,* ed. M. Redknap, 121–28. Oxford: Oxbow
       Books.

Gale-Morant Papers
1731–1925 "The Gale-Morant Papers 1731–1925 in the Library University of Exeter." In
       British Records Relating to America in Microform, ed. W. E. Minchinton, Section
       3, Papers Relating to York Plantation and Gale's Valley Plantation, University of
       Florida, Caribbean and Latin American Studies Collection, Gainesville.

Galliou, Patrick
1984   "Days of Wine and Roses? Early Armorica and the Atlantic Wine Trade." In
       Cross-Channel Trade between Gaul and Britain in the Pre-Roman Iron Age, ed. S.
       Macready and F. Thompson, 24–36. London: Society of Antiquaries.

García Arévelo, Manuel A.
1986   "El Maniel de José Leta: Evidencias arqueológicas de un posible asentamiento
       Cimarrón en la Región Sudoriental de la Isla de Santo Domingo." In *Cimarrón,*
       ed. J. J. Arrom and M. A. García Arévelo, 33–76. Santo Domingo, Dominican
       Republic: Fundación García Arévelo.

Garman, James C.
1998   "Rethinking 'Resistant Accommodation': Toward an Archaeology of African-
       American Lives in Southern New England, 1638–1800." *International Journal of
       Historical Archaeology* 2(2): 133–60.

Garman, James C., and Paul A. Russo
1999 "'A Disregard of Every Sentiment of Humanity': The Town Farm and Class Realignment in Nineteenth-Century Rural New England." *Historical Archaeology* 33(1): 118–35.

Gaspar, David Barry
1985 *Bondmen and Rebels: A Study of Master-Slave Relations in Antigua*. Durham, N.C.: Duke University Press.

Gefou-Madianou, Dimitra, ed.
1992 *Alcohol, Gender, and Culture*. London: Routledge.

Geggus, David Patrick
1991 "Haitian Voodoo in the Eighteenth-Century: Language, Culture, Resistance." *Jahrbuch für Geschichte von Staat, Wirtschaft und Gesellschaft Lateinamerikas* 28: 21–51.

1992a "La cérémonie du Bois Caïman." *Chemins Critiques* 2(3): 59–78.

1992b "Marronage, Voodoo, and the Saint Domingue Slave Revolt of 1791." In *Proceedings of the 15th Meeting of the French Colonial Historical Society*, 22–35. Lanham, Md.: University Press of America.

Geismar, Joan M.
1993 "Where Is Night Soil?: Thoughts on an Urban Privy." *Historical Archaeology* 27(2): 57–70.

Gibb, James G., and Julia A. King
1991 "Gender, Activity Areas, and Homelots in the Seventeenth-Century Chesapeake Region." *Historical Archaeology* 25(4): 109–31.

Gluckman, Max
1954 *Rituals of Rebellion in South-East Africa*. Manchester: Manchester University Press.

Goggin, John
1960 *The Spanish Olive Jar: An Introductory Study*. Yale University Publications in Anthropology no. 62. New Haven: Yale University Press.

Gollannek, Eric F.
2007 "Circumnavigating the Punch Bowl: Sociable Drinking and the Consumption of Empire in the Atlantic World." Paper presented at the International Workshop, Alcohol in the Atlantic World: Historical and Contemporary Perspectives, York University, Toronto.

Goodman, Jordan, Paul E. Lovejoy, and Andrew Sherratt, eds.
1995 *Consuming Habits: Drugs in History and Anthropology*. London: Routledge.

Goodwin, Conrad M.
1982 "Archaeology on the Galways Plantation." *Florida Anthropologist* 34(4): 251–58.

1994 "Betty's Hope Windmill: An Unexpected Problem." *Historical Archaeology* 28(1): 99–110.

Goodwin, Lorinda B. R.
1999 *An Archaeology of Manners: The Polite World of the Merchant Elite of Colonial Massachusetts*. New York: Kluwer Academic/Plenum.

Gragg, Larry
2003 *Englishmen Transplanted: The English Colonization of Barbados, 1627-1660.* Oxford: Oxford University Press.

Green, Chris
1999 *John Dwight's Fulham Pottery, Excavation 1971-79.* London: English Heritage.

Greenwood, Richard
2005 "Uneasy Spirits: Salvage Archaeology at an Early Distillery." Paper presented at the 34th annual meeting of the Society for Industrial Archaeology, Milwaukee.

Griggs, Heather J.
1999 "GO gCUIRE DIA RATH AGUS BLATH ORT (God Grant that You Prosper and Flourish): Social and Economic Mobility among the Irish in Nineteenth-Century New York City." *Historical Archaeology* 33(1): 87-101.

Groover, Mark D.
1994 "Evidence for Folkways and Cultural Exchange in the Eighteenth-Century South Carolina Backcountry." *Historical Archaeology* 28(1): 41-64.

Grulich, Anne Dowling
2004 *Façon de Venise Drinking Vessels on the Chesapeake Frontier: Examples From St. Mary's City, Maryland.* St. Mary's City, Md.: Historic St. Mary's City.

Gums, Bonnie L.
2002 "Earthfast (Pieux en Terre) Structures at Old Mobile." *Historical Archaeology* 36(1): 13-25.

Gusfield, Joseph R.
1986 *Symbolic Crusade: Status Politics and the American Temperance Movement.* Urbana: University of Illinois Press.
1987 "Passage to Play: Rituals of Drinking Time in American Society." In *Constructive Drinking: Perspectives on Drink from Anthropology,* ed. M. Douglas, 73-90. Cambridge: Cambridge University Press.

Haine, W. Scott
1996 *The World of the Paris Café: Sociability among the French Working Class, 1789-1914.* Baltimore: Johns Hopkins University Press.

Hall, Neville A. T.
1992 *Slave Society in the Danish West Indies: Saint Thomas, Saint John and Saint Croix.* Ed. B. Higman. Mona, Jamaica: University of the West Indies Press.

Hamilton, D. L., and Robyn Woodward
1984 "A Sunken Seventeenth-Century City: Port Royal, Jamaica." *Archaeology* 37(1): 38-45.

Hancock, David
1998 "Commerce and Conversation in the Eighteenth-Century Atlantic: The Invention of Madeira Wine." *Journal of Interdisciplinary History* 29(2): 197-219.

Handler, Jerome S.
1963a "A Historical Sketch of Pottery Manufacture in Barbados." *Journal of the Barbados Museum and Historical Society* 30(3): 129-53.
1963b "Pottery Making in Rural Barbados." *Southwestern Journal of Anthropology* 19: 314-34.

1967 "Father Antoine Biet's Visit to Barbados in 1654." *Journal of the Barbados Museum and Historical Society* 32: 56–76.

1989 *Searching for a Slave Cemetery in Barbados, West Indies: A Bioarchaeological and Ethnohistorical Investigation.* Research Paper no. 59. Carbondale: Southern Illinois University at Carbondale Center for Archaeological Investigations.

1997 "Escaping Slavery in a Caribbean Plantation Society: Marronage in Barbados, 1650s–1830s." *New West Indian Guide* 71(3–4): 183–225.

1998 Research Notes and Related Materials Shipped to the Barbados Department of Archives, January 1998; Box 1: Archaeology Projects (1971, 1972, 1973, 1987).

Handler, Jerome S., Arthur C. Aufderheide, Robert S. Corruccini, Elizabeth M. Brandon, and Lorentz E. Wittmers Jr.

1986 "Lead Contact and Poisoning in Barbados Slaves: Historical, Chemical, and Biological Evidence." *Social Science History* 10(4): 399–425.

Handler, Jerome S., and Ronald Hughes

2001 "The 1816 Slave Revolt in Barbados and the Petition of Samuel Hall Lord." *Journal of the Barbados Museum and Historical Society* 47: 267–86.

Handler, Jerome S., and Frederick W. Lange

1978 *Plantation Slavery in Barbados: An Archaeological and Historical Investigation.* Cambridge, Mass.: Harvard University Press.

Handsman, Russell G.

1981 "Early Capitalism and the Center Village of Canaan, Connecticut: A Study of Transformations and Separations." *Artifacts* 9(3): 1–22.

Hardesty, Donald L.

1994 "Class, Gender Strategies, and Material Culture in the Mining West." In *Those of Little Note: Gender, Race, and Class in Historical Archaeology*, ed. E. M. Scott, 129–45. Tucson: University of Arizona Press.

Harrington, J. C.

1972 *A Tryal of Glasse: The Story of Glassmaking at Jamestown.* Richmond: Dietz Press.

Harrington, Spencer P. M.

2000 "Fine Wine and a Piss-Poor Vintage." *Archaeology* 53(6): 24.

Harris, Jane E.

1979 *Bouteilles françaises bleu-vert du XVIIIe siècle récupérées à la Forteresse de Louisbourg, Nouvelle-Ecosse*, Histoire et Archéologie 29. Ottawa: Parks Canada.

Haselgrove, Dennis, and Jan Van Loo

1998 "Pieter van den Ancker and Imports of Frechen Stoneware Bottles and Drinking Pots in Restoration London c.1660–1667." *Post-Medieval Archaeology* 32: 45–74.

Haynes, Barrington E.

1959 *Glass through the Ages.* Harmondsworth, U.K.: Penguin.

Haynes, Maree Lee, Fiona Baker, and Richard Tipping

1998 "A Still Worm From Excavations at Carrick Castle, Argyll." *Post-Medieval Archaeology* 32: 33–44.

Heath, Barbara J.

1997 "Slavery and Consumerism: A Case Study from Central Virginia." *African-American Archaeology* 19: 1–8.

1998 "Engendering Choice: Slavery and Consumerism in Central Virginia." Paper presented at the 31st annual meeting of the Society for Historical and Underwater Archaeology, Atlanta.

Heath, Barbara J., and Amber Bennett

2000 "'The little Spots allow'd them': The Archaeological Study of African-American Yards." *Historical Archaeology* 34(2): 38–55.

Heath, Dwight B.

1976 "Anthropological Perspectives on Alcohol: An Historical Review." In *Cross-Cultural Approaches to the Study of Alcohol: An Interdisciplinary Perspective*, ed. M. Everett, J. Waddell, and D. Heath, 41–101. The Hague: Mouton.

1987 "A Decade of Development in the Anthropological Study of Alcohol Use, 1970–1980." In *Constructive Drinking: Perspectives on Drink from Anthropology*, ed. M. Douglas, 16–70. Cambridge: Cambridge University Press.

2000 *Drinking Occasions: Comparative Perspectives on Alcohol and Culture*. Philadelphia: Brunner/Mazel Publishing.

Heldman, Donald P.

1973 "Fort Toulouse of the Alabamas and the Eighteenth-Century Indian Trade." *World Archaeology* 5(2): 163–69.

Herd, Denise

1991 "The Paradox of Temperance: Blacks and the Alcohol Question in Nineteenth-Century America." In *Drinking: Behavior and Belief in Modern History*, ed. S. Barrows and R. Room, 354–75. Berkeley: University of California Press.

Herskovits, Melville J.

1966 *The New World Negro: Selected Papers in Afro-American Studies*. Ed. F. Herskovits. Bloomington: Indiana University Press.

Heuman, Gad

1994 *"The Killing Time": The Morant Bay Rebellion in Jamaica*. Knoxville: University of Tennessee Press.

Higman, Barry W.

1988 *Jamaica Surveyed: Plantation Maps and Plans of the Eighteenth and Nineteenth Centuries*. Kingston: Institute of Jamaica Publications.

1998 *Montpelier, Jamaica: A Plantation Community in Slavery and Freedom, 1739–1912*. Mona, Jamaica: University Press of the West Indies.

Hildyard, Robin

1985 *Browne Muggs: English Brown Stoneware*. London: Victoria and Albert Museum.

Hill, Sarah H.

1982 "An Examination of Manufacture-Deposition Lag for Glass Bottles from Late Historic Sites." In *Archaeology of Urban America: The Search for Pattern and Process*, ed. R. S. Dickens, 291–328. New York: Academic Press.

Hodges, Mary Ellen N.

1993 "The Archaeology of Native American Life in Virginia in the Context of European Contact: Review of Past Research." In *The Archaeology of Seventeenth-Century Virginia*, ed. R. Reinhart and D. Pogue, 1–65. Richmond: Dietz Press.

Hoffman, Charles A.

1987 "Archaeological Investigations at the Long Bay Site, San Salvador, Bahamas." In *Proceedings of the First San Salvador Conference: Columbus and His World*, ed. D. T. Gerace, 237–45. Fort Lauderdale, Fla.: CCFL Bahamas Field Station.

Hoffman, Kathleen

1997 "Cultural Development in *La Florida.*" *Historical Archaeology* 31(1): 24–35.

Holme, Randle

1688 *The Academy of Armory.* London.

Holt, Cheryl A.

1991 "Plants, Humans, and Culture: An Edible Model of Consuming Behavior." *Historical Archaeology* 25(2): 46–61.

Holt, Mack P., ed.

2006 *Alcohol: A Social and Cultural History.* Oxford: Berg Publishers.

Honeysett, Elizabeth A., and Peter D. Schulz

1990 "Burned Seeds from a Gold Rush Store in Sacramento, California." *Historical Archaeology* 24(1): 96–103.

Honychurch, Lennox

1997 "Crossroads in the Caribbean: A Site of Encounter and Exchange on Dominica." *World Archaeology* 28(3): 291–304.

Hoover, Robert L.

1992 "Some Models for Spanish Colonial Archaeology in California." *Historical Archaeology* 26(1): 37–44.

Horning, Audrey J.

1995 "'A Verie Fit Place to Erect a Great Cittie': Comparative Contextual Analysis of Archaeological Jamestown." Ph.D. diss., University of Pennsylvania.

2002 "Myth, Migration, and Material Culture: Archaeology and the Ulster Influence on Appalachia." *Historical Archaeology* 36(4): 129–49.

Horton, Donald

1943 "The Functions of Alcohol in Primitive Societies: A Cross-Cultural Study." *Quarterly Journal of Studies on Alcohol* 4: 199–320.

Howson, Jean E.

1990 "Social Relations and Material Culture: A Critique of the Archaeology of Plantation Slavery." *Historical Archaeology* 24(4): 78–91.

Hudson, J. Paul

1961 "Seventeenth-Century Glass Wine Bottles and Seals Excavated at Jamestown." *Journal of Glass Studies* 3: 79–89.

Hughes, Griffith

1750 *The Natural History of Barbados.* London.

Hull-Walski, Deborah A., and Frank L. Walski
1994 "'There's Trouble a-Brewin'': The Brewing and Bottling Industries at Harpers Ferry, West Virginia." *Historical Archaeology* 28(4): 106–121.

James, Stephen R., Jr.
1988 "A Reassessment of the Chronological and Typological Framework of the Spanish Olive Jar." *Historical Archaeology* 22(1): 43–66.

Jamieson, Ross W.
1995 "Material Culture and Social Death: African-American Burial Practices." *Historical Archaeology* 29(4): 39–58.
2000 *Domestic Architecture and Power: The Historical Archaeology of Colonial Ecuador.* New York: Kluwer Academic/Plenum.

Jankowiak, William R., and Daniel Bradburd, eds.
2003 *Drugs, Labor, and Colonial Expansion.* Tucson: University of Arizona Press.

Janowitz, Meta F.
1993 "Indian Corn and Dutch Pots: Seventeenth-Century Foodways in New Amsterdam/New York." *Historical Archaeology* 27(2): 6–24.

Johannsen, Christina
1980 "European Trade Goods and Wampanoag Culture in the Seventeenth Century." In *Burr's Hill: A Seventeenth-Century Wampanoag Burial Ground in Warren, Rhode Island*, ed. S. Gibson, 25–33. Providence: Haffenreffer Museum of Anthropology.

Johnson, Matthew
1996 *An Archaeology of Capitalism.* Oxford: Blackwell.

Jones, Olive R.
1971 "Glass Bottle Push-Ups and Pontil Marks." *Historical Archaeology* 5: 62–73.
1981 "Essence of Peppermint: A History of the Medicine and Its Bottle." *Historical Archaeology* 15(2): 1–57.
1986 *Cylindrical English Wine and Beer Bottles, 1735–1850.* Studies in Archaeology, Architecture, and History. Ottawa: Environment–Canada Parks.
1993 "Commercial Foods, 1740–1820." *Historical Archaeology* 27(2): 25–41.

Jones, Olive R., and E. Ann Smith
1985 *Glass of the British Military ca. 1755–1820.* Studies in Archaeology, Architecture, and History. Ottawa: Environment–Canada Parks.

Jones, Olive R., and Catherine Sullivan
1989 *The Parks Canada Glass Glossary for the Description of Containers, Tableware, Flat Glass, and Closures.* Studies in Archaeology, Architecture, and History. Ottawa: Environment–Canada Parks.

Kahn, Lisa C.
1996 "Beer and Brewing." In *The Oxford Companion to Archaeology*, ed. B. Fagan, 90–91. New York: Oxford University Press.

Karskens, Grace
2003 "Revisiting the Worldview: The Archaeology of Convict Households in Sydney's Rocks Neighborhood." *Historical Archaeology* 37(1): 34–55.

Katz, Solomon H., and Fritz Maytag
1991   "Brewing an Ancient Beer." *Archaeology* 44(4): 24–27.

Katz, Solomon H., and Mary M. Voigt
1986   "Bread and Beer: The Early Use of Cereals in the Human Diet." *Expedition* 28(2): 23–34.

Keller, Mark
1979   "The Great Jewish Drink Mystery." In *Beliefs, Behaviors, and Alcoholic Beverages: A Cross-Cultural Survey*, ed. M. Marshall, 404–13. Ann Arbor: University of Michigan Press.

Kelly, Kenneth G.
1997   "The Archaeology of African-European Interaction: Investigating the Social Roles of Trade, Traders, and the Use of Space in the Seventeenth- and Eighteenth-Century Hueda Kingdom, Republic of Benin." *World Archaeology* 28(3): 351–69.

Kelso, Gerald K.
1993   "Pollen-Record Formation Processes, Interdisciplinary Archaeology, and Land Use by Mill Workers and Managers: The Boott Mills Corporation, Lowell, Massachusetts, 1836–1942." *Historical Archaeology* 27(1): 70–94.

Kelso, William M.
1982   "Jefferson's Garden: Landscape Archaeology at Monticello." *Archaeology* 35(4): 38–45.

1984   *Kingsmill Plantations 1619–1800: Archaeology of Country Life in Colonial Virginia.* San Diego: Academic Press.

2006   *Jamestown: The Buried Truth.* Charlottesville: University of Virginia Press.

Kelso, William M., Nicholas M. Luccketti, and Beverly A. Straube
1999   *Jamestown Rediscovery V.* Richmond: Association for the Preservation of Virginia Antiquities.

Kelso, William M., and Beverly A. Straube
2000   *Jamestown Rediscovery VI.* Richmond: Association for the Preservation of Virginia Antiquities.

Kent, Susan
1983   "The Differential Acceptance of Culture Change: An Archaeological Test Case." *Historical Archaeology* 17(2): 56–63.

Kerns-Nocerito, Mechelle L.
2003   "Trade in Colonial Anne Arundel County: The Tobacco Port of London Town." *Maryland Historical Magazine* 98(3): 325–44.

Kerns-Nocerito, Mechelle L., and Paul F. Mintz
2000   "Thriving Trade, Thirsty Travelers: A Look at Rumney's Tavern in London Town." Paper presented at the 30th annual meeting of the Middle Atlantic Archaeology Conference, Ocean City, Md.

King, Julia A.
1984   "Ceramic Variability in Seventeenth-Century St. Augustine, Florida." *Historical Archaeology* 18(2): 75–82.

1988   "A Comparative Midden Analysis of a Household and Inn in St. Mary's City, Maryland." *Historical Archaeology* 22(1): 17–39.

1990   "An Intrasite Spatial Analysis of the van Sweringen Site, St. Mary's City, Maryland." Ph.D. diss., University of Pennsylvania.

King, Julia A., and Henry M. Miller
1987   "The View from the Midden: An Analysis of Midden Distribution and Composition at the van Sweringen Site, St. Mary's City, Maryland." *Historical Archaeology* 21(2): 37–59.

Kleij, Piet
1997   "The Identification of a Ship's Place of Departure with the Help of Artefacts." In *Artefacts from Shipwrecks: Dated Assemblages from the Late Middle Ages to the Industrial Revolution*, ed. M. Redknap, 181–90. Oxford: Oxbow Books.

Knight, James
1932   *Archaeological Survey of Foundations at King's Arms Tavern Uncovered in Williamsburg, Virginia, 1932*. Report of the Colonial Williamsburg Foundation, Department of Archaeological Research, Williamsburg, Va.

Kozakavich, Stacy C.
2006   "Doukhobor Identity and Communalism at Kirilovka Village Site." *Historical Archaeology* 40(1): 119–32.

Labat, Jean-Baptiste Père
1724   *Nouveau voyage aux isles de l'Amérique*. 2 vols. La Haye, France.

Lange, Frederick W., and Jerome S. Handler
1980   "The Archaeology of Mapps Cave: A Contribution to the Prehistory of Barbados." *Journal of the Virgin Islands Archaeological Society* 9: 3–17.

Langton, Marcia
1993   "Rum, Seduction, and Death: Aboriginality and Alcohol." *Oceania* 63: 195–206.

La Rosa Corzo, Gabino
2003   *Runaway Slave Settlements in Cuba: Resistance and Repression*. Trans. M. Todd. Chapel Hill: University of North Carolina Press.

Las Casas, Bartolomé de
1971   *History of the Indies*. Trans. A. Collard. New York: Harper and Row.

Laudan, Rachel
2000   "Birth of the Modern Diet." *Scientific American* 283(2): 76–81.

Law, Robin
1999   "On the African Background to the Slave Insurrection in Saint-Domingue (Haïti) in 1791: The Bois Caiman Ceremony and the Dahomian 'Blood Pact.'" Paper presented at the Harriet Tubman Seminar, Department of History, York University, Toronto.

Layfield, Dr.
1906   "A Large Relation of the Port Ricco Voiage; Written, as Is Reported, by That Learned Man and Reverend Divine Doctor Layfield, His Lordships Chaplaine and Attendant in That Expedition; Very Much Abbreviated." In *Hakluytus Postumus or Purchas His Pilgrimes*, ed. S. Purchas, vol. 16, 44–106. Glasgow.

Leacock, Seth
1964   "Ceremonial Drinking in an Afro-Brazilian Cult." *American Anthropologist* 66: 344–54.

Leath, Robert A.

1999 "'After the Chinese Taste': Chinese Export Porcelain and Chinoiserie Design in Eighteenth-Century Charleston." *Historical Archaeology* 33(3): 48–61.

LeeDecker, Charles H., Terry H. Klein, Cheryl A. Holt, and Amy Friedlander

1987 "Nineteenth-Century Households and Consumer Behavior in Wilmington, Delaware." In *Consumer Choice in Historical Archaeology*, ed. S. Spencer-Wood, 233–59. New York: Plenum.

Lenik, Edward J.

1972 "The Truro Halfway House, Cape Cod, Massachusetts." *Historical Archaeology* 6: 77–86.

Leone, Mark P.

1995 "A Historical Archaeology of Capitalism." *American Anthropologist* 97(2): 251–68.

Leone, Mark P., and Silas D. Hurry

1998 "Seeing: The Power of Town Planning in the Chesapeake." *Historical Archaeology* 32(4): 34–62.

Leslie, Charles

1740 *A New and Exact Account of Jamaica.* 3rd ed. Edinburgh.

Levin, Jed

1985 "Drinking on the Job: How Effective Was Capitalist Work Discipline?" *American Archaeology* 5(3): 195–201.

Levy, Philip, Mary-Cate Garden, Nicole M. Hayes, Lisa Fischer, Joanne Bowen, Donna Sawyer, and David F. Muraca

2007 "Life at Richard Charlton's Coffeehouse: A Story of Archaeology, History, and Hot Drinks in Eighteenth-Century Williamsburg, Virginia." Report of the Colonial Williamsburg Foundation, Department of Archaeological Research, Williamsburg, Va.

Lewis, Clifford M.

1978 "The Calusa." In *Tacachale: Essays on the Indians of Florida and Southeastern Georgia during the Historic Period*, ed. J. Milanich and S. Proctor, 19–49. Gainesville: University Press of Florida.

Lightfoot, Kent G.

1995 "Culture Contact Studies: Redefining the Relationship between Prehistoric and Historical Archaeology." *American Antiquity* 60(2): 199–217.

Lightfoot, Kent G., Thomas A. Wake, and Ann M. Schiff

1993 "Native Responses to the Russian Mercantile Colony of Fort Ross, Northern California." *Journal of Field Archaeology* 20(2): 159–75.

Ligon, Richard

1673 *A True and Exact History of the Island of Barbadoes.* 2nd ed. London.

Link, Marion C.

1960 "Exploring the Drowned City of Port Royal." *National Geographic* 117(2): 151–82.

Lister, Florence C., and Robert H. Lister

1974 "Maiolica in Colonial Spanish America." *Historical Archaeology* 8: 17–52.

1976   *A Descriptive Dictionary for 500 Years of Spanish-Tradition Ceramics (13th through 18th Centuries)*. Special Publication Series no. 1. Society for Historical Archaeology, Columbia, S.C.

1981   "The Recycled Pots and Potsherds of Spain." *Historical Archaeology* 15(1): 66–78.

1987   *Andalusian Ceramics in Spain and New Spain: A Cultural Register from the Third Century B.C. to 1700*. Tucson: University of Arizona Press.

Loftfield, Thomas C.

1991   "The Bendeshe/Byde Mill Sugar Factory in Barbados: The Ceramic Evidence." In *Proceedings of the 14th International Congress for Caribbean Archaeology*, ed. A. Cummins and P. King, 408–15. Barbados: Barbados Museum and Historical Society.

1992   "Unglazed Red Earthenware from Barbados: A Preliminary Analysis." *Journal of the Barbados Museum and Historical Society* 40:19–36.

2001   "Creolization in Seventeenth-Century Barbados: Two Case Studies." In *Island Lives: Historical Archaeologies of the Caribbean*, ed. P. Farnsworth, 207–33. Tuscaloosa: University of Alabama Press.

Long, Edward

1774   *The History of Jamaica; or, General Survey of the Antient and Modern State of That Island*. 3 vols. Reprinted 1970, London: Frank Cass.

Lorrain, Dessamae

1968   "An Archaeologist's Guide to Nineteenth-Century American Glass." *Historical Archaeology* 2: 35–44.

Lucas, Michael

2007   "'Our common drinke is syder, which is verry good': The Social and Material Context of Ordinaries in Early Prince George's County, Maryland." Paper presented at the 40th annual meeting of the Society for Historical Archaeology, Williamsburg, Va.

Luccketti, Nicholas M.

1990   "Archaeological Excavations at Bacon's Castle, Surry County, Virginia." In *Earth Patterns: Essays in Landscape Archaeology*, ed. W. M. Kelso and R. Most, 23–42. Charlottesville: University Press of Virginia.

MacAndrew, Craig, and Robert B. Edgerton

1969   *Drunken Comportment: A Social Explanation*. Chicago: Aldine Publishing.

MacMahon, Darcie, and Kathleen Deagan

1996   "Legacy of Fort Mose." *Archaeology* 49(5): 54–58.

Mancall, Peter

1995   *Deadly Medicine: Indians and Alcohol in Early America*. Ithaca, N.Y.: Cornell University Press.

2003   "Alcohol and the Fur Trade in New France and English America, 1600–1800." In *Drugs, Labor, and Colonial Expansion*, ed. W. R. Jankowiak and D. Bradburd, 89–99. Tucson: University of Arizona Press.

Maniery, Mary L.

2002   "Health, Sanitation, and Diet in a Twentieth-Century Dam Construction Camp: A View from Butt Valley, California." *Historical Archaeology* 36(3): 69–84.

Markell, Ann, Martin Hall, and Carmel Schrire
1995 "The Historical Archaeology of Vergelegen, an Early Farmstead at the Cape of Good Hope." *Historical Archaeology* 29(1): 10–34.
Marken, Mitchell W.
1994 *Pottery from Spanish Shipwrecks, 1500–1800.* Gainesville: University Press of Florida.
Marshall, Mac
1976 "A Review and Appraisal of Alcohol and Kava Studies in Oceania." In *Cross-Cultural Approaches to the Study of Alcohol: An Interdisciplinary Perspective,* ed. M. Everett, J. Waddell, and D. Heath, 103–18. The Hague: Mouton.
Marshall, Mac, ed.
1979 *Beliefs, Behaviors, and Alcoholic Beverages: A Cross-Cultural Survey,* Ann Arbor: University of Michigan Press.
Marshall, Mac, and Leslie B. Marshall
1975 "Opening Pandora's Bottle: Reconstructing Micronesians' Early Contacts with Alcoholic Beverages." *Journal of the Polynesian Society* 8: 441–65.
1979 "Holy and Unholy Spirits: The Effects of Missionization on Alcohol Use in Eastern Micronesia." In *Beliefs, Behaviors, and Alcoholic Beverages: A Cross-Cultural Survey,* ed. M. Marshall, 208–36. Ann Arbor: University of Michigan Press.
Martin, Ann Smart
1989 "The Role of Pewter as Missing Artifact: Consumer Attitudes toward Tablewares in Late Eighteenth-Century Virginia." *Historical Archaeology* 23(2): 1–27.
1997 "Complex Commodities: The Enslaved as Producers and Consumers in Eighteenth-Century Virginia." Paper presented at the Annual Conference of the Omohundro Institute of Early American History and Culture, Winston-Salem, North Carolina.
Marx, Robert F.
1967 *Pirate Port: The Story of the Sunken City of Port Royal.* Cleveland: World Publishing Company.
1968 *Wine Glasses Recovered from the Sunken City of Port Royal: 1 May, 1966–31 March, 1968.* Kingston: Jamaican National Trust Commission.
Maxwell, D.B.S.
1993 "Beer Cans: A Guide for the Archaeologist." *Historical Archaeology* 27(1): 95–113.
McAllister, Patrick A.
2005 *Xhosa Beer Drinking Rituals: Power, Practice and Performance in the South African Rural Periphery.* Durham, N.C.: Carolina Academic Press.
McCary, Ben C.
1962 "Artifacts of Glass Made by the Virginia Indians." *Quarterly Bulletin of the Archaeological Society of Virginia* 16: 59–62.
McClelland, David C., William N. Davis, Rudolf Kalin, and Eric Wanner
1972 *The Drinking Man: Alcohol and Human Motivation.* New York: Free Press.
McDonald, Maryon, ed.
1994 *Gender, Drink and Drugs.* Oxford: Berg Publishers.

McEwan, Bonnie G.
1991 "San Luis de Talimali: The Archaeology of Spanish-Indian Relations at a Florida Mission." *Historical Archaeology* 25(3): 36–60.
1992 "The Role of Ceramics in Spain and Spanish America during the Sixteenth Century." *Historical Archaeology* 26(1): 92–108.

McGovern, Patrick E.
1998 "Wine for Eternity: How Molecular Archaeologists Identified the Contents of Vessels Found in the Tomb of an Egyptian King." *Archaeology* 51(4): 28–32.
2003 *Ancient Wine: The Search for the Origins of Viticulture*. Princeton: Princeton University Press.

McGuire, Randall H., and Mark Walker
1999 "Class Confrontations in Archaeology." *Historical Archaeology* 33(1): 159–83.

McInnis, Maurie D.
1999 "'An Idea of Grandeur': Furnishing the Classical Interior in Charleston, 1815–1840." *Historical Archaeology* 33(3): 32–47.

McLearen, Douglas C., and L. Daniel Mouer
1993 *Jordan's Journey II: A Preliminary Report on the 1992 Excavations at Archaeological Sites 44PG302, 44PG303, and 44PG315*. Report on file at the Virginia Department of Historic Resources, Richmond.

Merrifield, Ralph
1955 "Witch Bottles and Magical Jugs." *Folklore* 66(1): 195–207.
1987 *The Archaeology of Ritual and Magic*. London: Batsford.

Miller, George L., and Catherine Sullivan
1984 "Machine-Made Glass Containers and the End of Production for Mouth Blown Bottles." *Historical Archaeology* 18(2): 83–96.

Miller, Henry
1988 "Baroque Cities in the Wilderness: Archaeology and Urban Development in the Colonial Chesapeake." *Historical Archaeology* 22(2): 57–73.

Mintz, Sidney W.
1985 *Sweetness and Power: The Place of Sugar in Modern History*. London: Penguin.

Mintz, Sidney W., and Richard Price
1992 *The Birth of African-American Culture: An Anthropological Perspective*. Boston: Beacon Press.

Monks, Gregory G.
1992 "Architectural Symbolism and Non-Verbal Communication at Upper Fort Garry." *Historical Archaeology* 26(2): 37–57.

Mora de Tovar, Gilma Lucia
1988 *Aguardiente y conflictos sociales en la Nueva Granada durante el siglo xviii*. Bogotá: Universidad Nacional de Colombia, Centro Editorial.

Mouer, L. Daniel
1993 "Chesapeake Creoles: The Creation of Folk Culture in Colonial Virginia." In *The Archaeology of Seventeenth-Century Virginia*, ed. R. Reinhart and D. Pogue, 105–66. Richmond: Dietz Press.

Mouer, L. Daniel, Douglas C. McLearen, R. Taft Kiser, Christopher P. Egghart, Beverly J. Binns, and Dane T. Magoon

1992 *Jordan's Journey: A Preliminary Report on Archaeology at Site 44PG302, Prince George County, Virginia, 1990–1991.* Report on file at the Virginia Department of Historic Resources, Richmond.

Mouer, L. Daniel, and Frederick H. Smith

2001 "Revisiting Mapps Cave: Amerindian and Probable Slave Occupation of a Sinkhole and Cavern, St. Philip Parish, Barbados." In *Proceedings of the 18th International Congress for Caribbean Archaeology*, 301–07. Basse-Terre, Guadeloupe: L'Association Internationale d'Archéologie de la Caraïbe Grenada West Indies.

Moussette, Marcel

1994 *Le site du palais de l'intendant à Québec: Genèse et structuration d'un lieu urbain.* Sillery, Quebec: Les éditions du Septentrion.

1996 "The Site of the Intendant's Palace in Québec City: The Changing Meaning of an Urban Space." *Historical Archaeology* 30(2): 8–21.

Mrozowski, Stephen A.

1984 "Prospects and Perspectives on an Archaeology of the Household." *Man in the Northeast* 27: 31–49.

Mrozowski, Stephen A., Grace H. Ziesing, and Mary C. Beaudry

1996 *Living on the Boott: Historical Archaeology at the Boott Mills Boardinghouses, Lowell, Massachusetts.* Amherst: University of Massachusetts Press.

Muckelroy, Keith

1976 "The Integration of Historical and Archaeological Data concerning an Historic Wreck Site: The 'Kennemerland.'" *World Archaeology* 7(3): 280–90.

Mullins, Paul R.

1999 *Race and Affluence: An Archaeology of African America and Consumer Culture.* New York: Kluwer Academic/Plenum.

Murdock, Catherine Gilbert

1998 *Domesticating Drink: Women, Men, and Alcohol in America, 1870–1940.* Baltimore: Johns Hopkins University Press.

Nassaney, Michael S., William M. Cremin, and Daniel P. Lynch

2004 "The Identification of Colonial Fort St. Joseph, Michigan." *Journal of Field Archaeology* 29: 309–21.

Nassaney, Michael S., and Carol A. Nickolai

1999 "Selective Memories and the Material World: The Changing Significance of the Warren B. Shepard Site, Battle Creek, Michigan." *Material History Review* 50: 76–85.

Nassaney, Michael S., Deborah L. Rotman, Daniel O. Sayers, and Carol A. Nickolai

2001 "The Southwest Michigan Historic Landscape Project: Exploring Class, Gender, and Ethnicity from the Ground Up." *International Journal of Historical Archaeology* 5(3): 219–61.

Nichols, Elaine

1988 "No Easy Run to Freedom: Maroons in the Great Dismal Swamp of North Carolina and Virginia, 1677–1850." M.A. thesis, University of South Carolina.

Noël Hume, Ivor

1961 "The Glass Wine Bottle in Colonial Virginia." *Journal of Glass Studies* 3: 91–117.

1968 "A Collection of Glass from Port Royal, Jamaica, with Some Observations on the Site, Its History, and Archaeology." *Historical Archaeology* 2: 5–34.

1969a *Archaeology and Wetherburn's Tavern.* Archaeological Series no. 3. Williamsburg, Va.: Colonial Williamsburg Foundation.

1969b *Glass in Colonial Williamsburg's Archaeological Collections.* Archaeological Series no. 1. Williamsburg, Va.: Colonial Williamsburg Foundation.

1969c *A Guide to Artifacts of Colonial America.* New York: Alfred A. Knopf.

1974 *All the Best Rubbish.* New York: Harper and Row.

1982 *Martin's Hundred.* New York: Alfred A. Knopf.

Olsen, Stanley

1965 "Liquor Bottles from Florida Military Sites." *American Antiquity* 31(1): 105–7.

Orser, Charles E., Jr.

1985 "The Sorghum Industry of a Nineteenth-Century Cotton Plantation in South Carolina." *Historical Archaeology* 19(1): 51–64.

1993 *In Search of Zumbi: The 1993 Season.* Report of the Midwestern Archaeological Research Center, Illinois State University, Normal.

1994 "Toward a Global Historical Archaeology: An Example from Brazil." *Historical Archaeology* 28(1): 5–22.

1996 *A Historical Archaeology of the Modern World.* New York: Kluwer Academic/Plenum.

2007 *The Archaeology of Race and Racialization in Historic America.* Gainesville: University Press of Florida.

Orser, Charles E., Jr., and Pedro P. A. Funari

2001 "Archaeology and Slave Resistance and Rebellion." *World Archaeology* 33(1): 61–72.

Ortiz, Fernando

1947 *Cuban Counterpoint: Tobacco and Sugar.* Trans. H. de Onís and reprinted 1995, Durham, N.C.: Duke University Press.

Otto, John S.

1984 *Cannon's Point Plantation, 1794–1860: Living Conditions and Status Patterns in the Old South.* Orlando: Academic Press.

Outlaw, Merry Abbitt

2002 "Scratched in Clay: Seventeenth-Century North Devon Slipware at Jamestown, Virginia." In *Ceramics in America,* ed. R. Hunter, 17–38. Milwaukee: Chipstone Foundation.

Paddock, John Miles

1992 "A Fulham Pottery 'Hunt' Tankard from Cirencester." *Post-Medieval Archaeology* 26: 91–93

Painter, Floyd

1980 "An Early Eighteenth-Century Witch Bottle: A Legacy of the Wicked Witch of Pongo." *Chesopiean* 18: 62–71.

Pan, Lynn

1975   *Alcohol in Colonial Africa.* Vol. 22. Helsinki: Finnish Foundation for Alcohol Studies.

Parker Pearson, Mike

1997   "Close Encounters of the Worst Kind: Malagasy Resistance and Colonial Disasters in Southern Madagascar." *World Archaeology* 28(3): 393–417.

Peacock, D.P.S., and D. F. Williams

1986   *Amphorae and the Roman Economy: An Introductory Guide.* White Plains, N.Y.: Longman Press.

Pegram, Thomas R.

1998   *Battling Demon Rum: The Struggle for a Dry America, 1800–1933.* Chicago: Ivan R. Dee.

Peña, Elizabeth S., and Jacqueline Denmon

2000   "The Social Organization of a Boardinghouse: Archaeological Evidence from the Buffalo Waterfront." *Historical Archaeology* 34(1): 79–96.

Pendery, Steven R.

1999   "Portuguese Tin-Glazed Earthenware in Seventeenth-Century New England: A Preliminary Study." *Historical Archaeology* 33(4): 58–77.

Perry, Warren R., Jean E. Howson, and Barbara A. Bianco, eds.

2006   *New York African Burial Ground Archaeology Final Report.* 4 vols. Washington, D.C.: Prepared by Howard University for the United States General Services Administration, Northeastern and Caribbean Region.

Perttula, Timothy K.

1994   "Material Culture of the Koasati Indians of Texas." *Historical Archaeology* 28(1): 65–77.

Petersen, James B., and David R. Watters

1988   "Afro-Montserratian Ceramics from the Harney Site Cemetery, Montserrat, West Indies." *Annals of the Carnegie Museum* 57(8): 167–87.

Petsche, Jerome E.

1974   *The Steamboat "Bertrand": History, Excavation, and Architecture.* National Park Service Publications in Archaeology no. 11. Washington, D.C.: Government Printing Office.

Pineau, Virginia

2007   "The Use of Alcoholic Beverages as a Shortcut to Conquer the Argentinean Territory (XIXth Century)." Presented at the International Workshop, Alcohol in the Atlantic World: Historical and Contemporary Perspectives, York University, Toronto.

Pittman, William

1990   "Morphological Variability in Late Seventeenth- and Early Eighteenth-Century English Wine Bottles." M.A. thesis, College of William and Mary.

Pope, Peter E.

1989   "Historical Archaeology and the Demand for Alcohol in Seventeenth-Century Newfoundland." *Acadiensis* 19(1): 72–90.

1997   "Fish into Wine: The Historical Anthropology of Demand for Alcohol in Seventeenth-Century Newfoundland." In *The Changing Face of Drink: Substance, Imagery, and Behaviour*, ed. J. S. Blocker and C. K. Warsh, 43–64. Ottawa: Les Publications Histoire Sociale/Social History.

2004 *Fish into Wine: The Newfoundland Plantation in the Seventeenth Century.* Chapel Hill: University of North Carolina Press.

Powers, Madelon

1998 *Faces along the Bar: Lore and Order in the Workingman's Saloon, 1870–1920.* Chicago: University of Chicago Press.

Praetzellis, Adrian

1999 "The Archaeology of Ethnicity: An Example from Sacramento California's Early Chinese District." In *Old and New Worlds: Historical/Post Medieval Archaeology Papers*, ed. G. Egan and R. L. Michael, 127–35. Oxbow: Oxford University Press.

Praetzellis, Adrian, and Mary Praetzellis

2001 "Mangling Symbols of Gentility in the Wild West: Case Studies in Interpretive Archaeology." *American Anthropologist* 103(3): 645–54.

Praetzellis, Adrian, and Mary Praetzellis, eds.

2004 *Putting the "There" There: Historical Archaeologies of West Oakland.* Rohnert Park, Calif.: Sonoma State University Anthropological Studies Center.

Praetzellis, Mary, and Adrian Praetzellis

1997 *Historical Archaeology of an Overseas Chinese Community in Sacramento California.* Rohnert Park, Calif.: Sonoma State University Anthropological Studies Center.

Prestwich, Patricia E.

1997 "Drinkers, Drunkards, and Degenerates: The Alcoholic Population of a Parisian Asylum, 1867–1914." In *The Changing Face of Drink: Substance, Imagery, and Behaviour*, ed. J. S. Blocker and C. K. Warsh, 115–32. Ottawa: Les Publications Histoire Sociale/Social History.

Pulak, Cemal

1998 "The Uluburun Shipwreck: An Overview." *International Journal of Nautical Archaeology* 27: 188–224.

Pulsipher, Lydia M.

1982 "Resource Management Strategies on an Eighteenth-Century Caribbean Sugar Plantation: Interpreting the Archaeological and Archival Records." *Florida Anthropologist* 35(4): 243–50.

Pulsipher, Lydia M., and Conrad M. Goodwin

2001 "'Getting the Essence of It': Galways Plantation, Montserrat, West Indies." In *Island Lives: Historical Archaeologies of the Caribbean*, ed. P. Farnsworth, 165–203. Tuscaloosa: University of Alabama Press.

Purser, Margaret

1992 "Consumption as Communication in Nineteenth-Century Paradise Valley, Nevada." *Historical Archaeology* 26(3): 105–16.

Reckner, Paul E., and Stephen A. Brighton

1999 "'Free from All Vicious Habits': Archaeological Perspectives on Class Conflict and the Rhetoric of Temperance." *Historical Archaeology* 33(1): 63–86.

Redknap, Mark, and Edward Besly
1997   "*Wreck de mer* and Dispersed Wreck Sites: The Case of the *Ann Francis* (1583)."
       In *Artefacts from Shipwrecks: Dated Assemblages from the Late Middle Ages to the
       Industrial Revolution*, ed. M. Redknap, 191–207. Oxford: Oxbow Books.
Reeves, Matthew
1996   "'To vex a teif': An African-Jamaican Ritual Feature." Poster presented at the 31st
       annual meeting of the Society for Historical Archaeology, New Orleans.
Reinhard, K. J., S. A. Mrozowski, and K. A. Orloski
1986   "Privies, Pollen, Parasites, and Seeds: A Biological Nexus in Historic Archaeol-
       ogy." *MASCA Journal* 4(1): 31–36.
Renfrew, Jane M.
1996   "Wine." In *The Oxford Companion to Archaeology*, ed. B. Fagan, 755–58. New
       York: Oxford University Press.
Rice, Prudence M.
1996a "The Archaeology of Wine: The Wine and Brandy Haciendas of Moquegua,
       Peru." *Journal of Field Archaeology* 23(2): 187–204.
1996b "Peru's Colonial Wine Industry and Its European Background." *Antiquity* 70(270):
       785–800.
1997   "Wine and Brandy Production in Colonial Peru: A Historical and Archaeological
       Investigation." *Journal of Interdisciplinary History* 27(3): 455–79.
Rice, Prudence M., and Greg C. Smith
1989   "The Spanish Colonial Wineries of Moquegua, Peru." *Historical Archaeology*
       23(2): 41–49.
Rice, Prudence M., and Sara L. Van Beck
1993   "The Spanish Colonial Kiln Tradition of Moquegua, Peru." *Historical Archaeology*
       27(4): 65–81.
Rockman, Diana Diz., and Nan A. Rothschild
1984   "City Tavern, Country Tavern: An Analysis of Four Colonial Sites." *Historical
       Archaeology* 18(2): 112–21.
Rorabaugh, W. J.
1979   *The Alcoholic Republic: An American Tradition*. New York: Oxford University
       Press.
Ross, Alice
1993   "Health and Diet in Nineteenth-Century America: A Food Historian's Point of
       View." *Historical Archaeology* 27(2): 42–56.
Ross, Lester A.
1985   "Sixteenth-Century Spanish Basque Coopering." *Historical Archaeology* 19(1):
       1–31.
Rotman, Deborah L., and John M. Staicer
2002   "Curiosities and Conundrums: Deciphering Social Relations and the Material
       World at the Ben Schroeder Saddletree Factory and Residence in Madison, Indi-
       ana." *Historical Archaeology* 36(2): 92–110.

Rubertone, Patricia E.
2001   *Grave Undertakings: An Archaeology of Roger Williams and the Narragansett Indians.* Washington, D.C.: Smithsonian Institution Press.

Ruhl, Donna L.
1997   "Oranges and Wheat: Spanish Attempts at Agriculture in *La Florida.*" *Historical Archaeology* 31(1): 36–45.

Runnels, Curt
1975   "A Note on Glass Implements from Greece." *Newsletter of Lithic Technology* 4(3): 29–30.
1976   "More on Glass Implements from Greece." *Newsletter of Lithic Technology* 5(3): 27–31.

Rush, Benjamin
1790   *An Inquiry into the Effects of Ardent Spirits upon the Human Body and Mind with an Account of the Means of Preventing and of the Remedies for Curing Them.* Boston.

Russell, Aaron E.
1997   "Material Culture and African-American Spirituality at the Hermitage." *Historical Archaeology* 31(2): 63–80.

St. John's Historical Society
1999   "Annaberg Plantation Historic Trails" (guide pamphlet). St. John, Virgin Island.

Salamanca-Heyman, Maria
2007   *Historical Archaeology at the Sixteenth-Century Spanish Port of Nombre de Dios, Panama.* Report on file at the College of William and Mary, Department of Anthropology, Williamsburg, Va.

Salinger, Sharon V.
2002   *Taverns and Drinking in Early America.* Baltimore: Johns Hopkins University Press.

Samford, Patricia M.
1996   "The Archaeology of African-American Slavery and Material Culture." *William and Mary Quarterly* 53(1): 87–114.
2007   *Subfloor Pits and the Archaeology of Slavery in Colonial Virginia.* Tuscaloosa: University of Alabama Press.

Sayers, Daniel O.
2005   *The Results of Ongoing Intensive Excavations at Several Sites in the Great Dismal Swamp National Wildlife Refuge, North Carolina and Virginia.* Interim report, U.S. Fish and Wildlife Service, Northeast Regional Office, Hadley, Mass.

Sayers, Daniel O., P. Brendan Burke, and Aaron M. Henry
2007   "The Political Economy of Exile in the Great Dismal Swamp." *International Journal of Historical Archaeology* 11(1): 60–97.

Scaramelli, Franz, and Kay Tarble
2003   "Caña: The Role of *Aguardiente* in the Colonization of the Orinoco." In *Histories and Historicities in Amazonia,* ed. N. L. Whitehead, 163–78. Lincoln: University of Nebraska Press.

Scaramelli, Franz, and Kay Tarble de Scaramelli
2005 "The Roles of Material Culture in the Colonization of the Orinoco, Venezuela." *Journal of Social Archaeology* 5(1): 135–68.
Schaefer, James M.
1976 "Drunkenness and Cultural Stress: A Holocultural Test." In *Cross-Cultural Approaches to the Study of Alcohol: An Interdisciplinary Perspective*, ed. M. Everett, J. Waddell, and D. Heath, 287–322. The Hague: Mouton.
Schávelzon, Daniel
2000 *The Historical Archaeology of Buenos Aires: A City at the End of the World*. New York: Kluwer Academic/Plenum.
Schoenwetter, James, and John W. Hohmann
1997 "Landuse Reconstruction at the Founding Settlement of Las Vegas, Nevada." *Historical Archaeology* 31(4): 41–58.
Schrire, Carmel
1991 "The Historical Archaeology of the Impact of Colonialism in Seventeenth-Century South Africa." In *Historical Archaeology in Global Perspective*, ed. L. Falk, 69–96. Washington, D.C.: Smithsonian Institution Press.
1995 *Digging through Darkness: Chronicles of an Archaeologist*. Richmond: University of Virginia Press.
Schulz, Peter D., and Sherri M. Gust
1983 "Faunal Remains and Social Status in Nineteenth-Century Sacramento." *Historical Archaeology* 17(1): 44–53.
Schulz, Peter D., Betty J. Rivers, Mark M. Hales, Charles A. Litzinger, and Elizabeth A. McKee
1980 *The Bottles of Old Sacramento: A Study of Nineteenth-Century Glass and Ceramic Retail Containers*. California Archaeological Reports no. 20. Sacramento: State of California, Department of Parks and Recreation.
Schuyler, Robert L., and Christopher Mills
1976 "The Supply Mill on Content Brook in Massachusetts: An Example of the Investigation of Recent Historic Sites." *Journal of Field Archaeology* 3(1): 61–95.
Scott, Elizabeth M.
1991 "A Feminist Approach to Historical Archaeology: Eighteenth-Century Fur Trade Society at Michilimackinac." *Historical Archaeology* 25(4): 42–53.
Sears, William H.
1955 "Creek and Cherokee Cultures in the Eighteenth Century." *American Antiquity* 21(2): 143–49.
Seasholes, Nancy S.
1998 "Filling Boston's Mill Pond." *Historical Archaeology* 32(3): 121–36.
Seifert, Donna J.
1991 "Within Sight of the White House: The Archaeology of Working Women." *Historical Archaeology* 25(4): 82–108.
Shackel, Paul A.
2000 *Archaeology and Created Memory: Public History in a National Park*. New York: Kluwer Academic/Plenum.

Shanks, Michael, and Christopher Tilley
1994   *Re-Constructing Archaeology: Theory and Practice*. 2nd ed. London: Routledge.

Sheridan, Richard B.
1974   *Sugar and Slavery: An Economic History of the British West Indies, 1623–1775*. Barbados: Caribbean Universities Press.

Sherratt, Andrew
1991   "Sacred and Profane Substances: The Ritual Use of Narcotics in Later Neolithic Europe." In *Sacred and Profane: Proceedings of a Conference on Archaeology, Ritual and Religion*, ed. P. Garwood, D. Jennings, R. Skeates, and J. Toms, 50–64. Monographs no. 32. Oxford: Oxford University Committee for Archaeology.

Shulsky, Linda R.
2002   "Chinese Porcelain at Old Mobile." *Historical Archaeology* 36(1): 97–104.

Singleton, Theresa A.
2006   "African Diaspora Archaeology in Dialogue." In *Afro-Atlantic Dialogues: Anthropology in the Diaspora*, ed. K. Yelvington, 249–87. Santa Fe: SAR Press.

Skowronek, Russell K.
1992   "Empire and Ceramics: The Changing Role of Illicit Trade in Spanish America." *Historical Archaeology* 26(1): 109–18.

Sloane, Hans
1707–25   *A Voyage to the Islands Madera, Barbados, Nieves, S. Christophers, and Jamaica*. 2 vols. London.

Smith, E. Ann
1983   "Drinking Practices and Glassware of the British Military, ca. 1755–85." *Northeast Historical Archaeology* 12: 31–39.

Smith, Frederick H.
2001a   "Alcohol, Slavery, and African Cultural Continuity in the British Caribbean." In *Drinking: Anthropological Approaches*, ed. I. de Garine and V. de Garine, 212–24. New York: Berghan Press.

2001b   "Volatile Spirits: The Historical Archaeology of Alcohol and Drinking in the Caribbean." Ph.D. diss., University of Florida.

2004a   "Holetown: Archaeological Investigations at the Site of the First British Settlement in Barbados." *Journal of the Barbados Museum and Historical Society* 50: 49–65.

2004b   "Spirits and Spirituality: Enslaved Persons and Alcohol in West Africa and the British and French Caribbean." *Journal of Caribbean History* 38(2): 279–309.

2005   *Caribbean Rum: A Social and Economic History*. Gainesville: University Press of Florida.

2006   "European Impressions of the Island Carib's Use of Alcohol in the Early Colonial Period." *Ethnohistory* 53(3): 543–66.

Smith, Frederick H., and Karl Watson
2007   "Western Bridgetown and the Butchers' Shambles in the Seventeenth-Nineteenth Centuries: New Insights from the Jubilee Gardens Archaeological Investigations." *Journal of the Barbados Museum and Historical Society* 53: 185–98

Forthcoming   "Urbanity, Sociability, and Commercial Exchange in the Barbados Sugar

Trade: A Comparative Colonial Archaeological Perspective on Bridgetown, Barbados in the Seventeenth Century." *International Journal of Historical Archaeology.*

Smith, Greg Charles

1997   "Hispanic, Andean, and African Influences in the Moquegua Valley of Southern Peru." *Historical Archaeology* 31(1): 74–83.

Smith, Hale G., and Mark Gottlob

1978   "Spanish-Indian Relationships: Synoptic History and Archaeological Evidence, 1500–1763." In *Tacachale: Essays on the Indians of Florida and Southeastern Georgia during the Historic Period*, ed. J. Milanich and S. Proctor, 1–18. Gainesville: University Press of Florida.

Smyth, Adam, ed.

2004   *A Pleasing Sinne: Drink and Conviviality in Seventeenth-Century England.* Cambridge: D. S. Brewer.

Snow, George E.

1991   "Socialism, Alcoholism, and the Russian Working Classes before 1917." In *Drinking: Behavior and Belief in Modern History*, ed. S. Barrows and R. Room, 243–64. Berkeley: University of California Press.

Sonnenstuhl, William J.

1996   *Working Sober: The Transformation of an Occupational Drinking Culture.* Ithaca, N.Y.: Cornell University Press.

South, Stanley

1977   *Method and Theory in Historical Archaeology.* New York: Academic Press.

South, Stanley, Russell K. Skowronek, and Richard E. Johnson

1988   *Spanish Artifacts from Santa Elana.* Anthropological Studies no. 7. Columbia: Institute of Archaeology and Anthropology, University of South Carolina.

Spradley, James P.

1970   *You Owe Yourself a Drunk: An Ethnography of Urban Nomads.* Boston: Little, Brown.

Spude, Catherine Holder

2005   "Brothels and Saloons: An Archaeology of Gender in the American West." *Historical Archaeology* 39(1): 89–106.

Stahl, Ann B.

1994   "Change and Continuity in the Banda Area, Ghana: The Direct Historical Approach." *Journal of Field Archaeology* 21(2): 181–203.

2001   "Historical Process and the Impact of the Atlantic Slave Trade on Banda, Ghana, 1800–1920." In *West Africa during the Atlantic Slave Trade: Archaeological Perspectives*, ed. C. DeCorse, 38–58. London: Leicester University Press.

Stanbury, Myra

1974   *Batavia Catalogue.* Perth: Department of Maritime Archaeology, Western Australian Museum.

Staniforth, Mark

2003   "*Annales*-Informed Approaches to the Archaeology of Colonial Australia." *Historical Archaeology* 37(1): 102–13.

Staski, Edward
1983 "Patterns of Alcohol Consumption among Nineteenth-Century Irish- and Jewish-Americans: Contributions from Archaeology." Ph.D. diss., University of Arizona.
1984 "Just What Can a Nineteenth-Century Bottle Tell Us?" *Historical Archaeology* 18(1): 38–51.
1990 "Site Formation Processes at Fort Fillmore, New Mexico: First Interpretations." *Historical Archaeology* 24(3): 79–90.
1993 "The Overseas Chinese in El Paso: Changing Goals, Changing Realities." In *Hidden Heritage: Historical Archaeology of the Overseas Chinese*, ed. P. Wegars, 125–50. Amityville, N.Y.: Baywood Publishing.

Stone, Garry Wheeler
1988 "Artifacts Are Not Enough." In *Documentary Archaeology*, ed. M. Beaudry, 68–77. Cambridge: Cambridge University Press.

Stoner, Michael J.
2003 "Material Culture in the City: Barbadian Redwares in Bridgetown." *Journal of the Barbados Museum and Historical Society* 49: 254–68.

Switzer, Ronald R.
1974 *The Bertrand Bottles: A Study of Nineteenth-Century Glass and Ceramic Containers.* National Park Service Publications in Archaeology no. 12. Washington, D.C.: Government Printing Office.

Tatton-Brown, Veronica
1991 "The Roman Empire." In *Glass, 5000 Years*, ed. H. Tait, 62–97. New York: Harry N. Abrams.

Taylor, William B.
1979 *Drinking, Homicide, and Rebellion in Colonial Mexican Villages.* Stanford, Calif.: Stanford University Press.

Teague, George A.
1980 *Reward Mining and Associated Sites, Historical Archaeology on the Papago Reservation.* Publications in Anthropology no. 11. Tucson, Ariz.: National Park Service, Western Archaeological Center.

Thomas, Brian W.
1994 "Inclusion and Exclusion in the Moravian Settlement in North Carolina, 1770–1790." *Historical Archaeology* 28(3): 15–29.

Thompson, Robert Farris
1984 *Flash of the Spirit: African and Afro-American Art and Philosophy.* New York: Vintage Books.

Tlusty, Beverly Ann
1997 "Gender and Alcohol Use in Early Modern Augsburg." In *The Changing Face of Drink: Substance, Imagery, and Behaviour*, ed. J. S. Blocker and C. K. Warsh, 21–42. Ottawa: Les Publications Histoire Sociale/Social History.

Torbenson, Michael, Robert H. Kelly, Jonathon Erlen, Lorna Cropcho, Michael Moraca, Bonnie Beiler, K. N. Rao, and Mohamed Virji

2000 "Lash's: A Bitter Medicine: Biochemical Analysis of an Historical Proprietary Medicine." *Historical Archaeology* 34(2): 56–64.

Toulouse, Julian

1970 "High on the Hawg: Or How the Western Miner Lived, as Told by Bottles He Left Behind." *Historical Archaeology* 4: 59–69.

Tracy, Sarah W., and Caroline Jean Acker, eds.

2004 *Altering American Consciousness: The History of Alcohol and Drug Use in the United States, 1800–2000*. Amherst: University of Massachusetts Press.

Turner, Victor W.

1969 *The Ritual Process: Structure and Anti-Structure*. Chicago: Aldine Publishing.

Tyrrell, Ian R.

1979 "Temperance and Economic Change in the Ante-Bellum North." In *Alcohol, Reform, and Society: The Liquor Issue in Social Context*, ed. J. S. Blocker, 45–68. Westport, Conn.: Greenwood Press.

1991 *Woman's World/Woman's Empire: The Woman's Christian Temperance Union in International Perspective, 1880–1930*. Chapel Hill: University of North Carolina Press.

Underwood, A.J.V.

1935 "The Historical Development of Distilling Plant." *Transactions of the Institution of Chemical Engineers* 13: 34–62.

Unwin, Tim

1991 *Wine and the Vine: An Historical Geography of Viticulture and the Wine Trade*. London: Routledge.

Van Bueren, Thad M.

2002 "Struggling with Class Relations at a Los Angeles Aqueduct Construction Camp." *Historical Archaeology* 36(3): 28–43.

Van Buren, Mary

1999 "Tarapaya: An Elite Spanish Residence Near Colonial Potosí in Comparative Perspective." *Historical Archaeology* 33(2): 108–22.

Van der Pijl-Ketel, C. L.

1982 "Very Fine Porcelain." In *The Ceramic Load of the "Witte Leeuw," 1613*, ed. C. L. Van der Pijl-Ketel, 143–45. Amsterdam: Rijksmuseum.

Veit, Richard, and Paul W. Schopp

1999 "Who's Been Drinking on the Railroad?: Archaeological Excavations at the Central Railroad of New Jersey's Lakehurst Shops." *Northeast Historical Archaeology* 28: 21–40.

Veth, Peter, and Jo McDonald

2004 "Can Archaeology Be Used to Address the Principle of Exclusive Possession in Native Title?" In *After Captain Cook: The Archaeology of the Recent Indigenous Past in Australia*, ed. R. Harrison and C. Williamson, 122–32. Walnut Creek, Calif.: Altamira Press.

Vlierman, Karel

1997 "The Galley, Galley Utensils and Cooking, Eating, and Drinking Vessels from an Armed 'Tjalck' Wrecked on the Zuiderzee in 1673: A Preliminary Report." In

Artefacts from Shipwrecks: Dated Assemblages from the Late Middle Ages to the Industrial Revolution, ed. M. Redknap, 157–66. Oxford: Oxbow Books.

Von der Porten, Edward P.

1972 "Drake and Cermeno in California: Sixteenth-Century Chinese Ceramics." *Historical Archaeology* 6: 1–22.

Walker, Iain C.

1976 "Alternative Uses for Clay Tobacco Pipes and Tobacco Pipe Fragments: Some Notes." *Historical Archaeology* 10: 124–27.

Walker, Mark

1996 *"The receptacles were emptied of their contents": Archaeological Testing of Area II-B of the Carlyle Property and Excavation of the Shutter's Hill Brewery Site (44AX35), Alexandria, Virginia.* Report prepared for the Norfolk/Southern Corporation, Engineering Science, Inc., Fairfax, Va.

Walthall, John A.

1991 "Faience in French Colonial Illinois." *Historical Archaeology* 25(1): 80–105.

Warner, Jessica, and Frank Ivis

1999 "'Damn you, you informing Bitch': *Vox Populi* and the Unmaking of the Gin Act of 1736." *Journal of Social History* 33(2): 299–330.

Waselkov, Gregory A., and John A. Walthall

2002 "Faience Styles in French Colonial North America: A Revised Classification." *Historical Archaeology* 36(1): 62–78.

Watters, David R.

1987 "Excavations at the Harney Site Slave Cemetery, Montserrat West Indies." *Annals of Carnegie Museum* 56(18): 289–318.

1994 "Mortuary Patterns at the Harney Site Slave Cemetery, Montserrat, in Caribbean Perspective." *Historical Archaeology* 28(3): 56–73.

Watters, David R., and Desmond V. Nicholson

1982 "Highland House, Barbuda: An Eighteenth-Century Retreat." *Florida Anthropologist* 35(4): 223–42.

Watters, David R., and James B. Petersen

1991 "The Harney Slave Site Cemetery, Montserrat: Archaeological Summary." In *Proceedings of the 13th International Congress for Caribbean Archaeology, Curaçao*, ed. E. N. Ayubi and J. Haviser, 317–25. Willemstad: Archaeological-Anthropological Institute of the Netherlands Antilles.

Weik, Terry

1997 "The Archaeology of Maroon Societies in the Americas: Resistance, Cultural Continuity, and Transformation in the African Diaspora." *Historical Archaeology* 31(2): 81–92.

Welsh, James

1589 "A Voyage to Benin beyond the Country of Guinea." Reprinted 1978 in *Richard Hakluyt, Voyages*, 6: 291–97. 8 vols. London: Everyman's Library.

Whitehouse, David

1997 "Looking through Roman Glass." *Archaeology* 50(5): 79–82.

Wilcoxen, Charlotte

1987 *Dutch Trade and Ceramics in America in the Seventeenth Century*. Albany: Albany Institute of History and Art.

Wilkie, Laurie A.

1996 "Glass-Knapping at a Louisiana Plantation: African-American Tools?" *Historical Archaeology* 30(4): 37–49.

1997 "Secret and Sacred: Contextualizing the Artifacts of African-American Magic and Religion." *Historical Archaeology* 31(4): 81–106.

2003 *The Archaeology of Mothering: An African-American Midwife's Tale*. New York: Routledge.

Williams, David F.

1989 "The Impact of the Roman Amphora Trade on Pre-Roman Britain." In *Centre and Periphery: Comparative Studies in Archaeology*, ed. T. Champion, 142–50. London: Unwin Hyman.

Williams, Eric

1944 *Capitalism and Slavery*. Reprinted 1994, Chapel Hill: University of North Carolina Press.

Williams, Joseph J.

1932 *Voodoos and Obeahs: Phases of West Indian Witchcraft*. New York: Dial Press.

Williams, Patrick Ryan

2001 "Cerro Baúl: A Wari Administrative Center on the Tiwanaku Frontier." *Latin American Antiquity* 12(1): 67–83.

2004 "Ancient Brewery Discovered on Mountaintop in Peru." http://www.eurekalert.org/pub_releases/2004-07/fm-abd072704.php.

2005 "Burning Down the Brewery: Elite Women Brewed a Beer-Like Drink at Ancient Wari Site—The First Diplomatic Outpost between Andean Empires." http://www.eurekalert.org/pub_releases/2005-11/fm-bdt110905.php.

Williams, Patrick Ryan, Michael Moseley, and Donna J. Nash

2000 "Empires of the Andes: A Majestic Frontier Outpost Chose Cooperation over War." *Discovering Archaeology* 8: 68–73.

Williamson, Christine

2004 "Finding Meaning in the Patterns: The Analysis of Material Culture from a Contact Site in Tasmania." In *After Captain Cook: The Archaeology of the Recent Indigenous Past in Australia*, ed. R. Harrison and C. Williamson, 75–101. Walnut Creek, Calif.: Altamira Press.

Willmott, Hugh

2001 "A Group of Seventeenth-Century Glass Goblets with Restored Stems: Considering the Archaeology of Repair." *Post-Medieval Archaeology* 35: 96–105.

Wilson, C. Anne

1975 "Burnt Wine and Cordial Waters." *Folk Life* 13: 59–63.

Wilson, Peter J.

1973 *Crab Antics: The Social Anthropology of English-Speaking Negro Societies of the Caribbean*. New Haven: Yale University Press.

Wurst, LouAnn

1991 "'Employees Must Be of Moral and Temperate Habits': Rural and Urban Elite Ideologies." In *The Archaeology of Inequality*, ed. R. H. McGuire and R. Paynter, 125–49. Oxford: Blackwell.

1999 "Internalizing Class in Historical Archaeology." *Historical Archaeology* 33(1): 7–21.

Yamin, Rebecca

1998 "Lurid Tales and Homely Stories of New York's Notorious Five Points." *Historical Archaeology* 32(1): 74–85.

Yawney, Carol

1979 "Drinking Patterns and Alcoholism in Trinidad." In *Beliefs, Behaviors, and Alcoholic Beverages: A Cross-Cultural Survey*, ed. M. Marshall, 94–108. Ann Arbor: University of Michigan Press.

Yentsch, Anne

1990 "Minimum Vessel Lists as Evidence of Change in Folk and Courtly Traditions of Food Use." *Historical Archaeology* 24(3): 24–53.

1991 "Engendering Visible and Invisible Ceramic Artifacts, Especially Diary Vessels." *Historical Archaeology* 25(4): 132–55.

Zierden, Martha A.

1999 "A Trans-Atlantic Merchant's House in Charleston: Archaeological Exploration of Refinement and Subsistence in an Urban Setting." *Historical Archaeology* 33(3): 73–87.

Zierden, Martha A., and Jeanne A. Calhoun

1986 "Urban Adaptation in Charleston, South Carolina, 1730–1820." *Historical Archaeology* 20(1): 29–43.

Index

Alcoholics Anonymous (AA), 137
Alcohol production: by brewing, 29, 57, 87,
92, 95; changes in, 28; and class, 29; as commercial activity, 6, 29–30, 38, 41, 43, 45, 46,
57; by distillation, 36–43, 44, 45, 46, 57, 95,
96, 138; as economic activity, 41, 43, 45, 46;
equipment for, 29, 36–38, 39, 40, 41, 43, 44,
122–24; expansion of, 6, 27, 29–30, 38, 43,
46, 138; by fermentation, 29, 44, 51, 118, 120,
121–23, 124; and gender, 10, 29, 31, 51, 123;
immigrants and, 88; Indians and natives
and, 44, 48–49, 50, 51; ingredients for, 30,
40, 41, 43, 50, 51, 118, 120, 121, 122–23, 124;
and lead toxicity, 96; local, 81, 89; scholarship on, 134; slaves and, 103, 120, 124; and
trade, 33, 41, 45
Alcohol studies: anthropologists and, 1, 3–5,
58, 59, 73, 97; barriers to, 2, 3; definition of,
1; ethnohistorians and, 44; historians and,
5, 58, 73; historical archaeology and, 1, 6,
43–44, 49, 58, 59–61, 73, 79–80, 97, 101–3,
104, 133, 134–39
Ale. See Beer and ale
Alexandria, Va., 32
Allchin, F. R., 29
Amazonia, 52
American Revolution, 5, 63
Andes and Andeans, 35
Andrews, Anthony, 100
Anglo Americans, 96–97
Animals: birds, 111; cattle, 53; cocks, 69, 70, 131;
dogs, 113; draft, 62; fish, 53, 82; fruit bats,
110; hogs, 116; horses, 113; llamas, 35; mules,
35; oxen, 35; pigs, 113; rats, 119
Annapolis, Md., 54
Anne Arundel County, Md., 54
Anthropology and anthropologists: and
alcohol studies, 1, 3–5, 54, 58, 59, 73, 97; on
burial practices, 94; cultural, 3, 6, 59, 60, 75,
135–38; historical, 134
Antigua, 38, 131, 132
Apalachee, Fla., 89
Appalachia, 43
Archaeological features: illustrations of, 109;
latrines, 98; pits, 69, 110, 130; privies, 32,
33, 73, 100; root cellars, 33, 78; stairs, 109;
trash middens, 81; walls, 109, 110, 111; wells,
24, 76

Archaeological techniques: artifact dating,
7, 8–9, 11, 16–19, 20, 21; biochemical tests,
95–96; bone chemistry analysis, 101; chemical analysis, 19, 29; grid establishment,
108; infrared spectroscopy, 19; measured
drawing, 107; soil core sampling, 33; surface
collection, 107, 108; surveys, 40; testing, 105,
107, 108
Archaeology, historical. See under Alcohol
studies
Architecture. See Buildings and structures
Argentina, 26, 52
Argyll, Scotland, 44
Armstrong, Douglas, 119
Artifacts: adze/axes, 111; barrel hoops, 23, 33,
52, 72; beer cans, 19; bowls (unspecified material), 93; buttons, 109; casks, 23, 53; celts,
111, 116; clothing, 73; contact-era, 46–47;
copper and copper alloy, 23, 24, 30, 41, 44,
72; drinking cups (unspecified material), 86;
fans, 69; faucets, 72; faunal, 64; fermentation vats, 40; flatware, 61; fuel oil cans, 43;
greenstone, 111, 116; human bones, 69; iron,
23, 33, 52, 72, 111, 116; kegs, 81; kettles, 30;
nails, 111; organic items as, 120; pestles, 116;
pewter, 61; poker chips, 71; prehistoric, 116,
117; pub tokens, 64; punchbowls (unspecified type), 86; seashells, 74; shell, 109, 111,
116; spigots, 23, 24; stone, 116; Suzaoid type,
110, 117; tankards, 64; taps and cocks, 41;
tea caddies, 69; timekeeping devices, 77;
tools, 116; vessels (unspecified types and
materials), 79; wine cocks, 23; wooden, 23,
40, 53–54. See also Bottles, glass; Ceramics; Ceramics, forms of; Ceramics, types of;
Glass
Ashurst, Denis, 16
Asia, 29, 57, 138
Atlanta, Ga., 20
Atlantic Islands, 139
Atwood, Thomas, 129
Australia, 2, 26, 52, 53, 57, 62–63, 138
Avery, George, 10

Bacon's Castle (Va.), 25
Bahamas, 48, 85, 119, 123
Balicki, Joseph, 98
Ballard's Valley Plantation (Jamaica), 132

Baltimore, Md., 67

Band of Hope (temperance organization), 3

Barbados: 1816 slave uprising on, 104, 117, 125–26, 130, 132, 133; agriculture on, 106, 107, 112; alcohol on, 1, 119, 121–23, 124, 137; archaeology on, 38–39, 105–6, 118; architecture on, 114; British and, 112, 113, 116, 119, 125; caves on, 106, 113; cemeteries on, 94, 96; ceramics on, 123; churches on, 122; economy of, 107, 118; foods on, 123; government of, 113; health on, 96; indentured servants on, 112; Indians and natives on, 112; maps and illustrations of, 106, 112, 113, 117, 118; maroons on, 113; population of, 112, 113; slaves and slavery on, 94, 96, 104, 105, 112, 113, 115, 117, 120–21, 123, 128–29; Spanish and, 112; sugar production and estates on, 1, 38–39, 108, 112, 113, 117, 118, 125; trade with, 54; travelers on, 119, 122. *See also* Mapps Cave (Barbados)

Barbot, John, 121

Barbuda, 85

Barrows, Susanna, 5, 84

Battle Creek, Mich., 89

Bayley, F.W.N., 119

Bayleys Plantation (Barbados), 104, 105, 112, 117, 125, 126, 133

Beaudry, Mary C., 21, 61, 76, 102

Beer and ale: Africans and, 119; *chica* beer, 123; and class, 29, 77; Eastern Europeans and, 91; and farming, 29; and gender, 10, 29; grain, 29, 44; Indians and natives and, 31, 60, 97; ingredients in, 29, 30, 31, 123; lager, 31; mentioned, 121; production of, 10, 29, 30–32, 92; slaves and, 92, 119, 123; as trade goods, 30, 31, 56. *See also* Alcoholic beverages

Belize, 99, 138

Bellermino, Roberto, 11

Ben Schroeder Saddletree Factory (Ind.), 77

Bermuda, 19

Betty's Hope Plantation (Antigua), 38

Beverages. *See* Alcoholic beverages; Foods and nonalcoholic beverages

Bight of Biafra, 120, 121

Binghamton, N.Y., 78

Bittmann, Bente, 77–78, 81

Blacks: African Americans, 26, 72, 87–88, 96; Afro-Barbadians, 94; Afro-Brazilians, 125; Afro-Creoles, 26, 44, 93, 115; free, 53; maroons, 53, 113, 114–16, 130. *See also* Africans; Slaves

Bloomington, Ill., 96

Bois Caïman (St. Domingue), 126

Bolivia, 56

Bond, Kathleen, 81, 102

Boott Cotton Mill and boardinghouses (Mass.): alcohol restrictions at, 68, 76, 84; archaeology of, 75, 76, 77, 78, 79, 81, 84; and ethnicity, 80; owners and, 68, 76; workers and, 68, 75–76, 78, 84, 102

Boston, Mass., 41, 57, 99, 133

Boston Saloon (Nevada), 72

Bottles, glass: for beer and ale, 17, 19, 32, 56, 76, 90, 91, 94, 97; British, 16, 27; and class, 78, 81, 84, 85; colors of, 16, 19, 20, 22, 26, 64, 87, 108, 111, 117–18; dating of, 16–19, 20; Dutch, 17; essense of peppermint, 96; French, 17, 91; German, 73; in graves, 93–94; hand-blown, 14–15, 18, 20, 25, 27, 33, 64, 78, 108–9, 111, 117–18, 119; illustrations of, 14–15, 18, 25, 34; Indians and natives and, 25–26, 47–48, 49, 51, 52, 89; for liquor, 17, 49, 57, 73, 78, 79, 84, 95, 98; at logwood cutter sites, 99; machine-made, 17–19, 20–21; at Mapps Cave, 107–8, 133; medicinal, 79, 81, 96; mentioned, 41, 46; at military sites, 98, 99; mold-made, 17–19, 20–21; production of, 16, 17; recovered with contents, 19, 20, 33, 34, 95; recycling of, 19–20, 21, 25–26, 32, 80–81, 101–2; for rum, 100; scholarship on, 63; seals, markings, and scratches on, 16, 17, 18, 20, 56, 57, 99–100; shapes of, 16–17, 27, 28, 87; slaves and, 26–27, 100, 119; soda mineral water, 80; at tavern and saloon sites, 64, 74, 99; and temperance, 30, 101, 102; and trade, 53, 55; Turlington Balsam of Life, 93; uses of, 7, 16, 17–21, 25–28, 56, 71, 72, 87, 90, 94, 119, 120, 124; for vodka, 91; for whiskey, 90, 95, 97; for wine, 14–15, 19, 20, 33, 56, 89, 97; witch bottles, 27; at work sites, 76, 77, 78, 95. *See also* Glass

Bragdon, Kathleen, 66

Braidwood, Robert, 29

Bray's Littletown (Va.), 20

Brazil, 113, 115

Breen, Eleanor, 41

Bridgetown, Barbados, 13, 62, 85, 86, 94, 106

Brighton, Stephen, 78–79

Bristol, R.I., 40

British: as colonists, 82, 85, 88, 90–91, 112, 113; and glass production, 16–17; and Indians and natives, 48, 52; and military rank, 99; and privateers, 119; and slaves, 53; and Spanish, 53, 112; and trade, 48

British West Indies, 128

Brooklyn, N.Y., 78, 79

Brothels, 73–74

Brown, Marley R., III, 49, 61

Browne, Benjamin, 119

Buenos Aires, Argentina, 24, 43

Buffalo, N.Y., 68, 80

Buildings and structures: amenities in, 74; asylums, 80–81; bars, 119; boardinghouses, 67, 92, 100; *bodegas*, 10, 32, 89; boiling houses, 55; bottling plants, 31–32, 45; breweries and brew houses, 30, 31–32, 44, 88; brick, 30; brothels, 73–74; cafés, 64, 74; and ceramics, 24; churches, 96; and class, 71–72; coffeehouses, 66, 69–70, 72; convents, 89; distilleries, 38, 39–40, 41, 42, 44; domestic, 66; factories, 38–39, 77; fraternity houses, 64; fur trade outposts, 52; and gender, 64; glasshouses, 16; government, 70; homes and residences, 23; hotels, 71–72; houses and residences, 26, 27, 43, 78, 85, 86, 100, 105, 114, 117, 130; illustrations of, 39, 40, 42, 55; Indendant's Palace, 30; Indians and natives and, 60; inns, 64; jails, 71–72; lifesaving stations, 96; limestone, 30; liquor shops, 119; locomotive repair facilities, 76; masonry, 30; in medieval Europe, 62; military, 99; mills, 40; missions, 52; multi-use, 68; outbuildings, 30, 66; placement of, 67, 70; poorhouses, 97; root cellars, 33; sawmills, 57; servants' dwellings, 78; slave quarters and dwellings, 92, 105–6, 119, 123, 130; stone, 114; storehouses, 30, 125; stores, 43; tenements, 79; timber, 114; urban, 43, 67, 68, 71, 72, 85; windmills, 38–39; wine cellars, 33, 43; wineries, 32, 43, 44. *See also* Boott Cotton Mill and boardinghouses (Mass.); Saloons; Taverns

Burial practices and cemeteries, 48, 92, 93–94, 96, 119, 121

Burley, David, 94

Burr's Hill (R.I.), 48, 49

Busch, Jane, 20

Bush, David, 98

Bushnell, Amy, 54

Bussa (slave), 126

Bussa's Rebellion. *See* Barbados: 1816 slave uprising in

Cabak, Melanie, 96

Calhoun, Jeanne, 68

California, 49–51, 52, 77, 92, 95, 99. *See also* Sacramento, Calif.

Canaan, Conn., 67

Canada, 17, 30, 100

Cannon's Point Plantation (Ga.), 87, 93, 119

Cape Coast, 33, 52

Cape Cod, Mass., 64, 96, 100

Capitalism, 75–77, 134

Caribbean: Africans in, 131; alcohol drinking in, 104, 120, 128, 136; alcohol production in, 38, 41, 44, 45, 48–49, 54, 121, 122, 124; British, 54, 126, 127, 129, 130, 131, 132, 133; ceramics in, 35, 108, 111, 118; class in, 85–86; French, 55, 122; glassware in, 118; Indians in, 44, 112; missionaries in, 2; scholarship on, 104; slaves in, 55, 104, 118, 119, 120, 122, 126, 127–32; Spanish, 54, 122; sugar production in, 38–40; trade with, 40, 41, 45, 48, 54, 55

Caribbean Rum: A Social and Economic History (Smith), 104

Carley, Caroline, 95

Carolinas, 85, 88, 115. *See also* South Carolina

Carrick Castle (Scotland), 44

Carstairs, G. M., 4

Casks, 19, 23, 26, 46, 53

Celebrations. *See* Holidays, rituals, and celebrations

Cemeteries and burial practices, 48, 92, 93–94, 96, 119, 121

Central Africa, 44, 55, 94, 120–21, 129, 132, 137. *See also* Africa; West Africa

Central America, 2

Central Railroad of New Jersey, 76, 77

Ceramics: and artifact dating, 8–9; and class, 21, 61, 82, 85; colors of, 83, 86, 108, 111, 112; dating of, 7, 11–13, 16, 21; decoration, dates, and markings on, 10, 11–13, 16, 27, 35, 56, 82–83, 90, 102, 109, 111; and economic status,

Frederick H. Smith is assistant professor of anthropology at the College of William and Mary, Williamsburg, Virginia. He is author of *Caribbean Rum: A Social and Economic History* (Gainesville: University Press of Florida, 2005). He has also published numerous journal articles, including "European Impressions of the Island Carib's Use of Alcohol in the Early Colonial Period" in *Ethnohistory* (2006) and "Spirits and Spirituality: Enslaved Persons and Alcohol in West Africa and the British and French Caribbean" in the *Journal of Caribbean History* (2004).

Since 1995 Smith has regularly conducted historical archaeological investigations in Barbados. He has investigated the lives of early British colonists and enslaved peoples in the urban context of Bridgetown as well as in rural sugar plantation contexts.